BANKING *in* INDIA'S HINTERLAND

MOIN QAZI

INDIA • SINGAPORE • MALAYSIA

ISBN 979-8-89363-363-4

For

my colleagues in

State Bank of India

This book is more a diary than an instructive guide. It provides the flavour of the author's personal experiences as a rural banker and his engagement with people experiencing poverty in the remote crannies of India .The seed around which the book crystallises is poor rural women's intrinsic tenacity and grit that can become energetic powerhouses to drive our rural society onto the road to prosperity. The book carries in its pages the poignant nostalgia of the author for villages, but it has, at places, rage and despair. The message in this book is that there is no grand, universal formula for poverty reduction. The struggle involves several fronts, and what works in one place does not necessarily work everywhere. The way forward lies in grassroots field experiments for understanding the causal relationships between poor people's behaviour and learning by doing. The author's faith in poor people's ability to climb out of the rut is unshakeable, and his core belief is gradualism. The author believes that lasting social change most often—and perhaps permanently—comes slowly rather than in a burst of revolutionary fervour. It is this belief that has shaped his work. He also believes that lasting change can be successful only when women have equal opportunities for financial empowerment.

The author firmly believes that it is possible to eliminate poverty in our country—provided we re-examine the wisdom we have received from our assumptions. The poor are poor not because they are unskilled or illiterate but because they cannot retain the returns of their labour. They neither own capital nor does anyone give them access to credit, except on the most unreasonable terms. They live on the edge, constantly fearing a catastrophe or tragedy, but they have no insurance because insurance companies consider them a losing proposition. The State's social safety nets are grossly inadequate and mired in corruption and bureaucratic red tape.

During his efforts in development finance and rural development work for over three decades, the author has seen projects and strategies succeed and fail. He has seen misguided project designs, poor implementation and squandering of large sums of money. But he also witnessed incredible achievements. When development works well, he argues, it can transform lives by providing the underprivileged with the capital and knowledge that can open up opportunities for them and reduce their poverty. Good judgment is a quality everyone would like to have. But it isn't easy to define precisely, and many people are not sure whether they possess it.

The difference between what we do and what we are capable of doing would suffice to solve most of the world's problems.

– Mahatma Gandhi

CONTENTS

Acknowledgements 11

Introduction 13

1. A Banker to the Poor 27
2. Adventures in the Rural Planet 71
3. Finance for the Poor 99
4. A Livelihood of Her Own 136
5. Where People Plan Their Destinies 170
6. My Odyssey with Dairy Farmers 211
7. Vignettes From Villages 254

ACKNOWLEDGEMENTS

There is no greater agony than bearing an untold story inside you.

– Maya Angelou

I owe much to a lifetime of collegiality of steadfast colleagues, enthusiastic bosses, supportive peers and juniors who have helped me learn and practice development finance. I owe deep gratitude to so many people for their help, and if I were to put down their names, it would make a formidable list. They all shared the physical and emotional adventure in the workplace and the field. They also assisted me in building a compelling narrative out of the impassable maze of my notes built up over three decades of work in development finance, which took me to remote hinterlands and provided firsthand knowledge of the problems of the rural poor, particularly the women amongst them.

Before all, I must record my debt to the thousands of women in the villages and low-income urban neighbourhoods of developing countries who so lovingly shared their time and taught me about their enterprises, finances, and lives. Most were poor in economic terms but rich in wisdom and social responsibility. I primarily owe my knowledge of development finance to them.

I owe a special note of thanks to many colleagues who, for various reasons, were (and may still be) sceptical of my approach. Without that scepticism and scrutiny, this book and related works would have far more weaknesses and errors. Those who know me know I love a good argument and enjoy defending my theories. I hope this approach does not lack appreciation for the opposition to my favourite ideas. For that reason, this acknowledgement is incredibly heartfelt. We are an exceptional community in that, without debate, we would be much less than we are now. I hope we never lose that quality. In the same spirit, I hope this book provokes some strong reactions— positive or negative.

I feel blessed to have lived to tell you that even when my hours were at their darkest, I drew strength from the belief that one day, I could share my experiences with others. This book reflects my struggles; the battles have kept my spirit alive. To struggle is to strengthen my faith, hope, and belief in humanity.

My final thanks are to the institution at the centre of all my learning and practice: State Bank of India. I deem it my great fortune that I was part of it in several turbulent yet defining periods of India's development history. I am immensely grateful to it for allowing me complete freedom to deploy my talents and ideas while keeping within patterns and standards. I consider it a highly benign institution with much to teach those willing to learn. It is a vast fraternity, and I found an abode in the homes of legions of strangers. I can only thank them in Tagore's words:

THOU hast made me known to friends whom I knew not. Thou hast given me seats in homes not my own. Thou hast brought the distant near and made a brother of the stranger. I am uneasy at heart when I have to leave my accustomed shelter; I forget that there abides the old in the new and thou abidest.

Finally, I seek forgiveness for all those who have been with me over the years and whose names I have failed to mention. The gifts were yours, the gratitude mine.

* * * * *

INTRODUCTION

I shall now, therefore, humbly propose my thoughts, which I hope will not be liable to the slightest objection.

– Jonathan Swift

This book is more a diary rather than an instructive guide. It has my thoughts, but I admit they are liable to as many objections as possible. Fallibility has been the mark of all adventurers. My diary provides the flavour of my personal experiences as a rural banker, my professional safari through the jungles of my bank's vast and deep network and its engagement with people experiencing poverty in the remote crannies of India. My diary may serve as an antidote to much of the euphoria generated these days about the development programmes and the benefits of economic liberalization. I believe in the economic philosophy that guarantees equitable and just development. I have tried to portray the Indian rural development scene faithfully and document my experiences in various roles – grassroots worker, field officer, program manager, policy maker, and academic. I have presented the facts plainly without any colour or gloss of ideology. I ran the risk of rebuke from many quarters for my chilling honesty, but I had grown weary of the inane sophistry that marked the stance of my bosses, peers and fellow academics and was desperate to furrow a new path.

My journey through rural India and my three-decade development finance career was rough and stormy as I rebelled against traditional approaches. The goal of my heretical act of questioning certain conventional assumptions was to shed light on the actual practices of the development sector and to prompt changes that will skew the odds in favour of people with low incomes. My diary drifts and tacks like a sailboat but has a clear leitmotif. The seed around which the book crystallises is poor rural women's intrinsic tenacity and grit that become energetic powerhouses to drive our rural society onto the road to prosperity. The book carries my poignant nostalgia for villages in its pages, but in places, it also has rage and despair.

Rural banking in India has been a significant hurdle race ever since the government nationalized central commercial banks and mandated them to focus their thrust on villages. The directive involved barefoot banking and working in unfamiliar terrain to establish their flag posts. The players were untrained and unwilling participants in the marathon. Their captains were equally unprepared. Only the umpire was stubborn and unrelenting. He brought more players into the race and changed the game's rules many times. At some stages, it appeared he had lost interest in the race. But the race continues, proceeding in different directions. Though the roadmap of financial sector reforms bypassed rural banking, the barefoot bankers, reconciled now, continue to walk amidst the debris of the populist programmes.

While the positive social and economic impacts of nationalization are evident, the experiment also teaches us about the disaster that mindless bureaucratic programmes can cause. Most development programmes are a grim reminder of how mechanically trying to meet targets can completely undermine the integrity of a veritable economic and social revolution that a counter-revolution originated.

People with low incomes have skills, are politically conscious, and are aware of the need for schooling for the children, taking care of their health and planning a future for their families. However, their lack of income makes it impossible for them to monetise their skills and improve their quality of life. Providing investment capital for additional income generation can unlock their potential to solve many, if not all, of the manifestations of poverty.

During my efforts in development finance and rural development work for over three decades, I have seen projects and strategies succeed and fail. I have witnessed misguided project designs, poor implementation and squandering of large sums of money. But I have also seen incredible achievements. When development works well, it can transform lives by providing the underprivileged with the capital and knowledge to open up opportunities and reduce poverty.

The development community seems constantly and restlessly searching for a singular approach to 'solve' poverty, unveiling new buzzwords every few years only to toss them aside. The fundamental flaw with this system is that each new approach fails to break out of the underlying technocratic and specialized paradigm. We must understand that there is no precooked blueprint for replication. Individuals can make a difference in fighting poverty when we can institutionalize their creative ideas. An associated caveat when examining specific experiences with replication in mind is the personal charisma of inspirational leaders and organisational synergies, which are not readily transferable. We must respect that charisma and passion are natural and not inheritable traits. Similarly, there is a vast difference between being a rural banker by choice and being one by chance.

There is a glut of information on rural development. There is now a mountain of scholarship in rural development. There is a vast circuit in operation: dissecting statistics, burrowing through the library, wracking the brain and pontificating. Most development finance academics are researchers with little real-world experience. Leadership in rural development programmes is a clinical art; people need experience. The fact is that what works in Haryana does not seem to work well in Bihar. What works in India is not automatically transferable to Peru and vice versa. It is not particular about the exact reasons for the different disparities but is a product of cultural/societal, economic, and structural differences. In country X, lending to a group of wives living close to each other may be fine. In country Y, potential clients may not live in densely populated villages, husbands may feel uncomfortable having their wives take out loans and expand their businesses, and neighbours may be weary of borrowing altogether, not to mention a group.

These have been making points that if the consultants are so confident in their advice and plans, why don't they execute them? The adage about teachers changes slightly: "Those who can, do; those who cannot consult." I feel consultants must seek engagement with people with low incomes so that they have a more authentic feel of reality. We must remove our academic blinkers to understand the people we want to serve accurately. I have been inspired chiefly by people following their printed blasts with long, tiring journeys in inhospitable terrain to show their solidarity with these people. Consultants have never lived down the description of them in Robert Tomasend's *Up the Organization* as people who borrow your watch to tell you the time. Too many consultants are willing to give advice, most of which are descriptive and rarely contain prescriptions. It is the hubris of the consultant who believes he can wear down the problems with sheer studiousness. Consultants are like burnished glass: they live their whole lives off the reflected glory of the organisations they were privileged to provide consultancy. They keep on using the offensive word "holistic". It's the world's most pretentious word I have ever come across. Consultants have abused its original connotation and stripped it of its dignified place in the development lexicon. The indulgence in barren polemics remains just as ineffectual as it always was. Inevitably, the excess of hyperbole, metaphor and myth-making harm the cause.

Nevertheless, consultants do have a role to play. There is always something of continuing value about bringing an outsider in. If the consultant has a profound understanding, they can sniff out problems. A broad knowledge of how many other organizations have coped with similar issues can help provide solutions that the organizations themselves could never have encountered. In addition, consultants can act as disseminators to the real world of the latest thinking in the academic world and of their own often considerable inner research.

Poverty reduction is not a discipline. You can't get somebody from a university with a PhD in poverty reduction. Nor is there a talisman for eradicating poverty. It may not be possible to locate a common denominator for a thriving rural manager. It may also not be possible to lay down a standard blueprint for a rural development programme. From their experience, rural banking veterans can spell the recipe to be successful. However, the new managers must work out their recipes to blend these ingredients in the proper proportions. There is so much cultural diversity even in neighbouring villages that a blueprint for one village may need a drastic change for a town next to it.

The consultants live on a planet of their own in a total disconnect from the average citizen – dominated by fancy summits and conclaves indulging in steroidal hospitality at conferences. These are considered an essential saloon for designing unique and path-breaking solutions. The same big names on podiums, with lofty aspirations and oversized ambitions, preening and drooling the same set of figures, the exact weary phrases reverberating the halls, and the same residents chewing on the same cud. The same usual fanfare marks such events as development experts and barons of finance parade in their pinstripe suits, labour in their ivory towers, and ride in their jets as poor people continue to suffer the pangs of poverty. Glib talks about substitute rhetorical adrenaline. Public discourse is rarely nuanced. The public's attention span is short, and subtleties tend to confuse. It is better to take a clear, albeit incorrect, position, for at least the message gets through. The sharper and shriller it is, the more likely it is to get the public's attention, and the apparent focus is to frame the terms of the debate.

The failure in practice of so many typical professional solutions points to a re-examination of the perceptions and priorities of professionals — those standard, non-poor, urban-based and numerate members of elites who define poverty and what is necessary. The other is to examine the perceptions and priorities of people with low incomes themselves. Neither has received much attention in anti-poverty discussions. Most professionals — politicians, bureaucrats, scientists, academics and others, including ourselves — have plunged into debate and action in the middle without questioning what has brought us there, what we are supposed to see and believe, or what others see and accept. We have had neither time nor incentive to examine ourselves and our predispositions, nor people experiencing poverty and theirs.

There are development panjandrums, authors, and writers on rural development and planning who arrogate to themselves the right to hand out certificates on best practices. These people shut themselves from the world and give lengthy opinions based on journal reports and statistics. I have found even senior executives turning into glib talkers on poverty. Even publicly proclaiming their commitment to a public cause, they don't hesitate to speak in a different voice at internal forums.

The best advice I can proffer to young managers is not to drain themselves in sterile debates but to straight away plunge into the task:

Much to cast down, much to build, much to restore;
Let the work not delay, time and the arm not waste;
Let the clay be dug from the pit, let the saw cut the stone,
Let the fire not be quenched in the forge.

(*Choruses from the Rock* – T.S. Eliot)

I firmly believe it is possible to eliminate poverty in our country—provided we re-examine the wisdom we have received from our assumptions. The poor are poor not because they are unskilled or illiterate but because they cannot retain the returns of their labour. They neither own capital nor does anyone give them access to credit, except on the most unreasonable terms. They live on the edge, constantly fearing a catastrophe or tragedy, but they have no insurance because insurance companies consider them a losing proposition. The State's social safety nets are grossly inadequate and mired in corruption and bureaucratic red tape.

We need to bring in people with low incomes to the conversation. Interventions that consider the end user almost always have better success rates than top-down decision-making. However, many social enterprises are still not talking enough to their poor customers to find out what they want. Too often, policymakers have no idea what their end beneficiaries need. I hope that the expanding use of technology across all segments of society will help create platforms for exchanging ideas so that people can better express their needs.

Years of working on poverty issues in India teach one to be patient. It is a field with a great many experts. These experts are committed, knowledgeable, well-intentioned and used to speaking with authority. They are, perhaps understandably, a little impatient with upstarts who start talking about data and evidence and even sometimes implement large-scale interventions to fix things without necessarily having spent decades immersed in educational theory. Evidence-based insights help to open debate, broaden perspectives and catalyse progress.

People with low incomes are yet to find their voice, even as the media (for that matter, the entire establishment) have become the megaphones of the prospering classes. The preference for growth over social justice, indeed the argument that economic growth is the road to social justice, is advocated over and above increased spending and is required for accelerated growth to translate into inclusive growth. The answer, I fervently believe, lies in inclusive governance. In the absence of Inclusive governance, the people at the grassroots, the intended beneficiaries of poverty alleviation programmes, are left abjectly dependent on a bureaucratic delivery mechanism over which they have no effective control. The alternative system would be participatory development, where the people can build their future through elected representatives responsible to the local community and responsive to their needs.

The message in this book is that there is no grand, universal formula for poverty reduction. The fight has to be on several fronts; what works in one place does not necessarily work everywhere. The way forward lies in grassroots field experiments for understanding the causal relationships between poor people's behaviour and learning by doing. My faith in poor people's ability to climb out of the rut is unshakeable, and my core belief is gradualism. I believe that lasting social change most often—and perhaps permanently—comes slowly rather than in a burst of revolutionary fervour. It is this belief that has shaped my work. I also believe that lasting change can occur only when women get equal opportunities for financial empowerment. If you're poor, you're disadvantaged, but if you're poor and also a woman, you are doubly disadvantaged. A poor rural woman's finds the best expression in Maya Angelou's poignant words:

I've got the children to tend
The clothes to mend
The floor to mop
The food to shop
Then, the chicken to feed
The garden to weed
I've got shirts to press
The tots to dress
The cane to be cut
I got a clean up this hut
Then, see about the sick
And the cotton to pick
Shine on me, sunshine
Rain on me, rain
Fall softly, dewdrops
And cool my brow again

In this book, I have said things which may sound critical, wounding, and even angry. In expiation, I can say that I have been as bitter about many societies, including my own. I do not mean to be hurtful to warm and generous people who have never been other than kind to me, wherein I have seen things challenging. It is because they are cruel and hostile to India itself.

Speaking out, I felt, would relieve me of a load of agitated thoughts and emotions.

Speak, your lips are free.
Speak, it is your own tongue.
Speak, it is your own body.
Speak. Your life is still yours.

See how in the blacksmith's shop
The flame burns wild. The iron glows red;
The locks open their jaws,
And every chain begins to break.
(Faiz Ahmed Faiz)

It is not to say that I have been unhappy with my former employers. I set out to write this diary because I wanted to tell the story rather than let it ferment into anger and discontent. I firmly believe that my younger colleagues would be able to put the lessons herein to good worth. But the more critical part lies in the opportunity this diary affords to publicly acknowledge the debt I owe to so many people: villagers, volunteers and the staff of banks, government and development agencies who put up with some of my wild adventures in the rural planet and made serious attempts to give them both workable and doable shape.

This book is built entirely on anecdotal evidence. I never wanted to submerge the central idea in a deluge of statistics or swamp the readers with mind-boggling figures. These figures are available in tomes and tomes of government reports already. I was keener to profile the trajectory of individual lives of grit, tenacity, determination, and honesty, which has given the women in this book an exalted status in bankers' eyes. To quote the great TS Eliot:

Where is the life we have lost in living?
Where is the wisdom we have lost in knowledge?
Where is the knowledge we have lost in information?

How does one tell the story of a statistic? One man is a person, a thousand are a community, and a million are a statistic. Or, as Joseph Stalin exclaimed, "A single death is a tragedy; a million deaths is a statistic." I decided to write something that wouldn't reinforce the statistics that make India millions but would look instead for the faces behind the figures. As each face becomes a person, numbers cease being an abstraction. Facts have supplanted understanding, and knowledge can no longer generate wisdom. Every school of thought has contrived its language of clichés and jargon understandable only by its exclusive devotees who jealously guard the entry of any new initiate. Human knowledge has become too fantastic for the human mind; every science has begotten a dozen more, each subtler than the rest. But even after the knowledge explosion, all that remains is the scientific specialist who knows more and more about less and less and the philosophical speculator who knows more and less about more and more.

I am constantly reminded of *The Little Prince* by Antoine de Saint-Exupery, in which he makes the telling point that adults think that only those things that numbers can describe are accurate. In contrast, it is much more interesting to explain things the way they are:

'Grown-ups love figures. When you tell them you have made a new friend, they never ask you any questions about essential matters. They never say to you, 'What does his voice sound like? What games does he love best? Does he collect butterflies? Instead, they demand: 'How old is he? How many brothers has he? How much does he weigh? How much money does his father make?'Only from these figures do they think they

have learned anything about him. If you were to say to the grown-ups: 'I saw a beautiful house made of rosy brick, with geraniums in the windows and doves on the roof,' they would not understand that house. You must tell them: 'I saw a house that cost $20,000.' Then they would exclaim: 'Oh, what a pretty house that is!'

The problem is that anecdotal evidence often seems more compelling than dry statistics. Social scientists are wary about using stories as evidence for a claim. Anecdotes not backed up with systematic and rigorous comparative data are not trusted. Anecdotes are the weakest form of evidence, but they are often the most persuasive. Even scientists find a telling anecdote contradicting a mass of statistical evidence. Anecdotes need careful use because we are psychologically susceptible to them. Anecdotes are not analyses, nor should they be. Yet, as a way of taking a society's temperature, of prodding and seeing what gives, I cannot think of any better.

Can we get a better picture of the plight of the Indian farmer than the vivid portrait painted by Rudyard Kipling:

His speech if of mortgaged bedding,
On his kine he borrows yet.
At his heart is his daughter's wedding.
In his eye foreknowledge of debt
He eats and hath indigestion
He toils and he may not stop,
His life Is a long-drawn question
Between a crop and a crop

(The Masque of Plenty)

My diary provides neither macro-narrative nor any catch-all explanations. My intent and direction lie elsewhere. My overarching goal is to give a flavour of the evolving rural India through its people, through their hopes and passions, their opinions and their perceptions. Such an approach is unapologetically subjective.

All our development programmes give priority to mathematical analysis and computer remodelling. There is an overemphasis on technology. The top management feels that the investments in technology can address all development issues. Tech-savvy and business school boys seem to be the answer to the problems of managing and scaling development programmes. All this makes it hard for an average professional development worker to understand and serve rural life's local, complex, diverse, dynamic and unpredictable realities—all the issues field workers face need to be classified as fixed templates and solutions.

I had a little fascination for figures, and at least in the initial years, banking appeared more like a number cruncher's delight. I found it hard to cope with the tedious wading through lists of figures. I was delighted more by peering beyond dry, lifeless figures and observing the millions of human actions that these figures represented. Analysis is not my strong suit; still, one would expect a creative writer to seek out individual experiences to tell stories of the changes in people's lives and emotions wrought by broader historical processes. It is all too rarely that a sense of style and an eye for beauty co-exist with a head for facts and figures and a flair for statistical analysis. I was fortunate to be reasonably endowed with both. Numbers may have never amused me, but I had developed a fair degree of flair for them. Nevertheless, I was not uncomfortable with them.

Successful rural bankers do believe in writing intricate business plans. However, they focus their energy, intelligence, and skills on creating businesses that thrive in a challenging environment where social skills are as critical as financial skills. Even if it means deploying financial resources, rural development has social levelling as its overarching goal. Since you are part of an economic planet, you must work through equations honed by financial experts and then create your own. However, you cannot find convincing answers in spreadsheets and databases.

Human behaviour is far too complex to be captured by mathematical models. Forecasting does not require tremendous prescience; it only needs to connect the dots using theoretical frameworks thrown up by credit analysts. Business plans, which contain stereotypical optimism, all appear maddening. The old rule of forecasting was to make as many forecasts as possible and publicize the ones you got right. The new rule is to forecast so far into the future that no one will know you got it wrong. Experts, including the celebrated author of *The Black Swan*, Nassim Nicholas Taleb, and Stanford finance professor Anat Admati, have written that banks can twist data to make ungrounded predictions yet sufficient to pass government-mandated stress tests.

The biggest misconception about banking is that people think one should have a degree in business or finance to do well in this industry. Banking is a generalist profession dealing with diverse sectors. An educational background in economics or finance may help one understand banking concepts. However, the person with the right mix of personal qualities and managerial skills will rise above the rest in the long run. These include the ability to learn quickly and continuously, openness to new challenges, disciplined professionalism, an outgoing and inquisitive nature, an analytical and systematic mind, negotiation savvy and personal integrity.

In my early days, working in a bank seemed like intellectual vegetation. Figures held no fascination for me, and the initial flush of enthusiasm soon faded in the thick of mainstream banking, which had its then-prevalent focus on retail business and housing finance. The day-to-day pressures of the job and the weight of administrative responsibilities put my dream of full-time engagement with villages on hold. However, the building blocks for my future work were slowly evolving when I first experimented with my wildly adventurous development finance plans at Chandrapur almost two decades ago. My part-time experiments soon blossomed into full-time immersion in the world of India's villages.

Many authors, papers, institutions and country case studies have been seminal to our understanding of the theory and practice of development finance. There is, in fact, a mountain of scholarship. It will be vain to claim my book to be in the same league. It is not a scholarly work; if any reader is anticipating some rare and astounding revelations, he will be disillusioned. The book only reinforces the wisdom gleaned from the experiences of great bankers, sociologists, development experts and thousands of anonymous names across the country.

I hope that, in different ways for different readers, the book will challenge received wisdom and provoke richer understandings of political, social, academic, economic and financial institutions, combining lessons from the classroom and the field.

* * * * *

1. A BANKER TO THE POOR

I joined the rural banking bandwagon at a critical period in the history of development banking, during a time of unresolved conflict between two tendencies in developing countries: the emergence of a massive range of creative solutions to the problem of lending to poor people, all of which interfered with the market mechanism, and the universal pressure from global financial institutions for removing these interferences. I was fiery with passion and enthralled by the heady slogans of the period, encouraging youth to lend their hand to eradicating poverty.

When I started my banking career, many of the developing-country practitioners with whom we worked at the time put their finger on the key questions arising out of the conflict between those advocating market-led solutions for fighting poverty and those who believed that sustained grants and aid from the State. When and where is intervention at the bottom end of the financial market justified? Of what kind: direct intervention, subsidy, regulation or something else? The literature of that time, which consisted more of polemic and counter-polemic than empirical investigation, did not answer all these questions. All we could do was to get a flavour of the aggressive debate in the hope that it might stimulate us to forge solutions that might at least have validity within our local working environment.

While still at university, studying economics, politics, anthropology, journalism and sociology, I dreamt of a full-time career in research and academics, writing critical notes on development programmes. Only when I came in close contact with rural realities did I decide to start as a ditch digger and learn the ropes of rural development by myself. I remember Walt Disney's classic quote, "The way to get started is to quit talking and start doing." Che Guevara, whose handsome face I had seen on posters and tee shirts, also came to mind. I did not know who he was till I read this passage attributed to him, "The merit of Marx is that he suddenly produces a qualitative change in the history of social thought. He interprets history, understands its dynamics, and predicts the future. Still, besides predicting it, he expresses a revolutionary concept: "The world must not only be interpreted, it must be transformed."

That was the epiphany for me, an experience nearly universal for social entrepreneurs. It reinforces that their work is less about money and profits than innovating unique and revolutionary solutions to the challenging human problems that elude answers. The satisfaction derived was immense and was always deeply personal. Since then, my sole preoccupation has been working with development programmes focused on empowering low-income people, especially women. Like every social entrepreneur, I constantly tested and retaught ideas, processes, and procedures.

I was born into a family where hard work and education were paramount. I admire my parents for teaching their children the values of hard work, justice and commitment. My father was a highly successful jurist and public figure who taught me the values of professionalism, while my mother passed on to me her artistic sensibilities. They formed the twin strands of my genetic code, though other threads also bind us together. They taught me that life was a struggle to achieve excellence in every area one touched.

For a million reasons, my dad was my hero. He was a master of humorous anecdotes that turned into morality tales. He was my greatest coach and still appears in my head, forcing me to work harder to improve whenever I feel like quitting. He gave me a feedback loop for life. My parents taught me the importance of getting the argument right. I do not always measure up to the exact standards of precision they set for themselves, but I understood the proper standard. They instilled in me a sense of social justice and impatience with the injustice one saw in the world around oneself.

In particular, I knew what was fair and what was not. The notion that you can always question authority was wrong, and this belief was fundamental to my parents; they had worked their way up the hard way. You can always ask how things are and then try to do something about it. I grew up surrounded by talk of revolution and justice. I have consistently jousted with titans on behalf of people experiencing poverty, who have been my crucial constituency in my professional career. A part of me, which comes from my parents, always wanted to do something useful for the world. Working in the development sector is the only way to get an intuitive sense of how people live.

My entry into banking was more by providence than by intent. I wrote the examination, faced the interview, got through it, and decided to try it. I was fascinated by development finance and decided to stick to it. I owe my romance with rural banking to a posting as a credit manager at the State Bank of India, India's biggest bank. I first learned directly about the power of the formal finance sector for the social and economic development of low-income people from the famous 1954 All India Rural Credit Survey. While interviewed by the press, the great novelist Aubrey Menon had to name what he considered the most important book written in India since Independence. He replied: "The 1954 All India Rural Credit Survey." I was fortunate to have read it in college, and it dramatically affected me. The best part of the survey was not that it was highly understandable, but it was inexhaustible; it rewarded rereading. It taught me and changed me as I grew older with it.

This survey's recommendations foreshadowed initiatives by governments and international organizations across the developing world and emphasised expansion to access to formal credit in rural, unbanked locations. The report's rationale for such initiatives had two essential premises. First, supply-led, inexpensive formal credit was necessary to displace 'evil' moneylenders who exploited their monopoly to charge high-interest rates and were, therefore, net contributors to rural poverty. Second, state-led expansions of cheap credit were necessary to allow poor, rural households to adopt new technologies and production processes and thus escape the cycle of poverty and indebtedness.

My foray into rural banking was a radical move. If someone wants to work in a village, the formal education system is a discouragement. The mindset that this system inculcates in students is that going back to the villages is a losing proposition. Remaining in the city is considered a success.When I decided to take up a rural assignment in the bank, most of my friends thought I was crazy. My parents were appalled and aghast. "You can't possibly go and stay in a village for months and years. The very idea is preposterous. It's good as a tourist but not as one who will be working with them. You'll take the toddy, the staple hospitality drink served by the villagers, to drink. When broken in mind and body, you will creep back to the city, looking and behaving like a tropical tramp off a banana boat, with good intentions ridiculed and rejected. You'll be met with hostility and suspicion by co-workers, politicians, and even the intended aid recipients." When they saw my determination, my mother was reluctantly supportive, and my father, too, came around slowly. My bosses hesitated to let me go to a village but conceded when they found me passionately determined. They prodded, quizzed, needled and unsettled me for days until they finally stopped, satisfied that I knew what I was choosing.

I had always been on the side that criticized and evaluated the government and other public institutions, first as a journalist and then as a civil society activist. I was entering the very structure I had questioned all these years. Most people who knew me were surprised at my decision—"You and the establishment?" after all, a public sector institution was also a State-controlled body. To some extent, so was I. But beneath the trepidation, there was excitement. As a journalist, I was often frustrated at not being able to bring about a change. I could see, show, and give to hear, but that was what was ordained. After one particularly passionate outburst in which I felt like joining a protest rally against corruption, which I was covering for my newspaper, my mentor warned me, "You are a journalist, not an activist."

Something about rural India was calling me. I wished to connect with my roots and deeply explore my spiritual relationship with the villages. I have always had a passion for development and social service, so it was only natural for me to go to villages to work in this arena. At college, I visited villages concerning my reporting assignments as part of my National Service Scheme internship. However, my exposure to the intricacies of rural problems and social and economic tyrannies was sparse as I was already pursuing my agenda.

I was a city-bred youth educated in Cambridge-affiliated schools in Nagpur and Bombay. I had my education in the archaic curriculum of Shakespeare's sonnets with an elementary literacy in Marathi, the regional language. My Presbyterian school taught me the first introductory lesson of life—not to show off. If you do not acquire the fine art of suppressing your ego when you are young, that ego will surely overtake you when you are older, becoming an incurable disease. What is worse is that you become an incorrigible bore. Humans are not born humble, and the tendency to show off is quite natural. Still, that tendency has to be subdued and restrained, or else it usurps one's sensibilities and starts corroding those finer qualities of the heart that define an individual's aesthetic and humanist responses. As Groucho Marx said, "Humility is a strange thing; the moment you know you have got it, you have lost it."

I had the most snobbish, exclusive education imaginable and could have qualified for any lucrative job. "How can some people live in such penury—and we who go through the best education don't give anything back?" I wondered. This combination of a prickling conscience with compunction and anger drove me to seek a career in rural finance.

It didn't involve too much of a sacrifice. The bank for which I was working didn't have a very steep difference in salary between a posting in a metro centre and one in a village. The only difference was that the employees didn't think it was sufficient compensation for the discomfort and hardship a posting in a rural centre entailed. The city postings carried attractive allowances apart from incentives, such as having the status of financial philosopher kings in the making. You also got an opportunity to acquire a robust set of financial skills that could help you leapfrog ahead in your career; one also acquired an appendage of a heavenly nature: forex expert, wealth manager, corporate banker, and credit head.

The physical, intellectual and emotional adventures the job provided seemed adequate compensation for those passionate about serving villages, despite the monetary loss and mental and physical hardship one suffered. Most of my peers did not share this optimism and felt that the management ought to compensate those working in villages through additional career rewards. I must admit that the city bankers suffered disdain and envy in social and financial circles. Those days, we didn't have the new generation private banks we have today, and the so-called elite bankers in our organisation monopolised most financial events. They soon became perfumed young men with shiny attaché cases and were welcomed as banking yuppies. Their assignments were a sure passport to the charmed circles of the bank.

The rural and corporate branches of a bank were worlds apart. Rural bank officers were in stark contrast to this elite class, which sported the countenance of savvy and dapper princes. Visiting a rural bank office, you could expect to see the staff in casual street clothes instead of the flamboyant corporate bankers' impeccable three-piece pinstripe suits and Hermes neckties with matching pocket squares. You were more likely to find a rusty motor scooter leaning against a tree outside a minuscule archaic-looking, weather-beaten and sparsely furnished office than the polished marble counters, carpets and luxury cars parked in reserved spaces of metro offices.

While we rural managers survived on snacks infested with marauding flies followed by poisonous-looking syrupy tea, our glamorous colleagues cruised in fast cars. Their entertainment ideas were Jazz Yatra concerts. Men wore suits and fat-knotted ties, yellow and pink; women frilly dresses. Their assistants would be dressed preppily in polo shirts and khaki pants, hair tied into taut ponytails and speaking with a coolly British accent or the upper-crust Indian version. In contrast, rural bankers had to wear attire that was acceptable to the rural culture. Hazardous roads made sophisticated two-wheelers out of the way. Instead, the hardy but clumsy-looking Yamaha, used by dairy owners for carrying milk to nearby towns, was the staple transport for bank officers and all government staff working in villages.

I knew there were no rewards for working in villages. Even today, when unemployment rates have zoomed in, and amenities in rural areas have improved considerably, working in a town is still considered a stigma. In our time, you lost out on promotions and languished in obscurity on the matrimonial map. At worst, you suffered the image of being punished for barking at the management by being posted to God-forsaken places. I had known many who would make nothing out of rural careers except returning with headaches and blisters.

But there were brighter sides, particularly if you were imbued with an adventurous spirit of transforming the society around you and felt many outstanding development programmes were not reaching low-income people. If one could risk an adventure, there could be sure rewards for a determined individual. I had taken a rural assignment out of my desire for an engagement with development programmes in villages. I had spent my days in school and college in a metropolis. I may not have been professionally acceptable for rural work, but I had the confidence and the temperament to compensate for other deficiencies.I was a professional banker taught and trained in complex and coarse grammar. Still, at the same time, I knew I was a developmental worker, always keen to empathize with people experiencing poverty and their cause. I wanted to stretch my brain on something that genuinely excited me.

A college education is not always essential for being groomed as a banker. Still, if, besides the liberal culture gained at a university, a man acquires a unique knowledge of finance, economics, sociology, psychology, history and the science of governance, he is better fitted to handle the varied problems of traditional and modern banking. A social anthropology and agriculture background can immensely help bankers overlooking rural financial operations.Any achieving banker will soon find himself thrust out of a comfortably known field into an unfamiliar one. He must be open to challenges. He must learn the ropes before he can guide others. A banker must master and micromanage details. A banker knows the surface of many disciplines but the depths of none; he should be ready to unlearn certain theoretical assumptions if his life experience warrants him.

Although I began my career in the exciting and turbulent world of industrial finance, development finance (which in lay terms means financial services for people experiencing poverty here) became an abiding passion and a lifelong obsession for me in the years that came. Even when posted on assignments unconnected with development finance, I kept involved in the field and updated with newer developments through academic journals, workshops, and seminars. I would also use my annual Social Service Leave to join village rehabilitation camps. The roots I had put down were not so shallow that I could pull them up when my assignment ended. I have cart-wheeled across the country but have always remained anchored to thoughts of village life. When my bosses reminded me, "Well, then *don't* sit in air-conditioned rooms and make policies without knowing the people whose lives depend on them .," I knew I had found true kindred spirits.

My first banking assignment disillusioned me after the failure of a big cotton mill financed by our bank. I knew it was the type which would never allow me to sleep peacefully. If I were unlucky, it would also mean endless enquiries, charge sheets and lawsuits. It was then that I realized I'd find working for people with low incomes more satisfying as there were so many development programmes that provided both a learning opportunity and a chance to assist people experiencing poverty, particularly in rural areas.

But this job was not without its bagful of hazards. You can understand my family's hardships, aside from the mental acrobatics needed to adapt to an alien culture, where one had to spend several nights without electricity, potable water, proper food grains and cooking oil. In those days, villagers were not so health conscious, nor did their income levels permit the quality of products they now afford. Wheat and rice, now consumed even by the poorest, were then a luxury for even the wealthiest in the villages.

It was my love and passion for books and literature that sustained me. It helped keep my communication skills alive, enabling me to compete with officers who waxed eloquently on rural development at seminars and conferences, even when none stayed overnight in a village. When the bank made rural postings mandatory, the blue-eyed staff of the management got industrial and forex branches situated barely outside the municipal limits of urban centres. However, they qualified as rural centres because their location was beyond the city limits. They did not serve people experiencing poverty but rather the prominent industrialists. It facilitated their completion of mandatory rural assignments. In this way, the bank made a sham of so-called rural assignments. The management and unions, generally at loggerheads, would always strike a truce on postings for their buddies at convenient centres.

I knew full well that I was an outsider in a strange civilisation. I would never be able to understand the area as well as a local person. However,

I also had unique experiences and a critique of development processes born from varied experiences. My academic studies in anthropology gave me an insight into rural and tribal societies. A stint as a journalist equipped me with valuable insights into the realpolitik of the country's development programmes and familiarized me with the rural ecosystem. I was going without any mental baggage of biases and prejudices which could colour my worldview.

In a mood of adventure, I took the bus for my first rural job in the village of Bina in the district of Nagpur. A man hanging on the back of the bus constantly yelled our route. Near a town, he screamed, "Refreshment and freshening halt; strictly five minutes." The driver coasted to the curb, yanked the hand brake and parked the bus to let passengers off at a little thatch-roofed tea shack where a smell of cooking oil and tobacco hung in the crisp air. On the highway, a "dhaba" is a catchall term that can include truck stops, car parks and sometimes nothing at all, with string cots lined up so you can lie down and relax after a happy meal. We discovered that our "dhaba" was a cafe. The cafe owner brought us sweet tea, puris, pakora dollops of chutney and pickles, and watery tomato sauce, which he frequently leaked from the plastic bottle.

Finally, the bus stopped and the driver shouted, "Bina". "Bina"! Get down here." I realized it was my turn to disembark. The bus roared away, leaving me on the roadside in the dark. There was no sign of any village, let alone one called "Bina". I had planned to arrive during daylight, but the bus left late and then spent two hours in a greasy mechanic's yard on the plains, as the exhaust pipe had detached from the engine.

We arrived in a small village about 30 minutes later, clearly not my destination. Though my Marathi was a little rusty, I asked the driver where he had taken me. He told me he had brought me the wrong way and tried to extort money to take me to my destination, but finally drove me to the right signpost. I gave the auto-rickshaw driver a considerable tip for not murdering me. It was pitch dark. Not a soul in sight. Even the stars had forgotten to light up the sky. To my relief, I could see somebody flashing a torch—my caretaker.

My first shock did not appear in my office but rather during the first night of my homestay. It was so quiet I could hear the goat's hooves clattering on the cobblestones and the murmuring of the distant monkeys. A long bulb glowed dimly, threatening to go out at any moment, casting surreal shadows on the walls. I writhed on the mattress, succumbing to all the aggressors: the heat, the mosquitoes, the stabbing bedsprings. I woke up scratching the blisters on my shoulders. The night had been a frantic experience, and all morning, the nostalgia lingered, making the house seem dreamlike, dreary, looming, like a set of a great mystery film.

The first-morning contact with a village is usually pleasing. I vividly remember my first day in the town, where I spent two years managing a village bank. It looked like a painting of an old pastoral village, with tiled roofs jigsawed together and mud-brick houses faded. It was a dusty warren of thatched huts, tiled roofs and brightly painted temples. I followed a footpath down the hill, deserted but for a herd of goats, and crossed the stream where women washed laundry, whacking clothes on boulders and drying them on shrubs. Older men, not entirely put out to pasture, cogitated while supervising small herds of cows.

I found the change – the slow pace of life, the stillness and silence, the smoky fire, the stones in the rice and the domestic chores – hard to adapt. The zeal of a volunteer in the village can erode quickly. That incredible stoicism is everywhere. It appeared to be a bitter medicine, but I needed it. I quickly grew impatient with poignant snapshots of Indian squalor: the ribby children with flies in their eyes and other emblems of abjectness that one can't help but see within five minutes of walking into a village. Sometimes, he gazes at his open palms with a questioning look, expecting the lines there to tell him something or his hands to explain how they have been left empty.

I had arrived in Bina with an overblown sense of my nobility and preparedness and, more naïvely, under-equipped for the responsibilities. I also profoundly underestimated the cultural baggage I unwittingly carried everywhere with me. I started my work in the village driven by the notion that I would help people experiencing poverty. Still, I discovered that noble missions do not necessarily add to extraordinary achievement. The usual linguistic faux pas and cultural gaffes contribute today to my repertoire of comical stories to tell at gatherings, but there were more severe mistakes.

I soon saw what happened when the 'educated' tried to 'help' the poor—how bureaucrats gave subsidized loans for high-yielding Jersey cows, which died in harsh drought conditions, leaving the poor worse off. How the veterinarians fleeced villagers, charging what top physicians and surgeons in cities didn't dare to charge affluent patients. How education failed to prepare poor children for getting a job yet alienated them from their traditional economies. The whole experience purged me of pretensions and made me realize my inadequacies. My mind had flabby conclusions drawn from sloppy reading. I substituted journals, books and films on rural projects for the fiction I intended to read in the coming months.

Going into my internship, I was unclear about what rural development entailed. Unprepared, with no road map, tools, insufficient gear, and protective layering, I decided to spend time with the people and listen to the communities. Early into my journey, I realized that my preconceived notions hindered my understanding of the issues and concerns. Instead, I needed to look at the problems of people experiencing poverty through their eyes. My pre-departure vision was one of heroically entering remote villages and, after briefly surveying the issues, rapidly coming up with solutions to better the lives of the villagers. I did not realize how crucial any project's sustainability was for the villagers, not the "development experts", to plan their schemes.

I had always imagined that the poor were ignorant and uneducated. Most people I consulted before starting my rural mission admired my aspiration but moderated my enthusiasm with caveats. "They know a lot more than we do. You can, at best, learn from them." "Don't try suppressing their culture; that will be the greatest disservice." I initially wrote off these responses as an attempt to unnerve me. Later, I realized that these youthful exchanges were not pure banter.

My fertile, overheated conscience was further stung by my academic reading of the sufferings of people in Latin American countries. Driven by guilt, buried under the weight of my attractive job and the sight of excruciating poverty every day, I volunteered to spend the weekends off from my office with villagers, trying to make up for the fact that I had so much while they had so little.

I put away my books and immersed myself in the rhythms of villages, learning from people with low incomes, understanding their problems, and trying to see their culture and society through their eyes. I had to invert everything I'd learned in economics classes. My status as a qualified sociologist was worth zilch. The heaviness of success was replaced by the lightness of being a beginner again, less sure about everything. That status did make me a little ashamed of my inadequacies, yet it freed me to enter one of the most creative periods of my life. I was able to turn my ideas into workable goals. The humble beginnings taught me life as only a villager can know. It brought me to terms with the inadequacy of my learning. I realised I had to become part of the villagers' heartbeat to be in a position to help them.

The bookish definitions of poverty have never hooked me: this much income or that much calorie intake. Poverty is the absence of adequate nutrition, clean water, basic sanitation and health care, education, and enforced constitutional rights. Poverty is the inability to secure the minimum consumption requirements for life, health and efficiency. Poverty is an insufficient supply of those things that are requisite for an individual to maintain himself and those dependent upon him in terms of health and vigour. The problem of poverty is considered the biggest challenge to development planning in India. High poverty levels are synonymous with poor quality of life, deprivation, malnutrition, illiteracy and low human resource development. Poverty is a social phenomenon in which a section of society cannot fulfil even its necessities of life. When people with low incomes live on the edge of subsistence, a minuscule misfortune can push them down into a tailspin. With nearly four out of five Indians living in poverty, Illnesses become a financial sinkhole for village women; they often drop out of the labour force as they provide most of the care. TB has now at least gone from being a death sentence to a manageable illness. The government has been building awareness of malaria by popularising blood tests wherever anyone has a fever. Similarly, polio is almost on the verge of getting worse. Mosquito nets and repellents are being liberally used even in remote villages.

The real tragedy of people experiencing poverty is that their voices are unheard in forums, even those exclusively devoted to their problems. As the Madagasy proverb goes, "poverty won't allow him to lift his head, dignity won't allow him to bow it down". They are shouted down by those who consider them illiterate and uninformed and abrogate to themselves the wisdom and the right to speak for people experiencing poverty. The oppression of impatience only came to me when I was on the other side years later. It is unpleasant for anyone to get pushed away with an "All right, certainly, now sit down" when that person is halfway through expressing an issue of life and death. And, of course, the public places where such meetings occur are designed to keep people experiencing poverty from any scope for voicing their problems.

No amount of reading or instructions could have taught me what I learnt during the years I spent in the hinterland. Henry Miller once said, "One's destination is never a place, but a new way of seeing things." I had a rare opportunity to connect with my country and its people, to see and understand the everyday realities of the everyday lives of the rural poor. I learnt to be less judgmental. I saw first-hand the consequences of all that ails our system. Yet, for the first time, I realized how easy it was to blame the government for everything; stepping inside and instituting change was much more difficult. Despite being connected through the news and media, I recognized how isolated we all are. The peasants, I believe, might have a keener understanding of the development and its implications than the economists sitting in the rarefied atmosphere of Yojana Bhavan.

This distance that has grown between the manager and his clients in the rural matrix has plagued the rural financial system. Too much dependence on data and less direct engagement with low-income people have been the primary causes of failure for most state-mandated development programmes.

I sometimes feel that the younger managers are now reluctant to accept rural assignments because they lack mentoring. Something has gone askew somewhere in the alchemy. We have been unable to build a new generation of committed rural bankers. So, are development practitioners born or made? The answer has been following my instincts and being in an environment that cultivated and directed my talents. Banking claimed me but could not hold me hostage to its rules, as I craved innovative ways. I rarely worked within conventional possibilities and was never impressed by the rarefied starched-shirt world of banking officialdom. I was not a rebel, but I felt leading life the way one knows best was essential.

There was a famous adage, "A village could be known as uninhabitable only if it did not have a branch of a bank." The depth and outreach of the banking network in the late seventies grew at a sizzling pace because of onerous government mandates. It was when the transport and communication infrastructure in the country was abysmally weak, unlike today when mobile phones, email, SMS and Skype enable you to communicate anywhere, any time.

We used to spend evenings with the village headmen, trying to understand the local culture and how we could best tailor schemes to meet the local needs. The *Village Adoption Scheme*, introduced by the government country-wide, was an innovation that helped banks build up professional credit culture in villages and empower the rural population with information about new agricultural technologies and development finance. Fortunately, politics had still not seeped into the rural fabric, and few factions were in the villages. A consensus of village elders would select the village headman (sarpanch). The headman was usually a sober, just and committed individual. Unlike today, the village headman would ensure the villagers enthusiastically embraced our programmes.

Villagers may be uneducated, but they are incredibly clever and good at telling an outsider what they think the outsider wants to hear. The truth of a village may come out only slowly, with time for trust to build between the villagers and outsiders and time for the outsider to peel away all the layers to get at the truth. I was there in the villages during the blistering heat of May, the chilling cold of December, the spring harvest festival and the September election for the *sarpanch* (headman). When the electricity failed, as it so often did, I would scribble notes by candlelight. I would drive through the sodden winter fogs to be in time for the meeting with the villagers. Most of them would leave home quite early for their fields. A delay on my part would mean a meeting loss.

It could be a drive in the milky whiteness of the dawn or the blazing darkness of the night along rutted paths as the warm air swirled over my face, my thoughts whirling me into a trance. I might have to plod through rain and slush. My hair would get as chaotic as the thorn bushes we passed on the road, and the villagers wondered whether I'd combed it properly in the first place.

During my engagement with people with low incomes as a bank manager handling rural finance, I found in them a reservoir of grit, wisdom, tenacity and courage that enabled them to cope with severe adversities. I had not known how brutal poverty could be until I encountered it almost daily, but the memories haunted me over the years. How the sick went without medicines, how children dropped out of school because parents could not afford education, and how young children went cotton picking to add to the family's kitty. Amartya Sen argues in his book *Development as Freedom* that poverty is 'capability deprivation'. These adolescents, facing a volatile situation at an early stage of life due to economic insecurity, are not simply poor but rather 'incapable' individuals who lack the primary means to enjoy the rights and freedoms enshrined in the Indian Constitution. In highly patriarchal societies, sudden access to skills and money can alter the dynamics of a woman's relationship with the people around her in unpredictable ways.

I had always wondered why rural poverty had defied all solutions. My exploration led me to a unique conclusion: first, the poor lacked capital and second, insurance against tragedies wrought by nature, to which people experiencing poverty were particularly vulnerable. I learned this during my extension work for the National Service Scheme as a university student.

I have learned and understood many things about working with poor people, but nothing is more evident than that poor people do not have to remain poor forever. People experiencing poverty remain poor because they are powerless. Once empowered, people experiencing poverty can overcome seemingly impossible odds. But people cannot transform their lives all on their own. The first step is to change the overall perception of development academics and policy designers about poor people—from needy beneficiaries to active architects of their development.

I had set a clear vision: to create new spaces and terms for poor village women. I knew my limitations and decided not to extend my agenda beyond this limited horizon. I always clarified that I was not there to drive the existing agencies out of business. Nor was I going to supplant the government welfare departments. I always warmly embraced the various functionaries in the development apparatus. I felt this limited agenda should help me to endear myself even to my worst opponents. Prejudices exist in the most open cultures, so society requires tempered radicals which can act as catalytic agents, bringing change without tearing down established and respected structures and picking out rotten apples without upsetting the apple cart. I always felt that the best way to finish an enemy was to make him a friend. As events unfolded, I was happy to find that I had taken the correct route. My good relationship with the village leaders helped me get the government's help. With time, even the rage of political leaders had all but gone or mellowed.

I learnt the hard lesson that helping improve lives and fostering economic development is complex, often because of locals' scepticism about the work of 'development experts'. "We don't hate you," they would tell me, "What we hate is what you represent." As I grappled with rural realities, I began to view the village and its environs more like a native than an outsider. Not only did I get used to the smells, dirt, dust, winds, noise, insects and vermin and the lack of privacy, but I also learned to distinguish good land from evil, the various properties of the plants and trees in the area. I picked up insights into good veterinary practices. The canvas of the story was ready to stretch wider, move further and include new friends: villagers from the neighbouring village, local rural leaders and a massive planet of development practitioners.

I saw how some of the world's poorest and most oppressed people are changing our world. But nowhere was my journey through development more influenced than in an unassuming village where I stayed whenever

I had the chance over the last fifteen years. This village, Wanoja, became a microcosm of all I saw elsewhere, stuck as it was in centuries of tradition. Only the names changed. It provided me with friends and joyful moments and sometimes gave me hope for human progress. But, just as often, it crushed that hope in the nasty friction between irresolvable social divisions. Even in the violence that submerged my village, I saw the hope of people breaking the status quo and gaining a voice. I saw women grappling with intense poverty. I heard the struggles of the women at the grassroots. Initially, I often broke down in confusion, not knowing what contribution I could make. Still, over time, I decided that my future lay with these poor but tenacious women fighting daily misfortunes to build a decent future for their families.

More than any other professional unit, a rural bank branch requires unique skills, mainly when few people are willing to work in villages and when your priorities are not the affluent farmers but poor, helpless and disadvantaged women. There is no point in making anyone in your team feel needlessly inadequate. I was never a slave of my own opinion. Instead, I listened to others. We must focus on each person's strengths and manage around their weaknesses. We shouldn't try to perfect each person but help each cultivate their talents and become more of who they already are. Your team may have a moody person, but careful handling may enable him to deliver the most beautiful results. There are a lot of people who don't enjoy the work they do. They tolerate it under duress and wait for the weekend. I have also met people who love what they do and can't imagine doing anything else. The expression we use is that they're in their element. It's what ignites their energy. It's their enthusiasm that must parlayed into commitment.

A community will always make a better decision than an individual. An open system means more voices, discussion, and criticism, leading to better decisions. I always bounced my thoughts off my staff. That's why building consensus is vital to the process. I wanted all these voices to come together in my projects. It is essential to get all stakeholders to play a role in exploring a solution by giving them a voice in the process. It also helps to look at old problems in new ways, putting a new twist on something already done. Team-building, consensus-building and innovative solutions are the keys to success. I demonstrated both trust and faith in my team. Ralph Waldo Emerson once said: "Trust men, and they will be true to you; treat them greatly, and they will show themselves great."

People can do wonders if their energy is channelled and focused on a given task. People make tomorrows. I learned early in life that great leaders don't teach. They touch and transform. They don't instruct. Their conduct and disposition inspire them. They help people discover within themselves the strength to find the path to the stars. There is much innovation, even heroism, and sacrifice by the staff of banks and development agencies known only to villagers and other staff, which is not only left anonymous but undocumented. Even when programme results are declared, the names and actions of the individuals who made the process successful are seldom known.

The talents and skills of our people are underutilized. Our most significant task is to redefine our relationship with our employees. The objective must be to build a place where people have the freedom to be creative and feel a real sense of accomplishment—a place that brings out the best in everybody. Just as an artist has many colours on his palette, a leader has a palette of employees with different skills. Like the adequate mixing of colours helps the artist produce a work of art, the leader's effectiveness in channelling the skills of and obtaining the best results from each employee helps create an organisation that is always energised, enthusiastic and effervescent.

During the ten years I was manager of the rural branches of the bank, my staff never participated in strikes because I knew that strikes would shutter our business. It wasn't because we were against the management or the unions. Most of our clients were villagers—the majority of them illiterate—who could not have advance notice of the strike in an era when even basic connectivity was light years away. We didn't want to cause inconvenience or discomfort to clients. An equally important reason was that neither the management nor the unions ever bothered about the problems of staff working in remote rural areas.

The outsiders believe that living in a village is cheaper than in cities. Contrary to what people think, living costs in a village are higher than in the nearby town. You have to depend entirely on the nearest town for your groceries. The local agents ferry these items from nearby cities and charge a heavy premium. School, medical facilities, and proper housing are usually unavailable; the family must be in the nearest town. It entails maintaining two establishments at a reduced salary because all the significant allowances are for larger centres. I know of staff assistants who spent their entire lives in remote areas because the unions had leaders from the urban elite who protected the interests of those living in cities. I was proud of the relentless work put in by my staff despite the miserliness of the bosses in recognizing them. I always dinned just one instruction into my boys' heads, "If the organization doesn't care for you, build goodwill with clients. That way, the esteem and respect from the local population will neuter your frustrations."

I tried my best to shore up the morale and confidence of the staff and give them the confidence and courage to face reality and move on to change the face of villages. I even enlisted the support of their families due to the high cost of maintaining two establishments. Most managers prefer to commute from their homes in towns to their rural job centres. To fresh entrants in this field of development work, I can only suggest that one must live in a village and not merely drop by for the day if one wants complete insight into the society in which one has to operate. I think many of our ambitious development programmes have gone awry because development workers, particularly the senior bosses, never had the patience to understand the problems and needs of villagers. During official visits, they move through villages as if passing through revolving doors. They are rarely interested in dropping into a villager's house, afraid of catching an infection if they must taste the villager's hospitality.

Managers working in Naxalite areas who have shown personal courage and ingenuity in creating safe spaces in which they can pursue development work. Their reward is not early promotion or early transfer out of these disturbed areas; usually, these boys would be the last to qualify for promotions because they have neither amenities nor instructors under whose tutelage they can prepare for departmental examinations. Many boys working in god-forsaken places are highly qualified and have been rank holders in universities. Their families stay far away in towns where the education and healthcare faculties are at least satisfactory. Their transfer doesn't occur because there are no replacements to relieve them, and management doesn't have the guts to post others who have spent their entire career in cities, at least for short periods. These unfortunate ones spend them in such abysmal conditions.

The management is helpless because they fail to take on the unions who want to create a haven for their chums. Someone who has spent a career in villages will tell you the discomforts and hazards one must face. Apart from the physical discomforts, one experiences a constant fear of physical insecurity. The government and corporations have been unable to induce their staff to agree to take up rural careers in villages in large numbers. All ambitious parents desire to give their children the best amenities and education, which is impossible if one opts for a rural career. Most individuals working in rural areas find leading a peaceful personal and family life challenging. The family stays at the nearest township where a semblance of at least bare primary health and education facilities are available, and the employee himself has to put up with the demanding rigours of village life: no toilets, erratic power supply, lack of primary health care and above all, lack of intellectual company.

The plight is similar to that of a voyager stranded on an island. Leave aside any guarantee of rewards; there is not even a token discomfort allowance. The lucrative allowances go to those already enjoying the luxury of the company of their kin and kin in regally furnished official apartments in big cities.

Before starting a full-time career in development banking, I worked as a journalist focusing on the development sector. I wrote extensively in national and international press and travelled extensively in remote hinterland. This experience provided me with a lot of insight into the problems of rural folk, and I decided to become a part of the development administration. As a journalist, I could never visualise the hazards of a career in villages. All along, I had a vital identity card, which gave me easy access to even the most powerful bureaucrats.

Most importantly, it gave me much-needed security and protection from local leaders. Too many conflicting ideologies serve a village, and your city breeding doesn't adequately equip you to deal with local leaders' crude and rustic manoeuvres. It is just basic common sense that you can use to navigate the rough terrain of village politics. In the heady world of policy and investment conferences, it is easy for policymakers to forget the incredible tenacity and endurance demanded of grassroots development workers.

Our exposure to villages came from our homestays. It was known as a 'night halt'. It was not just a paper fad. The bank's regional offices monitored these night halts, and we had to provide a monthly report. Rural branches were in such remote hinterlands that the bank manager was the only literate resident in some of these lonely islands. We lived the lives of the locals so that we would feel the pain the villagers felt. I remember a poor woman telling me, "Uncle, I will fetch rice from the village headman's house as what I cook is very dirty. It's so full of stones you'll crack your teeth if you eat it." When I checked the cavernous kitchen, I found her daughter trying to light the damp wood. She fingered the kindling gingerly for fear of the community of scorpions living, loving, and reproducing in the pile.

We had to tiptoe through a political minefield. It was a vibrant universe of fast-hatching leaders with diverse stripes and hues. Trying to patch up with these groups is like building relations between a wolf and a sheep. I had to play dumb on several occasions so that leaders didn't get irritated because earlier, when I tried to send them packing out of my office, they created a big uproar in the village the following night. The burly, moustachioed worthies who stalked me were ferocious and required diplomacy of a high order to pin them in their tracks. The temperature of the political rhetoric kept heating up. Bleeding the banks to aggrandize the wealthy farmers had become a favourite sport of the politicians. The politicians had been using banks as cash dispensers for populist programmes. A legacy of political interference hobbled most rural branches. The more significant part of the last decade of the twentieth century was spent by banks cleaning their branches of the avalanche of bad loans they had been buried. The upsurge of sloppy lending had left a vast hole in the balance sheets of rural banks.

I found rivalries between local leaders were poisonous, and the principle was that if one could not succeed, others had played foul. Each man sought to demonize the other. A war of attrition started between us and the syndicate of village power brokers. It would keep on rotting for weeks. People are only too ready to ascribe motives to you or even run you down. They would jeer us at meetings. One had to develop a thick hide to stand up to the mocking campaign of some of the villages' rowdy and conversational elements. I would always keep a joke ready to deflect any jeer.

Once I decided to remain a permanent creature of the planet of people with low incomes, I started religiously making myself part of the villagers' beats—interacting with people, speaking their earthy language, and rallying the masses for meetings. Without a common language, we communicated through gestures and occasional local words, which I had picked up from colleagues. Languages interest me greatly—as the basis of communication and their aesthetic right—but I have never been very good at learning them. My lingua franca was Hindustani, a mongrel of two hybrid languages, Hindi and Urdu. In remote villages, I spoke pidgin Marathi. I earnestly respected linguistic sentiments and avoided mangling culturally rooted communication modes.

Only through long and close contact with people with low incomes and our work with them could we gain a deeper understanding and more balanced view of the local society. In this way, our experience was not that of typical non-governmental organizations (NGOs), many of which work from within the confines of the project enclave in urban centres from where excursions are made out into the villages by jeep. Sadly, many NGOs are far removed from the realities of poverty and often fail to reach those most in need. The most surprising discovery was the simple human-to-human connection that let me overcome linguistic and cultural barriers.

We have to eliminate the pernicious notion that the roots of poverty are due to the cultural differences responsible for the gap between less-developed countries and the industrialized West. I found the villagers had many of the exact economic needs, beliefs and aspirations as the most capitalist of Westerners. Village artisans were keenly interested in profits, and entrepreneurship was in plentiful supply in rural India, having been part of the traditional culture for a millennium.

Underdevelopment in these communities resulted from a scarcity of capital, the allocation of which was a matter of politics, not culture. Anti-poverty programmes that ignored this reality had the potential, perversely, to exacerbate inequality because they would only reinforce the power of elites. Many government programmes inadvertently fostered stratification by channelling resources through village officials who used the money to fatten the existing wealthy classes. The fact that policies often fail for no good reason is annoying but is indeed less depressing than the view that they are a conspiracy against people with low incomes.

Now more than ever, it is essential to reaffirm that significant advances are attainable for the rural poor, who are potentially a source of great wealth and creativity but must first and foremost seek survival under present institutional, cultural and policy conditions. Their poverty deprives both themselves and the rest of us of the more excellent value they could produce under more conducive circumstances. The people who pioneered the various programmes that have become models recognised this potential and sought to evoke it. We must treat them fairly and respectfully. We must foster a collaborative and empathetic culture conducive to these people's interests, wit, and initiative.

We should not forget that poor villagers are not just statistics but people like you and me, and apart from the poverty that they share in common, there is as much variety of humankind among them as anywhere else in the world: the hardworking, the lazy, the shy, the outspoken, the honest, the devious, the intelligent and the dull, the myopic and the enterprising. The people with whom we worked were all of these, though, in my experience, the positive characteristics almost always stood out.

An essential piece of advice I would give the younger rural managers is that they must always have the desire and urge to produce a superior thing. How you think and handle relationships decides how well you communicate with your customers and relate to your team. Someone said that much of today's communications are like scrambled eggs—wholesome but messy. We must learn to be compelling and logical in our communications. I suffered from an irresistible urge to correct not only my drafts and letters but also those of others, much to the distress of my long-suffering typists, whom I must have driven up the wall many times and to whom I shall ever be grateful for their understanding and patience. With a low tolerance threshold for inefficiency, I confess to being intolerant of slipshod work and irritatingly insisting on pursuing excellence in tasks that hardly demanded it.

While the world is indeed complex, we see that constraining 'circles', even if they are not always 'vicious', can be broken by initiatives that are well thought out but adaptable, conceived by leadership that persisted and shared credit widely by melding so-called traditional and modern features into new attractive combinations.

Midway through my rural career, I realized I had collated a ragbag of half-cooked impressions, prejudices and preferences about the villages. I had no idea what my rambling outpourings of half-fangled ideas would amount to. I wrote to get things off my chest—a kind of catharsis. I was surprised that leading business newspapers gave prominent space to my despatches, presumably because I was the only writer reporting directly from the field. Quickly, I became a roving faculty member, lecturing at academies and a one-eyed denizen in a kingdom of blind people. I scribbled in my notebooks. With the onset of computers, I kept tapping away on my laptop, composing copious notes and sometimes angry missives; the words spawned from the depths of my rage and desperation. As an ex-journalist, I learned the craft's subtleties and the profession's sensitive nuances.

The word 'finance' conjured up images of cold-hearted bankers working with people they did not understand, an unwelcome stranger to the village. The rural banker seemed a remote figure: infinitely rational and too perfect to relate to mere human concerns. At worst, he would seem like a social naïf, if not an outright sociopath, a man who had intelligence and reason but was devoid of emotions. Yet bankers are not the horned, greedy villains the public tries to demonize them to be. They are decent, caring human beings. Because their business offers few anchors for their morality, their primary compass becomes how much money they make.

The real story of development finance is neither the numbers nor rapid growth. It is about the slow movement—a value-based, de-risked, diverse, widely-spread, bottom-up social transformation.As a society, we often look for models we hope will trickle down. Maybe it is just the right time for some lift. There are charlatans everywhere. There are also attempts to subvert the ethic, some by entrepreneurs pushing ultra-rapid growth and some by politicians who love to give away freebies at no cost to themselves. However, genuine attempts by innovative and committed managers have brought new hope for people with low incomes, particularly women. It is now accepted wisdom that villages present an ideal arena for improvising credit policies and procedures. I found innovative efforts at the village level easier, followed by rich dividends.

People with low incomes are yet to find their voice, even as the media (for that matter, the entire establishment) have become the megaphones of the prospering classes. The preference for growth over social justice, the argument that economic growth is the road to social justice, is advocated over and above increased spending. But is it required for accelerated growth to translate into inclusive growth? The answer, I fervently believe, lies in inclusive governance. In the absence of Inclusive governance, the people at the grassroots, the intended beneficiaries of poverty alleviation programmes, are left abjectly dependent on a bureaucratic delivery mechanism over which they have no effective control. The alternative system would be participatory development, where the people can build their future through elected representatives responsible to the local community and responsive to their needs.

Not only is responsive bureaucratic administration almost a contradiction in terms, but the Indian experience of the last six decades would appear to confirm that bureaucratic delivery mechanisms absorb a disproportionately high share of the earmarked expenditure: up to 85 paise in the rupee, said Rajiv Gandhi; perhaps 85 paise, says the

Planning Commission in a recent evaluation; not relatively so high, says the Prime Minister. We can leave it to experts to argue how many angels can dance on the head of a pin; for our purposes, it is enough to note that the delivery mechanism itself absorbs 75% to 85% of expenditure on poverty alleviation schemes. No wonder outcomes are so derisory.

In India, over a hundred schemes go to the same set of beneficiaries through mutually insulated administrative silos set up by central government ministries intent on jealously guarding their respective fiefdoms. Convergence of schemes at the delivery point becomes virtually impossible, thus depriving beneficiaries of the multiplier effect that would operate if the beneficiaries use their locally elected leaders to have the authority to plan and implement the utilisation of these resources in keeping with their respective priorities. So far, I am on well-trodden ground. However, the argument for a systemic reordering of the delivery mechanism to shift from bureaucratic delivery to participatory development runs much more profound.

The priorities of senior managers keep rapidly changing. Top managers often take their eye off the ball once it seems to be within the goal, and the whole thing tends to fall apart. However, successful micro-finance programmes in most banks are more individual-driven than institution-driven. The time has come when we must institutionalise the best practices by recognising individuals who have innovated them. I have seen that most senior managers are thrifty in praising juniors. Recognition is a way of indicating an organisation's approval. These seminars often resonate with buzzwords like *empowerment participation, sustainability, and marginalisation, and they end with* copious policy statements. They would arrange discussions and symposia on microfinance over glitzy parties at expensive hotels.

I had a quick eye for vanity and would perceive the frequent contradictions between how people talked and the realities of the situation. There has been much disservice to the cause of rural development because of this schizoid approach: alternating engagement and withdrawal. It is easy to dish out micro-finance lectures, but practising it is an arduous experience. Any debate about the economic policy for low-income people is usually tortuous, long-winded and insular. There is a tendency to stay away from the common ground for common goals for the development of desperately poor people. More than anything, it obscures issues. To cut through the fog, we have to lend our ear to the voice of the people who are the stakeholders. "God gives us nuts, but he doesn't crack them," says an Irish proverb. The world is not a finished product. We contribute to it with our sincere work to make it perfect and ideal. We work to bring out a new earth, which will arrive when our works promote a better order in human society, uphold human dignity and promote love, equality, freedom, beauty and creativity. In the process, we also perfect ourselves; thus, our work becomes a means for our self-actualisation.

Fortunately, these common beliefs are misconceptions—only a tiny part of the explanation of why people with low incomes are poor. In all corners of the world, the poor face structural challenges that keep them from getting their first foothold on the development ladder. Most societies with the right ingredients—good harbours, close contact with the rich world, favourable climates, adequate energy sources and freedom from epidemic disease—have escaped extreme poverty. The world's remaining challenge is not to overcome laziness and corruption but rather to take on the solvable problems of geographic isolation, disease and natural hazards and to do so with new arrangements of political responsibility that can get the job done. We need plans, systems, mutual accountability and financing mechanisms. But even before we have all that apparatus in place—the economic plumbing—we must understand more concretely what such a strategy means.

I must admit that I was considered a maverick, a heretic, a radical, an avant-garde and an anachronist in rural banking. I never toned down my ideas to ingratiate myself with the bosses, most of whom were parlour socialists. Many of my suggestions would spark dismissive snorts from them, who found my uncompromising rebelliousness not in keeping with the organisation's ethos. Honestly, I had grown tired of the traditional approach but was blissfully unaware of the power dynamics at our headquarters. I knew that the staid arena of rural banking could be improved and innovated. In the process, I trod on some pretty powerful toes. There were regular missives of stinging criticism and sharp-edged admonitions from my superiors. Every time a programme got grounded, I had to seek their patronage to nudge the processes down below. Then, several hard-line strands within the management were unwilling to see beyond the mould of traditional banking. The most inspiring mantra that sustained me through such trying phases was the one Mahatma Gandhi gave: "First they ignore you, then they laugh at you, then they fight you, then you win."

The excruciating hardliners remained stuck in a time warp. Many of them had an innate dislike for rural banking. My peers and my senior colleagues would label me a "freak", "leftist", "deranged", and "populist". The critics in my organization would often scoff at my notion of getting much traction for an initiative, but I persevered. But my close friends knew that deep within me, I harboured a sensitive heart guided by the poignant words of Che Guevara: "Let me say, at the risk of seeming ridiculous, that great feelings of love guide the true revolutionary." I am a professional banker trained in the complex and coarse grammar of banking. But at heart, I'm a developmental worker, always keen to do my bit for the underprivileged.

I would get chafed at the restrictions my managers would impose on me. Banking claimed me but could not hold me, hostage to its rules, as I craved relentlessly for innovative ways. I rarely worked within conventional possibility and was never impressed by the rarefied starched-shirt world of banking officialdom. I was not a rebel, but I felt leading the life one knows best was essential. It was a no-holds-barred, bottom-up approach that refused to accept 'no' and defied stuffy Anglicized sticklers for rules that put human relationships above everything. I kept pushing the idea of including people experiencing poverty in the dialogue, not doing what we (privileged outsiders) think is best but asking them what is best for them. Ask a non-swimmer what he needs before he gets in the pool. He might tell you that he wants to know how to keep his head above water. Maybe you give him arm-floats, but he wants you to tell him how to keep himself afloat without props.

That inability to put oneself in the shoes of the poor and to keep living the same way, thinking, "thank god I don't have to live THAT way", doesn't work. Berating or patronizing rural folks is both culturally and professionally the most undesirable extension of any rural development executive's trait. Unfortunately, most aid personnel have cultivated this mindset and approach. Since they never had extended homestays in the villages, they always carried the stereotyped notion of people experiencing poverty as helpless people who needed handheld through every stage.

Our clients lived miles apart down rutted dirt roads; travel between villages could take the better part of a day. It was before electronic contraptions appeared, and accounts had to be laboriously copied and recopied by hand in ledger books stored in giant stacks, with all the mistakes and inefficiencies that the process entailed. We had to page through hand-written ledgers to produce periodic reports and data sheets for our Management Information System (MIS). After unwrapping and counting wads of cash collected from borrowers, I would begin entering the instalments into their respective ledgers by hand, which would take nearly two hours. Computers have greatly relieved modern-day managers whose time went into writing account books.

My days in rural India were a colourful adventure. Puttering down dirt roads by motorbike to villages in the most remote of areas, with a cotton cloth wrapped around my head, tied below the chin, to protect me from the searing heat, interacting with people of cultures that seemed to exist on a different plane, long hours spent waiting at desolate, mice-infested bus stops in the middle of nowhere, greasy late suppers among the coloured neon lights and throbbing speakers of all-night "dhobis", the heat, the dust, the anxiety, the fatigue and the cold bucket-bath in a dismal flophouse at the end.

I met some of the poorest of my villagers, for whom life is a never-ending struggle, yet they have somehow survived. Some whom I knew as malnourished children have, against the odds, grown into adulthood, married and had children of their own. I marvel at their endurance and resilience. At the same time, I feel stirredby the immense loss of all the latent talent, skill and accomplishment of so many millions of people these inhabitants of another world could not reach their full potential. One glimpsed it in their innate skill, grace, artistry and physical stamina, but how much they might have been able to contribute to human knowledge and well-being will never be known.

I had the privilege of watching the women acquire a sense of dignity once they could get opportunities to reach self-sufficiency. I discovered the power of creating a business with honest accountability. And I learned, maybe most importantly, to listen with my heart. At every hospital, school or village where I would stop, people put their time on hold to provide me insights into how they lived. Even when recounting embarrassing truths (like not being able to pay a child's school tuition) or telling painful stories (like losing a baby in childbirth),

A manager's emotional weight depends on his sensitivity to the holes in his society. As far as a mentor or guide is concerned, a teacher helps only in the initial stage. Then, you have to discover the teacher in yourself. A teacher can inspire in the beginning and instruct somewhat, but then you have to listen to your inner response, your voice. Bumps may be along the road, but they are part of every career road. You have to learn to negotiate the shoals of myriad challenges.

No one in the government appeared to be bothered about the welfare of people with low incomes, about doing something to resurrect their lives, bring up their standard of living, and give them the basic amenities. Delivery systems of primary education, healthcare, rural roads and drinking water were rusty and decrepit. Hearing from Dalits, who had long sat at the bottom of the heap in nastily hierarchical villages, I observed that as more of them got a job, money or land, some of the old oppression visibly lifted.

I worked hard to acquaint myself with poor, rural India by making numerous visits to remote, neglected villages, where I spent hours listening to villagers, sometimes sleeping in their huts or sitting cross-legged on their dirt floors, sharing their meals in their dark, dingy, windowless kitchens, awkwardly inhaling smoke from the clay oven over which the poor women rotated slowly inflating chapattis with a pair of rusty iron tongs. I would duck into ramshackle farmhouses, pat dirt-smudged children on the head, and, with little prompting, nibble on a potato plucked from a twig-fuelled cooking fire. As the night wore on, blinking open my eyes, I took notes, anaesthetized by exhaustion and despair. I would roll down on the bare *dari* for a fabulous soiree under the canopy of a hotel that is not three – or five-star but a tremendous canopy studded with millions of stars.

My rumpled clothing and the stubble on my face would leave my origins unidentifiable to the few visitors I had from my native town. I got stuck in traffic jams with goats and their herders coming in the opposite direction on narrow, sloping tracks—technicolour butterflies lolloped by, as big as dolled-up bats. I remember often stopping to inspect giant spiders, bodies the size of blackened plums.As I travelled through rural and urban landscapes, too often devastated by the demands of development, I met people who have risked their homes, families and even their lives to effect real change in the world. The stories they shared so openly and warmly were not merely economic or political success but stories of empowerment and hope that dramatically portray the potency of collective action.

Tiny villages huddled beside the road, and when an automobile approached, naked children would cower in fright and then invariably, as panicky chickens do, dart into the car's path. Though kindness was quick, acceptance came slowly. One long-time native said, "You're only a stranger for five minutes, but you're a newcomer for 50 years."

Nevertheless, I was delighted to discover that I was welcomed d with an instant affection that had, as far as I could see, no qualifications from the first day we walked about the little compound together and shared our first food in the little house. I made it a point to address every village elder as 'uncle', the all-purpose Indian honorific for men even marginally older than yourself.

A village assignment is a unique experience despite the inconveniences one has to deal with. You can change lives and turn a shrivelled, stricken economy into a vibrant community where children go to school, health and nutrition improve, and poverty-driven horrors like starvation and prostitution are memories, not the future. Your vision and perspective of human development will be incomplete unless you have engaged with a village –the microcosm of the other and more exciting and creative India. It gives remarkable insight into the soul of honest India –an India we can't ignore. If we want to forget, we can do so only at our peril. In his book *The Prince of Tides*, Pat Conroy writes: '*Once you have travelled, the voyage never ends, but is played out repeatedly in the quietest chambers. The mind can never break off from the journey.*' Like the lion in the jungle, my natural habitat was the field. Even as I kept climbing the ladder in my professional career, making me bound to a desk, I always kept returning to the field as if the fields kept beckoning me. When posted to my administrative office, I told my boss why I didn't fit in. 'I'm a field person. I can't sit inside all day and study programmes. I need to be up and about, to see, hear and learn.'

There is a lack of clear understanding of rural India's social forces, the fundamental nature of caste systems, and the potential for institutional change. Some critics believe that since people with low incomes are so poor, we should not make them pay for things. My experience is that dignity is more important than anything else and that people experiencing poverty already pay for things, so let's find a way to provide them with things they can afford and want. That ethos underpins development finance. The mantra is, "Tell us what the poor want; don't tell us what you think is good for them."

Just as resistance movements need to reinvent themselves, to shed their weary, old slogans, development workers need to find new ways of doing what we've done in the past. And that includes me. Poverty is the biggest hurdle to empowerment. It is poverty that denies access to education, fails to create job opportunities, drives families to a demeaning life shorn of the barest dignity, and forces a mother to give away her girl child in marriage. People live in such seething poverty and crippling penury that they have stark choices: should they sell an animal and send a child to school?

In one village where an untouchable was, a few years ago, beaten, or worse, merely for letting his shadow pass over someone of a higher caste, I found castes could sit together for meals. That matters: social division may break down faster than economic inequality. During my school days, I did not have enough money to buy all the prescribed gear—textbooks, dissecting sets, rulers, compasses, carpentry tools, unique exercise books, pens, etc. I knew how deprivations could plague the educational trajectory of a creative mind.

It sounds ridiculous to say so, but it can be expensive to be poor. People at the bottom of the pyramid tend to face more risks than wealthier people because they cannot afford the same defences. Without efficient, formal markets, they pay more for services than those living at the top of the pyramid—a phenomenon known as the "poverty penalty": they have to spend more of their income on basics than people who live in high-income areas with decent infrastructure. They must buy water from roving vendors rather than turn on a tap to connect their in-home system to the water system. They miss work more often because of preventable illnesses caused by poor sanitation. They waste more hours commuting because of inadequate public transportation. Chances are that they don't have legal title to their land. And since they have nothing to put up for collateral, it's almost impossible for them to obtain a loan. In an emergency, they resort to loan sharks that charge usurious interest rates.

I have always felt that poor people have very short time horizons to think about—daily bread and daily needs. They can't think more than twenty-four hours at a time. They believe that by the following week, things may be better. Therefore, microfinance institutions have two options. For ultra-poor families, the Grameen Bank gives soft loans coupled with food grains and grants provided by the government. The institutions offer financial counselling for the marginally poor and try to tailor a daily or weekly loan collection schedule to the customers' daily cash flow. However, this sort of assistance is scarce in Indian microfinance institutions.

We could learn by bearing witness to the villagers' way of life. Their entire mental model is different—the primary fulfilment of human needs replaces the multiplication of wants. A farmer explained it to us thus, "You cannot make the clouds rain more, and you cannot make the sun shine less. They are just nature's gifts—take it or leave it."A villager is, at several levels, a philosopher, too. When the things around you appear as gifts, they are no longer a means to an end; they are the means and the end. Thus, a cow-herder will tend to his animals with the compassion of a father, a village woman will wait three hours for a delayed bus without a trace of anger, a child will spend countless hours fascinated by stars in the galaxy, and finding his place in the vast cosmos. Life has changed inexorably in the two decades the Internet has powered, but the same hoary pattern still governs remote tribal belts.

All development programme managers must understand that the magic that goes with our immediate successes may disappear after we move to the next assignment. Our successor is already stung by the praises we have received, and he examines every action of ours under a microscope. All my successors, without exception, painted me in harmful colours during my career.

I was always stubborn about what I thought was right—whether confronting powerful bureaucrats, fighting land sharks or helping flood-affected fishermen. I feel satisfied that my pugnacity and courage have given heart to many friends and colleagues. Being a maverick and an iconoclast in an ossified culture can help you. Yet being a loner can be a considerable handicap when tearing down that culture, facing powerful, entrenched forces fighting you every step of the way. Despite the loneliness, my unshakable self-confidence, unwillingness to compromise, courageous hard work, steadfast heart and steely stomach enabled me to push my plans. It also helped me to insulate myself from the controversies around me and focus on the work instead. My action would leave many eyebrows arched in the corporate office of my bank. Many seniors were keen to write my banking obituary.

I must thank Providence for having survived many attempts by my detractors to trap me. It was not baseless police complaints filed by local goons but the stinkers and warnings I received from the immediate bosses that sank me into depression. Sometimes, when the government departments rejected subsidy claims because of my disrespect, I would go on the defensive, trying to mend fences and swallowing painful admonitions because I couldn't afford to have my poor clients lose government largesse. I had to keep colleagues to my point—the superior, the peers and the subordinates, to push my agenda. Every time a programme got grounded, I had to seek their patronage to nudge the processes down below. I honestly wouldn't trade this experience for anything else.

I firmly believe that a sensitive official alone cannot smoothly manage and drive a grassroots programme. Vision is one thing; creativity is another. But what can you do when you are up against a calcified bureaucracy, fickle-minded villagers who change their opinions faster than they change their clothes and local drunkard goons who can stab you without provocation?

Several development successes have occurred in less-than-optimal settings, often under appalling conditions: weak governance, widespread corruption, minimal infrastructure, deep-rooted social divisions and a poorly functioning judicial system. In each case, creative individuals saw possibilities, whereas others saw only hopelessness and imagined a way forward that considered local realities and built on regional strengths.

When we want to help people experiencing poverty, we usually offer them charity to avoid recognizing the problem and finding the solution. Charity becomes a way to shrug off our responsibility, but charity only perpetuates poverty by taking the initiative away from people experiencing poverty. It allows us to go ahead with our own lives without worrying about the lives of people with low incomes.

My background has taught me a lot about the power of investing in people experiencing poverty, particularly women because you feed a family and not just an individual. For a solution to intractable poverty, we need a massive cultural shift. Foundations, universities, NGOs, and financial institutions must contribute educational, social, and economic programmes that deliver tangible, measurable progress and define clear policy and position points.

I did not belong to the tribe of development-mavens wanting to rock the boat of established development practices. Nor am I a development expert. I am certainly not a proselytizer for the philosophy that breeds contempt for customs and traditions symbolic of the old order, but one shouldn't hesitate to make room for innovation. I always tried to resist the traps that could make traditions toxic: the temptation to use them as cover for prejudice and conformity, a refusal to change or stretch—we'll do it this way because we always have. In India, the public sector's general impression is of bureaucratic insensitivity and bland indifference, with executives preferring to conform to Byzantine traditions.

From the drawing board to delivery, you must inhabit the product and the programme, living every detail like a living, breathing organism. You put so much of your life into this thing. There are such rough moments that I think most people give up. I don't blame them. You must be burning with an idea, a problem, or a wrong that you want to right. You'll never stick it out if you're not passionate enough from the start.

First, the grand design of most development projects, typically hatched by outside development professionals, makes local ownership of this difficult. Second, the hierarchical structure of most public sector agencies in low-income countries, coupled with the implicit rules for allocating credit and blame, make committing to performance goals unappealing for middle managers and frontline staff. Third, in many low-income countries, the public views public sector workers as incompetent or corrupt, while public sector workers view themselves as victims of a dysfunctional system that encourages corruption and rewards inefficiency. Consequently, public sector workers assume an identity that does not promote accountability and professionalism.

It is against my natural inclination to present an idyllic picture of the villages I served or to view its inhabitants through rose-tinted glasses.

I knew very well that some of the peasants I befriended were shrewd, calculating, cunning and often deceitful: they took satisfaction from turning the tables on a naïve urban banker. Yet, despite all the tribulations I suffered—physical hardships, lack of privacy, and monotonous food—I came from the villages with feelings of warmth towards their men, women, and children, which I retain even now.

Today, the most critical need for a development worker posted in a rural area is the need to listen. Listen to people's wants instead of assuming one knows the problems and solutions. Listen to those who work in the field and live the day-to-day challenges. Respect opens many doors. Economic development and social change cannot occur without the cooperation of people experiencing poverty. They must be sought and grasped by the individual pursuing opportunities for self-realization. Lasting change comes about so slowly that you may not even notice it until one day; people and Individuals don't want to be taken care of—they must have the option to fulfil their potential. If we can inspire people worldwide to think differently about what it means to be poor, we will have made a real impact.

We have a real chance to end poverty when we design solutions that recognize people experiencing poverty as clients or customers and not as passive recipients of charity. And I believe we can do that in our generation. This logic comes from the importance of empathy—not a form of empathy that comes from superiority, but one born from a profound humility. Unfortunately, there is a significant lack of empathy in our world; too often, our better-off citizens choose to ignore the woes of the rest of humanity. This trend has become pronounced recently because of the emergence of several unrepeatable fault lines in the development space.

In recent years, a development worker has had to wrestle with political leaders, deal with lobbying by various groups, tolerate allegations of one's lack of personal integrity, and overcome opposition from government departments. The political arena in villages is no longer binary—the ruling party and the opposition party. Today, we have a kaleidoscope of political parties of different hues and stripes. Yet it is true that if one is sincere about bringing about change or development, one will have to ride through these storms. The nitty-gritty of the development process is much messier than what people expect.

Poverty and vulnerability are not purely economic phenomena reflecting what people have but social phenomena reflecting who they are. Caste ethnicity and religion exacerbate the financial dimensions of poverty and vulnerability through processes of cultural devaluation, which assign certain groups of people a lower position in the social order. In the introduction to their book *Super Freakonomics*, Levitt and Dubner wrote, "If you had the option of being born anywhere in the world today, India might not be the wisest choice. Despite its vaunted progress as a major player in the global economy, the country remains excruciatingly poor. Life expectancy and literacy rates are low; pollution and corruption are high. In the rural areas, where more than two-thirds of Indians live, barely half of the households have electricity, and only one in four homes has a toilet." I cannot contest this statement factually. However, being an Indian, I can say if I had a choice to be reborn, I would choose India as my place of birth. Not because I have had an excellent existence in the country but because of the challenges to which it exposed me that made my life richer.

With age comes wisdom, and now I realise that reason must prevail over emotions. I will have to make hard choices that go against the grain of my conscience shaped by the eternally held values I cherish. People may advise that positive thinking and big dreams can help us accomplish significant tasks. One has to bow before the altar of destiny and realise that we must navigate our ambitions within the realms of divine will. Each of us has a moral compass that shows us the limits of our talents and abilities. I think that is a more authentic guide than the well-meaning advice of well-wishers.

At specific turning points in my life, when I would have made the wrong decisions with my limited intelligence, I felt guided by some higher power that saved me:

There's a divinity that shapes our ends,
Rough-hew them how we will

(Shakespeare, Hamlet*)*

Malcolm Muggeridge says in his autobiography, "In all the larger shaping of a life, there is a plan already, into which one has no choice but to fit." Ruskin's famous quotation has remained an enduring touchstone for me: "Quality is never the result of an accident. It is always the result of intelligent effort."

Now, my voyage is over. And I return home. The reclining moon floats high in the sky and has lost its dome, little by little tattering away from above. I don't feel I am returning from another world but rather from an inner world whose arcane existence is outside us. The world from which time departs and to which it returns, its waves caught in countless manifold simultaneity. Recollections keep filtering back to me, some sharp and stark, some a little hazy, others faint and blurred.

For the first couple of days after returning to a compulsory metropolitan assignment as a policymaker and advisor, I felt remorse whenever I opened the fridge or flipped on the TV. But it's hard for a city-bred boy who has only ever attended excellent schools and lived comfortably to be genuinely thankful without a healthy dose of perspective. I lacked a proper perspective and took my education and possessions for granted.

Now that I've been back long enough to reflect a little, I see that there's a more constructive path to take. That path boils down to one word: "thanks". The words of the brave Steve Jobs keep resonating in my daily world—

I'm convinced that the only thing that kept me going was that I loved what I did. You've got to find what you love. And that is as true for your work as it is for your lovers. Your job will fill a large part of your life, and the only way to be truly satisfied is to do what you believe is great work. And the only way to do great work is to love what you do. If you haven't found it yet, keep looking. Don't settle. As with all matters of the heart, you'll know when you find it. And, like any great relationship, it just gets better and better as the years roll on. So keep looking until you find it.

* * * * *

2. ADVENTURES IN THE RURAL PLANET

When I entered banking, I thought it was a high-profile job with an aura of greatness in which one could bask the whole day. The bank branches I had seen were in swanky contrast to government offices, which always presented a sad and mournful look through the dank corridors. My view of the career as a fancy job turned wrong when I found bankers so often hauled up for loans gone wrong for frauds perpetuated by clients whose culpability one could never know. I immediately forsook this bright career for an adventure in rural India through the vast but highly inactive rural network. It was an extensive, highly abhorred backwater with extremely bleak prospects for a career. It had both physical and mental discomforts. I found solace in the philosophy of Leibman. If I have been able to realize in full measure the bar set by Leibman, it is because I took the less travelled path. A belief in Frost's prophetic verse made all the difference in my life.

Two roads diverged in a wood, and I—
I took the one less travelled by,
And that has made all the difference.

The village is chock-a-block with a variety of resourceful talent: postman, schoolteacher, Anganwadi (village nursery) worker, and the staff of the local Primary Health Centre. Through years of exposure to visitors, these people have developed an independent worldview and are neutral players on the village turf. They have been waiting in the wings to be empowered to play a role in the making of their village.

We as practitioners must learn to shun entrenched vested interests that stubbornly resist reformation in the existing social order that perpetuates their feudal tyrannies. We must seek out people at the lowest rungs of society; these are the ones who matter to the success of our development initiatives. At the same time, experienced veterans who have spent several years in villages and thereby learned a great deal about those villages too can serve as a prism into the worldview of a town.

Our repayment culture

It is strange that repayment ethics, so deeply ingrained in Indian culture, have been made foul words by politicians. The sanctity of repayment, no matter how deceitfully the debt was contrived and how cruel the costs, has been drilled into the Indian consciousness since the time of *Manusmruti*. Manu listed eighteen main categories of law for the king to decide on. Of those, wrote Manu, "The first is non-payment of debts." Manu held: "By whatever means a creditor may be able to obtain possession of his property, even by those means may he force the debtor and make him pay." Manu's code has twelve chapters, and in the eighth chapter, there are stipulated rules on the eighteen subjects of law, including civil and criminal law.

Sir William Jones, who came to India in 1774 as one of the first judges of the Supreme Court of Judicature of Bengal, learnt Sanskrit and undertook an authoritative translation of the *Manusmriti*. He wrote in the preface of the translated work (published in 1794):

"The style of the Manusmriti *has a certain austere majesty that sounds like the language of legislation and exhorts a respectful awe; the sentiments of independence on all being but God, and the harsh admonitions even to kings are truly noble."*

What about disputes and debt recovery? Manu specified the punishments in case of disputes arising about loan repayment and listed eighteen types of disputes. When a creditor sued the debtor for recovery of money, it was the king's duty to ensure that the creditor returned his money. Manu permitted the king to employ all means, fair or foul, to recover the dues, including killing the debtor's wife, children and cattle or obstructing his movements. Manu believed that a defaulter could not absolve himself of his debt burden even by death.

Chanakya said sons should pay a deceased person's debt, co-debtors, or sureties with interest. Was a spouse responsible for the debts incurred by a person to whom they were married? Yes and no. A wife was exempted from the debt burden of her husband if she had not given her consent to his borrowings. However, for the debt incurred by a wife, her husband was liable for repayment. Perhaps this was the background in which one of the committees on rural indebtedness concluded that "the Indian farmer is born in debt, lives in debt and dies in debt".

I do not want to make a case for the moneylender. We cannot have outlandish justifications for stratospheric interest rates. However, the loans banks offer for small loans in India are pretty affordable. Added to this is the government subsidy. It will undoubtedly be an interest subsidy if it is not a capital subsidy. The legal system in India is a product of the English language and heritage, both borrowed from abroad. Originally an English transplant with Anglo-Saxon roots, the legal system in India has grown over the years, nourished in Indian soil. What was considered an English oak has turned into an Indian banyan, whose dangling trellises are as big as independent plants.

* * * * *

We had to make frequent trips to the Block Development Office at Warora and the Collector's Secretariat in Chandrapur to discuss various rural development projects our bank branch undertook. We believed that instead of individual clients sorting out issues, we would be wise to meet the Collector and discuss the problems collectively. My first visit was a unique experience. I had a young, agile youth volunteer, Moreshwar Chikankar, who would join me on my trips to these government offices.

In the 1990s, India had some of the hardest-working bureaucrats in the world, but its administration had an abysmal record of serving the public. The sclerotic bureaucracy had plagued all development programmes. Vijay Bhoge, a fifty-three-year-old civil servant, woke each morning to the screeching of peacocks outside his bedroom window. A scuffling attended him as an armed guard, peons, gardeners and orderlies—tasked with catering to Mr Bhoge's various needs—hopped to attention. After a simple breakfast, he would leave his residence, a Victorian-style bungalow once used by a senior British police officer, and get into his car, a white Ambassador—the curvaceous clone of the 1948 Morris Oxford, complete with siren and flashing yellow light, which has symbolized officialdom in India for decades. Mr Bhoge would take the back seat, a policeman riding a machine gun in the front, and in a few minutes, they would arrive at Mr Bhoge's main office, the Collectorate.

For the next four hours, beneath a portrait of a beaming Mahatma Gandhi, Mr Bhoge would receive a stream of poor people. A turbaned flunkey would regulate the flow, letting in a dozen at a time. Many were old and ragged or blind. Most brought written pleas: for the resumption of a widow's pension that had mysteriously dried up, for money for an operation, a tube well or a sprinkler. Many bore complaints against corrupt officials. Mr Bhoge listened, asked questions and, in red ink, scrawled his response on the petitions. For desperate cases, he ordered an immediate payment of rehabilitation grants. He often wrote a note to the official and appeared to address: "Act upon this according to the law." If he noticed a particular case of injustice, his usual remark was, "Kindly do what is needed."

Supplicants had already besieged the Collector's office when I arrived that morning. Two greasy clerks presided over his antechamber, their desks overflowing with papers loosely bound in crumbling files held together with strings. Three phones rang intermittently, and the responses were in various tones, ranging from uncooperative to phoney, depending on who was calling. Outside, a nervous line of saluting adjutants waited for signatures, permissions and orders.

All eyes were on the closed teak door in the corner, bearing the brass nameplate of the Collector, behind which important decisions about people took place. The vast hall appeared to be a neglected warehouse; admin papers piled high on every employee's desk, paper-bound files held down by paperweights, metal filling cabinets rimmed with dust, an old, rusty fan wheezing away, a single colossal padlock. We were seated in a tiny garret where the collector's assistant shooed away visitors like he was swatting mosquitoes. People crowded around the desks, seeking attention, thrusting slips of paper forward, folding hands in entreaty, shouting to be heard. The files were disposed of quickly, and a khaki-uniformed peon carried them to their destination. Occasionally, people have declined a meeting, though most seemed to proceed towards the hall where dozens were already waiting, wearily resigned on their faces, hoping for their problems to be resolved. We saw a small board hung at the entrance of a dilapidated hall reading "Staff Recreation Hall". Two men sat on each end of a wobbly pew, straddling the chessboard between their knobby knees, their noses directed at the chaos of pawns in the centre. We later realized that these were occupants of vacant chairs in different sections of the Collectorate. A man stood at the door to signal the likely entry of any official. Before we left, we witnessed one such signal. The players clattered pieces on the board and slipped through a broken window.

"It's hopeless," I said to Moreshwar, who had accompanied me. "I told you we should have tried to get an appointment. We'll be here all day."

"How would we have got an appointment?" Moreshwar explained we did not have a phone in the village, so we approached the boss directly. He answered with a cooperative approach, "Then, this is the only way.

You go and give them your card."I did not share Moreshwar's faith in the magical properties of this small rectangular advertisement of my status, but I battled my way to the front of one of the desks and thrust it at an indifferent clerk. "Please take this to the Collector Saab," I said, trying to look both important and imploring. "I must see him."

The clerk seemed unimpressed by my card. "You and everyone else," he said sceptically, putting the card aside. "Collector Saab is very busy today. You come back tomorrow, we will see."

At this point, Moreshwar insinuated a twenty rupee note into the clerk's palm. The man's eyes lit up and sparkled. "Send the card in," said Moreshwar, "It's important."

"I am doing as you wish," the clerk said grudgingly, "but you will still have to wait. Collector Saab is so very busy today."

"You've told us that already," I replied. "We'll wait." He then called a clerk hidden in a cubbyhole desk in front of him. A peon wandered in, bearing tea for the clerks. He added my card to the pile of papers he gave the peon to take into the Collector. "It will take some time," he repeated with a grin.

It didn't. Soon after the door had closed behind the peon, the black phone on the assistant's desk jangled peremptorily. "Yes, Sar. Yes, Sar," he said, sweating. "No, Sar. Not long. I have taken care of them. Yes, Sar. At once, Sar." He had stood up to attention during this exchange, and when he replaced the receiver, his eyes showed a new look of respect. "Collector Saab has called you in."

A long bank of windows ran along the side of the room. Mr Bhoge half rose to greet me, which consisted of bracing his hands on the side of the chair and raising his sloping shoulders in a quick jerk upward to shake my hand. I offered mine, robotically expecting him to have a commanding presence, but his demeanour was modest and his tone warm. He reeled out his priorities in village development projects in a subdued stream of equally-accented, putt-putt syllables. I couldn't resist the urge to broach the subject of corruption among lower babus, particularly those associated with development programmes. After a pause, he counteracted, saying that the whole culture had to share the blame for the situation. I mentioned that, because of the government's cranky programmes, we sanctioned loans and wrote them off ritually after three years. His eyes flashed with sardonic delight.

The leather top of his wooden desk was covered almost entirely by a dozen or more piles of documents arranged in neat rows; two telephones remained in the space. He leafed through the pages, signing some and pushing others to one side. A husky clerk came in, carrying a cache of documents and a clutch of papers. Yellow and orange sticky labels indicated which pages required signing. Mr Bhoge fished out a pen from the tray, scribbled his signature in the requisite places and shunted the files down the table. The clerk hobbled out.

When he promised to issue suitable instructions on my pending issues, I was happy to find a sensitive soul and a liberal analogue in the hard-fisted bureaucracy. The meeting turned out to be a forerunner for a lasting friendship. In the Collector, I found a source of enormous support for us.

Inside the World of Indian Moneylenders

Almost every farmer in India's massive rural swathes is tethered, in one way or another, to the *sahukar,* the Indian variety of the moneylender, the ubiquitous, ravenous loan shark.

For centuries, moneylenders have monopolized rural Indian credit markets. Families have lost land, farmers had to prostitute their wives to pay off debts, and when all else has failed, they have tied the noose to end their misery.

An inescapable cycle of debt continues to grip rural India, particularly its farming class. Yet the public image of menacing debt collectors does not reflect the actual plight of India's three million farmers. Moneylenders have been around for generations, but their business has boomed ever since India's economic priorities shifted, with globalization, from agriculture to industry. The arrival of high-cost seeds and pesticides and the attraction of bumper harvests have added to the debts. In farm belts, moneylenders operate under the guise of farm input sellers.

Unlike banks and other lending institutions, there is no steel and glass. Neither is a leather couch nor a coffee vending machine at the moneylender's workplace. Vithal Radke's business is registered as a shop because he hasn't met the legal standards to call it a finance agency.

After failing at several other companies, Vithal stumbled into the moneylending business eight years ago. He doesn't look like you'd imagine a loan shark would – which, to most, is cunning, challenging, maybe with a little streak of violence running underneath the refined exterior.

The socialist Indian;l; the lobby believed banks would become a trendy port of call for clients seeking loans. These financial institutions recorded a surge in the social banking era of the 1970s, but the populist policies left a cruel legacy of dud loans. This sour experience made bankers very wary, and they turned off the spigots. Institutional credit is red tape blocked by bankers bedevilled by a highly contaminated credit culture. Hence, moneylenders continue to thrive.

"It has been business as usual. Shylocks are still in demand," Vithal says."Shylocks give you that instant fix. You don't need security or guarantors. I borrowed again this year. It is going well. I think that because of the ease of it; borrowing becomes addictive," says a cash-strapped farmer.

Loan sharks also do not ask questions regarding your borrowing history, meaning the defaulters find a haven with them. Then, some are seeking to hide because of the shame of borrowing. As the transactions are quick and the requirements minimal, the moneylenders might seem like the perfect solution for those seeking a quick fix. Their customers agree they are a working solution if you do not default on your loan.

Moneylenders are a vital part of India's economy. They charge higher, sometimes usurious, interest rates but require few formal guarantees and offer hassle-free services. The nation has 13 bank branches per 100,000 people, and only about one in four people can access the internet. Single households comprise about 96 per cent of the nation's unincorporated non-farm enterprises, and only 1 per cent receive loans from the government. For most low-income households, moneylenders are the only dependable source of money when emergencies arise.

In Bina, a small farming village about 40 kilometres from Nagpur in central India, where I spent almost two years during my career in development finance, I relentlessly pursued a one-point agenda: banish the moneylender. But as all such social and economic experiments and policies have learned, a moneylender is an all-season creature whose unique DNA makes him resistant to all attacks. In every village, moneylenders are feared as their business lies in squeezing out poor farmers' blood. Yet villagers know there is no life without the loan shark. The rapacious moneylender, who plugs the gaps in rural financial services, is also the man they turn to in times of need. You can't banish him from the financial planet; he remains indelible.

I found that nearly all inhabitants in Bina had been compelled at some time or the other to call on the sahukar. No matter how much distaste he provoked, the sahukar was the key person in the village. He was its banker, moneylender, pawnbroker, and often its vampire. As I did while living in rural India, one must ask where the capital of the poor came from since that is the one permanent requirement of a capitalistic society. In poor countries worldwide, you will find most tiny businesses financed by moneylenders.

When asked, I would get the ubiquitous answer: "I get my money where everyone else does."

"Where is that?"

"Everyone knows. I get it from a five-six."

"What is a five-six?"

"It is where you borrow five rupees in the morning and pay back six in the evening." It is possible to get day loans in the vegetable market that provide 100 rupees in the morning and then repay with 10 rupees interest by dusk.

In Bina village, all dirt tracks converged at the house of the sahukar, like the threads in a spider's web. Along the tracks came desperate families. Some brought their wives' ornaments wrapped in bits of rags; others got the produce from their fields. Sometimes, women would walk in, remove their glistening nose studs, wedding chains, and bangles, and hand them to the moneylender. Others had nothing to pledge but their bodies. The moneylender swallowed everything, and nothing that entered came out; his house grew and bulged. The moneylenders had already sucked the poor dry of their assets, and their sleight-of-hand accounting had left the villagers' principal debt untouched by their repayments, which led to the recovery of the interest.

During my engagement with rural India, I found that moneylenders would survey potential customers with the sleepiness of crocodiles and pose an instant offer. Despite the heavy interest, the offer would be a tempting solution to the customer's financial woes. If you keep paying the moneylender's monthly interest on time, you will find him the sweetest person. All moneylenders carry the air of messiahs as long as you allow them to bleed you.

Farming distress has attracted a new breed of moneylenders. Anyone with some disposable cash — from shopkeepers, government officials, and police officers to village teachers — now lends in the hope of making a killing. They are willing to extend credit, but at highly extortionate rates – sometimes exceeding 50 per cent – keeping borrowers in lifelong poverty.

A current of dread runs through the country's suicide-ravaged farmlands as their debts pass from husband to widow, from father to children. Most villages get trapped into a bond with village moneylenders — an intimate bond, sometimes a menacing one. Popular cinema and classic literature tell many pathos-filled narratives of India's poor caught in that karmic cycle of poverty. Those stories inevitably end in tragedy.

Farmers who fall into the moneylending trap find themselves locked in a white-knuckle gamble, juggling ever-larger loans at usurious interest rates, hoping that someday a bumper harvest will allow them to clear their debts. So they can take out new ones. This pattern has left a trail of human wreckage.

The authors of a landmark study of the system of credit and household indebtedness published by the Reserve Bank of India (RBI) in the early 1950s, the All-India Rural Credit Survey, scrutinized the role and operations of the moneylender, who then enjoyed a dominant position as a source of finance. They did so on the premise that, in India, agricultural credit presented a "twofold problem of inadequacy and unsuitability."

The authors envisaged only a minor place for him in their proposed solution, which took the form of a system of cooperatives covering all villages: "The moneylender can be allotted no part in the scheme [of cooperatives] ... It would be a complete reversal of the policies we have been advocating ... when the whole object of ... that structure is to provide a positive institutional alternative to the moneylender himself, something which will compete with him, remove him from the forefront and put him in his place."

The authors of the Survey did not, of course, lay out a formal model of India's rural credit system as it then existed, nor did they provide a formal analysis of the effects of introducing a system of cooperatives upon its workings. The authors agreed that the moneylender possessed considerable market power, the exercise of which was made very profitable by the peasants' pressing needs. Despite legions of committees and reports that have outlined ways of replacing moneylenders by stepping up institutional credit, the moneylender remains the backbone of the rural financial system. It is a bitter truth which we have to swallow.

The picture which Nobel Laureate Gunnar Myrdal presented in his memoirs *Asian Drama* almost five decades ago remains the same, despite gigantic efforts from both the private and public sectors in bringing large swathes of people into the folds of formal finance.

"When the moneylender sees that he can benefit from the default of a debtor, he becomes an enemy of the village economy," Myrdal wrote. "By charging exorbitant interest rates or inducing the peasant to accept larger credits than he can manage, the moneylender can hasten the process by which the peasant is dispossessed."

Today, Bina is moneylender-free, which is heartbreaking for me. Some years back, the village struck coal, which signalled the financial death of the moneylender. Every inch of land has a price tag. Bina's 3,000-strong community is slowly abandoning the village, which coal barons are acquiring. Lalita Jangde, whom I lent 5,000 rupees to relieve her of a moneylender's debt, is a transformed woman now. I still remember her scared face and trembling body when she came barefoot to me without even the courage to speak. She now owns assets of around Rs 6 million. Her house is far worse and grander than mine. But she still values those 5,000 rupees I lent all those years ago more than her present fortune.

"It was a great event in my life. It liberated me from the chains of a moneylender," she exclaims with a great heave.

Wily borrowers

I have found in my career that most people have a psychological aversion to repaying bank loans. In most instances, the defaulters have sufficient assets and capital to redeem their debt but will use every possible means to renege on their debts. In many cases, defaulters of massive amounts have erected shrines to legitimize their new image as beneficent avatars. There was once a defaulter in a village close to my bank whose debts caused the banker who had processed this debtor's case to lose his job; the borrower had erected a magnificent temple on the highway and earned massive popularity for his so-called God-consciousness. Whenever I encountered the temple on my travels, I felt compelled to nail a board explaining that the bank metaphorically owned the temple.

Personal experience taught me that when villagers need a loan, they will make endless trips to the bank, sitting meekly in office halls, beseeching the manager for help with obsequious supplications. "You're our God, you're our saviour. God will bless you with a hundred children." However, once the loan is released, most start behaving like wily debtors who can be tamed only by the Cabuliwallah!

Villagers are often highly clever and cunning, contrary to popular urban notions of villagers being simpletons and dimwits. One reason for the villagers' recalcitrance could be that they have come to associate the signing of documents with cruelties and frauds. Stories are legion of fly-by-night operators duping villagers by posing as genuine financial agents and promising eye-popping returns. The villagers no longer wish to trust anybody, especially politicians and other authority figures.

Bank officials must often waste precious time obtaining a particular document from a borrower to ensure the bank doesn't lose its claim over the loan. The statute of limitation stipulates that, in case of default of debt, the claim must be invoked within a prescribed time limit, typically three years. Before the end of that third year, borrowers start performing vanishing tricks because they know that deferring the payment would permanently absolve them of their liability to the bank. Collecting these documents is one of a bank manager's most humiliating experiences. Villagers play clever hide-and-seek games with the manager, who may have to return empty-handed to his bank even after spending an entire day scouring the village. The process entails enormous costs for the banks, drains its precious workforce, and entails a mental struggle for the officials. I am sorry that even well-established businesses make much fuss about signing these documents. They use their signature as a negotiating tool to get part, if not complete, amnesty on the defaulted amount.

The essential spirit behind the statute is that there should be a reasonable period during which the bank may take action against the borrower. Bankers do not want to file lawsuits against erring borrowers, especially for smaller loans. Since lawsuits are time-consuming and drain precious workforce resources and other expenditures, banks use traditional methods to recover dues. Court proceedings will sometimes turn into such protracted odysseys that it is not unusual for the litigation to long survive the litigants themselves. The worst case is when farmers, particularly agricultural labourers, migrate to other villages. The manager has to do a lot of intelligence work to sniff out these borrowers. It is more complex at smaller bank branches, where a single officer handles hundreds of small loans. Since the farmers are in the fields all day, the manager has to visit the village in the early morning or late evening to meet them in person.

When the banker searches, there is no certainty that the borrower will be in the village. He may be labouring in the fields, shopping in the bazaar or groaning at the local hooch joint. Even if he is at home, the chances of meeting him there depend on his dwelling location. If it is in the deeper terrain, it is possible that word of the manager's visit has already travelled to him, and he has slipped out of the house. Waiting for the banker at the house's doorstep would instead be the wife or children, studiously parroted to recite the usual script. They would feign total ignorance, wearing a mournful look on their faces. "Sir, he is not at home. We will convey your message. He told us he plans to visit you to assure you of his commitment to relinquishing the debt." Or it could be, "Sir, he has just gone to the city doctor as he has had a fever for the last ten days. People say it *is chikungunia* (complex strain of malaria)." During those days, *chikungunya* claimed villagers were like monsters, and every borrower would proffer it as a standard excuse for not paying loans.

During one such visit, I tasted the villagers' fantastic ability to manipulate emotions. A particular borrower would give my staff the slip whenever they visited the village—the access to Charurkhati was a two-kilometre treacherous path. I met a farmer on the trail who immediately recognized me as the local bank manager. I inquired about the borrower's whereabouts. At first, he pleaded ignorance and fumbled. Then his face became deceptive, and he assertively asked, "What's the matter?" I told him that the borrower had not paid a single rupee and that the loan documents would expire in three days. I had to renew the documents and obtain a signature for the renewal token. He fixed me with a stern stare and started haranguing me, "Today's managers deserve such ordeals. They made us make many trips to the bank before we could get a loan. Officials in the local government steal the funds sent from the government for our benefit, leaving us with a two-hour hike to the nearest dirt track. The closest well is an hour's walk away, and the nearest hospital is four hours away. We don't even have a proper path to the cremation site. Our elders cannot get a decent funeral because the body keeps slithering on the slushy and broken path!"

It took me a while to recover from the sudden increase in his decibels. I felt hurt that he had lumped me with the stereotypical managers who had been posted here against their wishes and were therefore frustrated and ventilated their distress through harassment of clients. I assured him I would be gentler and more accessible than my predecessors. My gesture of courtesy softened the intensity of his rage, but I was already losing my patience as the evening wore on. I asked him if he could help me in locating the borrower. He wondered how severe the matter was, given that the bank manager himself had to come to the village. I emphasised to him it was severe enough and that I might lose my job if I could not locate the borrower. The unruffled farmer insisted it would be futile to identify the borrower, as the villagers were unsure of his whereabouts and that I should waive off the loan.

I have been an avid believer and practitioner of Thomas Alva Edison's great dictum, "Many of life's failures are people who did not realize how close they were to success when they gave up." If I persisted with the search, I would at least have the consolation of pursuing it to its logical conclusion. Like most astute villagers, who run their village administration more ably than B-school boys, this man tried to unnerve me, saying, "I think you better return, or else you'll get caught in the storm. It appears it will rain heavily." I told him I wouldn't abandon my pursuit and proceeded despite the hovering clouds that portended heavy rains.

I found a weary farmer with a pugilist's build, chain-smoking under a tamarind tree. Without cracking a smile, he asked why I'd chatted so long with such a crooked farmer. The man I'd been speaking to was the same farmer I had been relentlessly pursuing. I was stunned. Despite a half-hour conversation, he had tricked me, who enjoyed the reputation of being a great face reader. I sprang back on my bike to pursue the deceitful man, who had now slipped into the lanes crisscrossing the fields. I tried to put the ignition on. I tried to kickstart my machine, but nothing happened. It seemed my loyal and steadfast mobile, too, was in low spirits. I kicked again, and the machine whined. I tried harder: the old engine groaned to life, kept sputtering and finally gained traction. Lightening crackled and speared down explosively, and thunder shook the city like a bass drummer on LSD. The moon had already disappeared into a massive cloud of darkness. The battle appeared already lost. The experience was one of the most frustrating events in my life and has stuck firmly in my memory. It was a hair-raising exercise, and it eroded not just my self-confidence but my confidence in the innate goodness of villagers.

The village postman

Wait Mr. Postman
Please, Mr. Postman, look and see
Oh yeah
If there's a letter in your bag for me.

These lyrics, sung in the '70s by the Carpenters, immortalized the humble postman and his role in a lovesick teenager's life. Closer to home, Rajesh Khanna did pretty much the same in *Palkon ki chhaon mein* ('In the Shade of the Eyelids'), as he sang *Dakiya dak laya* ('Come, the mailman has brought the mail'). These films and songs reflected a reality many middle-aged Indians were familiar with—the ineffectual man in khaki, his pants clipped firmly at the bottom to keep the well-starched fabric from getting smudged by the greased cycle chain, pedalling his bicycle and putting letters and postcards into eager hands.

In a village, the postman enjoyed a status unrivalled by his urban colleagues. My experience of the city postman had not been very encouraging. The mailman would abandon the letters atop the boxes of residents, and sometimes the letters fell, were trampled, and were tracked back outdoors. For the villagers, the postman was a souvenir they treasured. The postman's social perimeter straggled around the constellation of villages he covered in his official errands. He had access to even the most intimate and private affairs of families; if the entire household were unlettered, he would read their letters aloud and write out replies on their behalf. When he brought good news, the recipient would reward him with whatever sweets in the house. During festivities, he would be an important guest and lavished with the family's goodies.

Gone are the days when he delivered picture postcards, letters to lovers, money orders from newly-employed sons, and goodies from doting grandparents. Gone is when he was the villagers' window to the world, a tenuous link with loved ones. In these high-tech times, lovers no longer write letters, instant banking has replaced money orders, and grandparents rely on courier companies to send love parcels. The ubiquitous telegrams have gone. The postman now visits the houses to drop off the official statements of the bank or the insurance company, the telephone or electricity bills, or printed pamphlets to promote consumer products. He is now part of the communication transmission called snail mail, even though it may still be the most trustworthy mail.

The postman at the village where I worked was Vithal Batte, a timid man with a knack for striking up friendships with any stranger. With his grey hair and gentle demeanour, he cut a grandfatherly figure, but, as I quickly learned, he was a postal employee with a workaholic edge. Money was not a high priority for him. His wife was a peon in a local school. The Battes didn't have children. For them, the entire village was their family. Batte had a unique calm ability for defusing tension; he was a natural mediator. He handled every visitor to the town with warmth and sobriety. On account of his generous nature and his charming manners, Vithal was a much-adored man. He was everybody's family friend, the fond uncle for the kids.

After every short ride on his bicycle, he would shuffle to a stop and lower his voluminous satchel, sending a few letters flying into the dust. Diligently, he would brush off the dust and return them to his stockpile, don his pouch again and resume his daily rounds—a process which I watched with pleasure through the large window in my office. A dedicated postal carrier, he spent most of his day weighed down by letters as he navigated treacherous paths to ensure the mail reached the remote villages on time. He would sit using the seal to cancel blank postage stamps on letters, putting them into his old, worn-out, discarded canvas bag bulging with letters with doomed addresses. It had also a seal, *'Returned Letters'.*

For me, the postman was more than just a benign messenger who delivered a trove of daily mail. He was an informal but highly resourceful member of the local bank family. He relieved us of several cumbersome and mundane tasks, made simple by his knowledge of the local geography and the social arcana. He didn't mind the long hours of work he had to put in despite his meagre salary. I think the most significant incentive for him was that he enjoyed the job and was able to realize his self-actualization needs. He always cared about the respect he could command. "Those who have known us continue to respect us. People trust us more than the courier guys," he would chuckle. "There have been many times when I have picked up letters dropped carelessly by the courier wallah and delivered them to the right address."

The postman was crucial in the village as he helped me with innovative solutions to intractable problems. One such problem was the difficulty experienced by the infirm and old customers when visiting the bank. Most of the villages in our block had no access to a river to be negotiated by mall canoes or by a swim to reach Bina, the larger village with the bank branch. The paths from other directions were treacherous and impassable for most of the year. People needed to be ferried across by canoes to transact business with the bank. A large number of depositors were illiterate and could not sign their cheques. They had to be escorted by a family member who had to forego a day's wage. I felt that a solution was necessary to mitigate the hardship of these people. I also lost precious time as I had to keep bobbing across villages on a fishing boat to get simple formalities completed by marginal farmers and agricultural labour.

At the suggestion of the postman, I worked out an innovative method for addressing this issue. I decided to use the postman's services to pay those depositors. My staff compiled a list of such ailing or elderly customers, and we decided to set apart a specified amount of cash to be delivered by the postman against cheques signed by the depositor.

For illiterate customers, the postman would attest to the thumbprints. There was no provision for drawing cash from the *suspense account*—an account usually debited in case of emergency expenses for the bank; so I decided to draw from my account. Once the cheques were received and the accounts debited, my cash would get replenished. Since the postman was a contractual employee of the post department, I had no qualms about engaging him for this work. However, as a matter of caution and to circumvent the possible complications of labour laws, I decided to pay in his wife's name.

It was Vithal again who inspired me to become a firm adherent and later a staunch champion of the experiments, which reinforced that even a small loan to a woman tends to have far more beneficial ripple effects for the family compared to one made similarly to a man. Sociologists may endlessly debate the reasons why men tend to spend money on themselves. In contrast, women tend to spend more on their families, especially their children, but an assignment in a village can reveal this truth in its starkest colours. Vithal's voice was not the only voice raised in the town in favour of women, but he was indeed the loudest, most persistent, and—cumulatively—the most persuasive. He was such a zealous believer in the theory that he tramped through almost all the villages with me to demonstrate the creative potential of poor rural women in money management.

Another area where his advice proved worthwhile was dealing with loan defaulters. Our everyday practice was to print tersely worded standard letters in which we would fill in the particulars of the borrowers and mail these letters to them. The postman observed me generating vast volumes of correspondence with unimpressive results. The mounting postal expenses for dispatching these letters blew holes in the balance sheet without yielding commensurate benefits. I happened to discuss my dilemma and anguish with the postman. He suggested I send postcards for small borrowers and telegrams for bigger ones.

What was so new about this strategy? The postcard is not a sealed cover; its contents are always open for public reading. The postman typically drops the mail in villages at the villager's doorstep. If the person is away, his neighbour or visitor will likely go through the contents. Similarly, the villagers get alarmed and curious when there is a telegram. A telegram in a village usually triggers an instant alarm. The informal communications network of any town is so efficient that even the bowel movements of every man are known to his fellowmen.

Losing face is devastating in a village context, and the villagers will do anything to avoid it. The news of the bank's notice catches immediate fire, and the borrower becomes the butt of the village gossip mill. The villagers come up with beautiful theories about the likely fate of the poor borrower. It builds tremendous social pressure on the borrower's family, forcing him to take immediate steps to regularize his loan. This strategy served me well for almost a decade during my professional career and would have continued to do so had the internet not decimated these channels.

A village has a variety of quaint characters. In Bina, we had a venerable *maulvi*, *Chacha*(uncle), who wrote out psalms from the Quran for the village folk to wear as charms or amulets and for the sick to swallow as medicine. He would use water tinted with saffron for the purpose. If this were not available, he would use ink of saffron colour. He had a fantastic fund of anecdotes and sayings that the peasants loved to hear, and he would keep reciting doggerels in Arabic. He would twirl a one rupee note around the head of the person to bless him, the amount used for charity.

Community resources

An ASHA (Accredited Social Health Activist) is a community worker appointed under India's National Health Programme to assist pregnant women in availing themselves of their health entitlements. There is one

ASHA for every 1,000 women. Her job is to spread awareness about antenatal care, ensure that women go to hospitals for deliveries, and receive proper care during childbirth and postpartum. Many ASHAs accompany women to a health facility for antenatal check-ups, delivery and postnatal check-ups.

Another cadre called *Anganwadi sevikas* (assistants at the village kindergarten). These *Anganwadi sevikas*(nursery assistants) help create awareness about the government's family planning programme in the lower strata of society. They also play an essential role in reducing child deaths due to malnutrition. The critical task that they perform, she says, is improving the human development index. Without *anganwadi sevika*, most people with low incomes would see no improvement in their living standards. These dedicated female health workers are India's primary tool against the menace of child malnourishment, infant mortality, illiteracy, and preventable diseases. They provide services to villagers, low-income families, and sick people nationwide, helping them access healthcare services, immunization, healthy food, and hygiene. They also provide healthy learning environments for infants, toddlers, and children.

In every village, the Anganwadi workers are the first point of contact for all issues related to women and children. The Anganwadi worker in my town, Meerabai Chaudhary, was a caring woman who was highly sensitive to the demands of her role, meticulous and efficient, not to mention well-versed in the nuances of official protocols. She would thread marigolds into garlands and stitch up bouquets made from local flowers. I bought her five spindles and various tinted threads, which she used to embellish their floral presentations.

As a rural bank manager, when I had several regular visitors from Indian and foreign donor agencies, the local women members of Self Help Groups would handle the local arrangements under Meera Chaudhary's supervision. At first, the alien culture of the visitors would bewilder them. Still, soon, they learned modern etiquette and treated visitors with fresh juice of fruits from local orchards—custard apple, guava, musk melon and mango—and dense *lassi*(clarified milk).

We once hosted a high-profile delegation comprising foreign visitors, tenured Indian bureaucrats and local officers. I was planning to have several tea-making teams to cater to the different profiles of guests. When Meerabai heard this, she laughed like I had devised a naïve strategy. She suggested she organize a single team that would brew tea without sugar. A half-teaspoon of sugar would be for foreign visitors, one teaspoon for Indian VIPs, one and one-half for local officials, and two for villagers. Despite the cost, villagers are never very meticulous about how much sugar they consume in tea.

Sclerotic legal system

Bank managers working in villages would tell you how an inefficient legal system has made their job drudgery. The Indian legal system is well known for its Dickensian delay in pushing for adjournments, appeals, and motions. Despite repeated proclamations from the government's throne and the lofty pedestals of courts for dispensing inexpensive and timely justice, the legal system remains dear and mired in interminable delays. The cost to Indian society of its sclerotic legal system is steep. No aspect of our social or national life remains untouched by this malaise, not the development sector. Unless all arms of administration—financial, legal, political and economic— move in tandem with each other, development programmes for people with low incomes will continue to move in a long-winded way.

One of India's ancient texts warns its readers of King Nuga, who was reborn as a lizard because he kept two litigants waiting too long over a cow dispute. Many lizards would be presiding over India's courtrooms if the myth became reality today. The laws are often so woolly and poorly enforced that legality means having the right lawyer to interpret the law according to the client's needs. The finery of law makes even standard rules a matter of debate and encourages a display of wits in the art of interpretation.

One of the most challenging tasks of a village bank manager is monitoring farm loans. A single officer has to take care of almost a thousand borrowers. It is physically impossible for him to meet each one of them personally. The only recourse, therefore, is to keep writing letters and sending notices, reminding the borrowers whenever the loan instalment becomes overdue. It may be difficult to assess whether the borrowers return with the instalment out of genuine good intentions or fear of the bank letter. Maybe it is a combination of both. Those clients who consult lawyers may be apt to delay their repayments because there will always be some legal point to whip the banker into granting concessions to the borrower. Lawyers thrive on promises, and farmers trust them more than their bankers.

A diverse crowd of rich, poor and middle-class had begun to gather in the hallway. I entered the courtroom and sat just below the judge's bench. Four dirty fans on long stems circled slowly above my head, with the subdued hum produced by low voltage. Lawyers wearing traditional black-and-white costumes came and went from the courtroom, bowing according to custom as they entered, filling several rows of chairs behind the front row, where they would wait all day long for their case to come up for hearing by the judge. Light green folders and crowded dockets were everywhere—stacked high on the judge's desk, piled on the litigant's table, stuffed into shelves on the wall. A long bulb glowed dimly in the hall, threatening to switch off anytime, casting surreal shadows on the walls.

Outside, under trees, documents were produced by men hunched over manual typewriters, copies made with the help of carbon paper. Lawyers worked out of open stalls, the more prominent ones laying claim to space with a roof, others merely posting a sign amid the weeds. Cows and goats wandered around listlessly, like the plaintiffs and defendants, trying to evade the sun.

Meanwhile, as I found my case was listed much lower than the cases already in progress, I walked into the main courtroom where a lady judge presided. The lady judge demonstrated an intelligent legal thinker in her written opinions and questions from the bench. She was also an excellent communicator with a crisp, direct style that made her persuasive among her colleagues and the court's broader audience.

When I returned to my courtroom, the keeper told me my case got listed ahead of others because the two previous litigants and their lawyers were absent. The third lawyer had sought an adjournment. My encounter in the witness box left my ideals evaporating. As I took my place in the dock, my lawyer hurried into the court, pulling on his robes. He saw me and raised his thumb. A dizzying number of exhibits—notices, bank vouchers, signed cheque correspondence—were placed before me as my lawyer and the defendant's lawyer sparred over legal issues.

The lawyer defending the defaulter proceeded to grill me in near-perfect theatrical slang with a cannon fire of questions: "Did the borrower sign in your presence?"; "Were the contents of the documents explained to him?"; "Can you produce any witnesses in support of your argument?" He tried to play an intelligent game and questioned every simple line of logic. Painfully aware of how words skate over and around truth, never having enough nuance to grasp it completely, I contested him equally forcefully, testifying in blunt terms. A loan of Rs.25,000 was at stake, and the lawyers were battling as if the country's sovereignty was at stake. He was gesturing with ferocious gravitas. He reminded me of the famous aphorism: *If the facts are against you, pound on the law. If the law is against you, pound on the facts. And if both are against you, pound on the table!*

My lawyer couldn't respond suitably. He kept skirting around the law. His usual refrain would be, "Your Lordship, this is a leading question." His strategy appeared to wear out the defending lawyer or elicit some favourable response from the Magistrate, who kept overruling the objections. The judge pronounced: "The court found no violations." Perhaps an individual judge may be biased, I thought at the time, but the judicial system can't ignore both the law and self-evident facts. My lawyer tried to inject some hysteria into the courtroom to impress me. He would keep banging the table while making his point. It is not surprising. The law deals with the same sort of questions as politics.

I tried to reason with the Magistrate that if I had known that each loan could generate a thriving cottage litigation industry, I would have moderated my enthusiasm and sense of commitment. I have a passion for helping people experiencing poverty, and now I have found that I have become trapped in a multiple helix in chasing this vain chimaera. My humble, polite voice chimed oddly amid the thundering perorations of top-rank lawyers. The Magistrate seemed offended by my remark, as if he sat on Vikramaditya's throne and lesser mortals like me dare not use his court for moral philosophizing. In front of me sat the philosopher king, the flag-bearer of the cloistered virtue of justice, holding the court in its majestic grandeur, and I was a supplicant who dared to dispense his version of wisdom. I hunched my shoulders forward to listen to the lawyers in the room, seeking a reprieve, rarely darting my eyes anywhere else. My attorney did stumble over the judge's questions.

He was conscious of being a deity in his tiny kingdom, where he exercised unbridled authority. He appeared pretty patronizing, dispensing justice the way a modern saint dispenses benedictions. For him, everyone who entered the witness box and stood across the stern tribune of justice. The judge grimaced at my audacity, and his mouth was a straight, grim line as if to say, "We know the law better." The regulations of the judiciary are broad enough to be used punitively by small-minded judges. Earlier in the day, a colleague of mine had to suffer the same fate. It was a field day for the Magistrate, slamming people from the banking fraternity to the undisguised delight of the chattering lawyers.

The courts continue their trend of sticking closely to the language of the governing statutes and rules and reining in creative efforts by lawyers. Everyone knows those who won't play ball with the prosecutor will be convicted. Their intransigence means they will have to serve their full terms. A litigant shot back a profanity to the judge, who deflected it calmly.

Standing in the hallowed precincts of the temple of justice, I shuddered, wondering whether the Magistrate would frame me for lowering the dignity and prestige of the court. Looming before me was the lofty majesty of law, whose shadow stood a puny creature. The judiciary should not move into such narrow straits and shallow shoals. St. Luke in the Bible abjured the physician thus—"Physician, heal thyself!"

In the 4th century BC, the wise Greek philosopher Socrates named four qualities required in a judge–"to hear courteously, to answer wisely, to consider soberly and to decide impartially". The magistrate appeared to disdain philosopher kings and was more at ease with his crude version of a judge.

The government must enhance the legal system and muster the political will to bolster contract enforcement because public sentiment often runs against bank loan recovery efforts. At first glance, more vigorous enforcement would appear to work against disadvantaged consumers, but it would improve their access to credit. Banks avoid these consumers in part because they find it difficult to collect debts from them.

A general problem affecting the banking system (both public and private sector banks) is the efficacy of the legal system in enforcing creditor rights. The legal procedure is tardy, and difficulties are associated with enforcing recovery through the seizure and sale of collateral or forced liquidation. The primary risk mitigation agency, the justice system, is dysfunctional. No crook who flees with a bank's money can be brought to book under the present system unless he is a small fry. Banks cannot send musclemen to throw acid, take away cars or burn crops as lenders in the informal system do to discipline borrowers.

The labyrinth of bureaucracy

For a young manager, rural India and its vast array of institutions, the people who man and service them and the equally vast number of unique characters one encounters in the labyrinths of the hallowed buildings.it is the laboratory where the primary democracy churns out inputs for the larger national governance agenda. There are miniature versions of all public institutions with all their heart and drama as vital elements that make up the national administrative architecture. It was an experience that made my later assignments at the national level much more accessible. With the knowledge of the processes at the lower bureaucracy, you can better understand and creatively provide broader and deeper values to the nuances that underpin national policies and programmes.

* * * * *

3. FINANCE FOR THE POOR

Historians will tell you that an explosion of creativity occurs when the world starts complaining that there is nothing left to invent or that the search for solutions to intractable problems has become futile. This explosion is fate's way of reminding us that there is always something just over the horizon of knowledge. 'Social entrepreneurs' now use their talent to foster social change and bring lasting solutions to the chronic problems confronting us. These wide-ranging problems relate, among other things, to infrastructure, health concerns, education, sanitation, connectivity and food insecurity. These new-age heroes have single-handedly spearheaded significant innovations and are transforming the lives of millions of ordinary people.

My tryst with a unique destiny

The rise of soloists signals the ultimate atomization of the modern world. It demonstrates that individual initiatives can be as powerful game-changers as collective efforts. The power and reach of individual creativity have grown in inverse proportion to the shrinking of the global village. The failure of conventional strategies to alleviate the problems that the marginalized face today has set the creative juices of shoals of the younger lot flowing. It has catapulted them to a cutting-edge vanguard position. This approach leaves no room for alibis and is highly committed to delivering results. Many of this new generation of innovators from Ivy League universities, IITs and IIMs are former bankers, academics, technocrats, bureaucrats and consultants. They have shown that our time-tested values—hard work and honesty, courage and fair play, humility and modesty, tolerance and curiosity—are as relevant today as they ever were. Their tribe believes in the power of ingenuity to solve problems and mitigate human suffering. They embrace world-changing entrepreneurship and do not shrink from tinkering with and reforming entrenched systems. They favour open-source solutions that share intellectual property–computer code or DNA sequences–so that others can improve and build on their creations.

Significant innovations have taken place in recent decades in finance. Earlier, we could only visualise social change in rural India, where villages were mired in caste conflicts earlier. These conflicts had engendered local tyrannies and subverted the social order, resulting in bondage and servitude for significant portions of the population for generations. In the 1970s, the locus of change shifted to other areas, which worked in levelling caste divisions and neutralising feudal overlords. Finance was the pivot of this process of change.

When I began life as a rural banker in the 1970s, outsiders rarely visited the villages. Those who did, other than the occasional anthropologist, government extension officer, family planning staff of the government or census worker, were missionaries of various religions. Over the years, I noticed that the balance shifted from outsiders bringing religion to outsiders bringing finance. Of course, those who lived in the villages already had both. As an ancient Indian proverb has it, a town can emerge wherever a river, a priest, and a moneylender come together. This gradual change in the profile of visitors and reformers was my first introduction to the then-embryonic revolution in development finance, which later grew into the niche of social banking.

With globalisation and liberalization, a shift from the socialist to the capitalist approach was evident. Banks had bled badly in the government-mandated programmes for the eradication of poverty. They realised that age-old nostrums of finance could not be compromised; a new initiative was necessary to engage with people with low incomes. Development finance emerged as the much-touted miracle for combating poverty. The eventual arrival of microfinance further strengthened the efforts of professionals and bankers to pursue solutions for issues facing people with low incomes. They attracted people with splashy projects.

The Self Help Group model of finance, the oldest and most authentic model of microfinance in India, arrived at a time when the poor villagers were already neck-deep in debt as a result of recurrent droughts throughout vast swathes of the country. Their values are collective beliefs and behaviours that strengthen the group's purpose and demonstrate where they want to be. The self-help group revolution made India a country widely seen as a bulwark of stability for the empowerment of rural women. For the average Indian farmer, the rain gods had long gone deaf. The hapless farmers had no energy left to appeal to the heavens. Even their tears had gone dry. The banking system needed to prevent bad loans from taking off again. Farmers were committing suicides. The success of the self-help group movement is a beacon of progress lit from the embers of farmers' mass suicides. It appeared that farmers' suicides might spiral into an immense tragedy, but the self-help group women averted that hazard.

The moneylenders' sleight-of-hand accounting procedures left the principal debt of the borrowers untouched by their repayments, mostly marked up against the interest. Government funds had started drying up, and the generous dollops of outside aid were thinning. The losses from bad loans took a massive bite of rural banks' earnings and cash flow. Bankers were looking for strategies to deflate the portfolios of bad loans, so they started retreating from rural areas. It was a regressive development for the village economy, limiting villagers' access to essential financial services. It alone could provide an economic toehold for villagers looking to escape the slough of poverty and debt.

Failure of development programmes

The poor performance of development programmes has already debunked the notion that subsidies could play a helpful role in hastening development. Political doles had only resulted in a devastated economy and severely restricted commercial opportunities. The people erroneously believed the state had all the answers to their problems. Governments, international financial institutions and non-governmental organizations (NGOs) threw vast amounts of money at credit-based solutions to rural poverty, particularly in the wake of the World Bank's 1990 initiative to put poverty reduction at the head of its development priorities. And yet those responsible for such transfers had, and in many cases continue to have, only the haziest grasp of the unique demands and difficulties of rural banking.

Another dampening development on the macro front was that, amid sizzling growth in cities in the past five years, India's largest institutions grumbled that their smaller, often unprofitable, branches in the poorer parts of the country crimped their ability to deploy adequate workforce and capital to urban operations. Foreign banks, which had little obligation to India's farmers, gained the all-important urban market share.

During this period, the idea took root in many countries that financial services could and should be made widely accessible to low-income people through the formal financial sector. The discrepancy between financial institutions' modes of operation and the economic characteristics and financial needs of low-income households resulted in a lack of access to credit for people with low incomes. Self-employed households rarely had either, and as a result, bankers tended to consider low-income households a lousy risk, imposing exceedingly high costs on collecting information on these households. Lenders preferred to deal with small numbers of large loans to minimize administration costs.

The bankers who began showing up in villages on their bicycles, motorcycles or jeeps in the 1970s and 1980s were usually employees of local branches of state-owned banks. Their mission, as assigned by their governments and assorted international donors, was to find trustworthy villagers to whom they could provide credit. It would help villagers start small businesses, thereby increasing rural economic growth while at the same time empowering people to climb out of poverty.

The bankers and the missionaries, who shared much of the same client pool, were curiously alike in some ways. Usually outsiders to the local community, members of both groups tended to discover their preconceptions in the villages rather than the local realities and dynamics. However, many genuinely cared about helping poor people increase their incomes and improve their lives. Some were even relatively successful. They came with powerful ideas, found other similarly powerful ideas already present, and often became catalysts for the cross-fertilization of their ideas of social and economic reforms and the wisdom of the locals.

A unique characteristic of bankers visiting villages was the refreshing change in their academic credentials and willingness to adapt to the harsh realities of rural life. Most of them were from technical backgrounds, endowed with a vision that focused more on the technical and practical rather than the financial aspects of the problems of people experiencing poverty. There were innovative agricultural practices, small dairy enterprises, and artisanry. Their overarching goal was energising the rural economy and promoting entrepreneurial approaches, and development finance was just one of the many sources into which they dipped.

They brought a range of weaponry to combat poverty and agricultural regress: high-yielding varieties of seeds, new techniques for pest management, and a modern range of fertilizers and equipment.

The veterinary doctors brought exotic cattle breeds, new drugs and nutritional supplements to combat mortality and improve cattle health. Artificial insemination techniques have helped use the l; loans to produce superior cattle breeds.

Bankers also started leveraging the voluntary sector in the villages to supplement finance with changes in the social dynamics of the village social order. Several new rural development entrepreneurs seamlessly adapted to the local culture and enjoyed enormous trust among the local population. These people revolutionised rural societies' cultural mindsets and harnessed their creative energies into extraordinary regional social and economic movements.

Financial inclusion

Access to finance is critical for a country's development—as much a part of its basic infrastructure as access to roads, electricity, or the Internet. Ample evidence indicates that economies with deep financial sectors and well-functioning financial systems perform better. Contrary to common impressions, poor people need and use the same variety of financial services for the same reasons as wealthier clients: to seize business opportunities, improve their homes, and cope with emergencies and other significant expenses.

A growing body of evidence confirms that access to finance has significantly improved household welfare. However, the financial services usually available to people with low incomes are limited in terms of cost, risk, and convenience, requiring people experiencing poverty to, on occasion, tap into other assets, such as livestock, building materials, and 'cash under the mattress', when the need arises. Cash saved under the quaint practice of hiding it, the mattress can be stolen or lost value due to inflation. A cow cannot be divided and sold in parcels to meet small cash needs. Certain types of credit, particularly those from moneylenders, are costly. Rotating savings and credit clubs (the international variant of the Indian *bishi*) are risky and don't allow much flexibility in loan amounts or the timing of deposits and loans. Deposit accounts of formal financial institutions require minimum quantities and may have inflexible withdrawal rules. Loans from these institutions have collateral requirements that exclude many poor borrowers.

Over the last two decades, however, successful experiences of development banks in providing finance to small entrepreneurs and producers demonstrate that poor people, when given access to responsive and timely financial services, even at market rates, repay their loans as promptly as wealthier clients and use the proceeds to increase their income and assets. It is unsurprising since their only realistic alternative is borrowing from the informal market at much higher interest than market rates. Barriers to formal savings are bank fees, lack of convenience in operating savings accounts, and the perception among the bankers that the sums available to these potential customers are too small to deposit.

The financial illiteracy of people experiencing poverty has exiled them from formal financial institutions, even though modern banking is over two centuries old. For decades, balancing one's chequebook has been the cornerstone of personal finance for conscientious adults in the developed world. I remember when I first opened an account of my own in my college days, I received a little booklet, the ubiquitous passbook, in which the bank staff acknowledged every deposit and withdrawal. I learned that keeping track of the bank balance was the personal hygiene of finance, like brushing your financial teeth. The implicit message, not just for me but for society, was that the bank account was the locus of money management. All one's foremost financial transactions would pass through the account, and the account would serve as a running financial statement showing income, expenses, and personal solvency. This philosophy, termed 'financial inclusion', has been the cornerstone of personal finance for adults in the developed world. And it is now the key focus of governments in developing countries. Financial institutions are now engaged in a vigorous battle to enlist people experiencing poverty as their clients, not just for their business but to open a window for the poor, allowing the global development winds to touch their lives.

Financial inclusion covers financial services that can lead poor people to the economic ocean. Formal accounts and savings may help poor people smooth their consumption and weather unexpected events such as unemployment, accidents, illnesses and deaths without using expensive debt instruments. Financial inclusion enables poor people to save and responsibly borrow—allowing them to build their assets, invest in education and entrepreneurial ventures and improve their livelihoods. Poor people save, borrow, and make payments throughout their lives, but to use these services to their full potential, protect their families and improve their lives, they need products well suited to their needs. Bringing this about requires attention to human and institutional issues, such as quality of access, affordability of products, sustainability for the provider of these services, and outreach to the most excluded populations.

However, financial inclusion is no new idea or philosophy; it is just that it has been retrieved from the financial backwaters and resurrected. A by-product of the drive towards financial inclusion is the radical idea that the thing people need, more than business loans, is a safe place to save money. Development expert Robert Vogel calls it the "forgotten half of rural finance."I remember that in the early eighties, all bankers were part of a financial inclusion revolution that was far more vigorous than we see now. The wave of commercialization put the brakes on this enthusiastic journey, and a great mission was abandoned and orphaned. The high-profit goals spurred bankers to design rabbit holes where people experiencing poverty would get trapped and lose their accounts. The introduction of penalties for not maintaining minimum balances and for accounts remaining inoperative (absence of transaction in the account) led to a mass-scale demise of the bank accounts of millions of poor account holders. Without informing the poor customers of policy changes, the bankers sheared and denuded the accounts of their bank balances by applying penalties, finally knocking them off the bank ledgers altogether.

Two decades back, a worldwide initiative was launched by the voluntary sector, later bolstered by commercial investors, to make credit accessible to the hitherto unserved population which remained out of the orbit of the financial planet. This approach was designated 'microcredit.' Microcredit later evolved into a larger basket of products, including savings, insurance, and remittance, with the entire bouquet of services falling under a common umbrella known as 'microfinance'.

The concept of microfinance

What exactly is microfinance? Microfinance refers to various financial services that target low-income clients, particularly women. The institutions that administer and provide microfinance are termed microfinance institutions (MFIs), and their services include loans, savings, insurance, and remittances. Microloans are given for a variety of purposes, frequently for microenterprise development. The diversity of products and services offered reflects that the financial needs of individuals, households and enterprises can change significantly over time, especially for impoverished people. Because of these varied needs and the industry's focus on people experiencing poverty, microfinance institutions often use non-traditional methodologies, such as group lending or other forms of collateral not employed by the formal financial sector.

Although microfinance has been around in various forms for years, it has become a global revolution under Mohammed Yunus, the founder of the Grameen Bank. In his autobiography, he describes how, as a Bangladesh professor, he understood the importance of finance for people experiencing poverty. Horrified by the consequences of a famine, he left the sheltered walls of the university to find out how people experiencing poverty made a living. When he started making small loans to local villagers in the 1970s, it was unclear where the idea would go. Around the world, scores of state-run banks had already tried to provide loans to poor households, and they had left a legacy of inefficiency, corruption and squandered subsidies running into millions of dollars. Economic theory also cautioned against lending to low-income families that lacked collateral to secure their loans. Yunus vowed to one day make profits and argued that his poor clients would repay the loans reliably. Yunus was one of the early visionaries who believed in poor people as viable, worthy and attractive clients for loans. That simple notion has put in motion a vast range of imitators and innovators who have taken that idea and run with it, improved on it, and expanded it.

In an episode that has now passed into the folklore of microfinance, Yunus encountered a woman who made bamboo stools, Sufiya Begum. The raw materials she needed to make one stool cost only twenty-two American cents, but she made a pitiful two American cents on every stool; because she had no capital, she had to borrow money from intermediaries to purchase supplies and sell the stools back to them to repay the loans. Yunus was appalled: 'I watched as the woman began to work again, her small brown hands plaiting the strands of bamboo as they had every day for months and years. How would her children break the cycle of poverty she had started? How could they go to school when Sufiya's income was barely enough to feed her alone, let alone shelter her family and clothe them properly?'

Yunus paid off the money she and other villagers owed to loan sharks. To his surprise, the borrowers paid him back in full. He discovered that while the credit market was the scene of the most brutal exploitation of people experiencing poverty with high-interest rates leading to persistent indebtedness ending in a forced sale of assets and subsequent deprivation, it was also the arena in which interventions to break the cycle of poverty were easiest. His pilot programme has now become a movement for both financial and social empowerment–particularly for poor rural women.

It was the start of the microcredit revolution. Traditionally, banks shunned the poorest as lousy credit risks since they have no collateral for loans. But with increasingly ambitious experiments–initially with himself as guarantor for bank loans–Yunus established that many of the poorest could be good borrowers: they knew a line of credit was their only chance to break out of poverty.

Yunus emphasises: "If you go out into the real world, you cannot miss seeing that the poor are poor not because they are untrained or illiterate but because they cannot retain the returns of their labour. They have no control over capital, and the ability to control capital gives people the power to rise out of poverty."

When Yunus formalized this loan-making arrangement as the Grameen Bank in 1983, it adopted its signature innovation: making borrowers take out loans in groups of five, with each borrower guaranteeing the others' debts. Thus, in place of the hold banks had on wealthier borrowers who did not pay their debts—foreclosure and a low credit rating—Grameen depended on an incentive at least as powerful for poor villagers: the threat of being shamed before neighbours and relatives. Since traditional credit ratings and past credit histories were unavailable for most microfinance borrowers, recovery of the loans is done through a process called "building and placing reliance on social capital". The collateral created through joint liability through group lending is termed "social collateral" or "moral collateral". With individual financial histories have evolved over the years, the borrowers realise the importance of making their loan repayments on time so that others are not starved of credit by their default and to keep up their reputation as honest borrowers for getting easy access to credit in future, the Grameen

Bank has now moved to individual loans, with the personal reputation of borrowers replacing the group guarantee.

The model of microfinance in Bangladesh, as it originated at Grameen Bank, involved tiny loans with fixed terms and amounts to women, group liability, weekly meetings, forced payments into a group savings account, and a set of 16 social pledges chanted each week while standing at attention. Yet the great revolution that fetched Yunus international acclaim angered politicians in his own country. Like all great reformers, he has become a target of a political vendetta in his country. The government of Bangladesh has played its trump card in its long-running campaign against Grameen Bank and Muhammad Yunus: legislators passed a law that effectively nationalizes the bank by wresting control of it from the millions of women who controlled it as a cooperative and divested Yunus of his position in the institution which he'd cradled since its inception.

Clasical model of microfinance

The Joint Liability Group (JLG) system, the basic unit of microfinance in Bangladesh, was, in its classical avatar, an operationally intensive model with a strong emphasis on adherence to simple yet well-designed processes. A group of borrowers form the basic unit–the Joint Liability Group; five is the most common number of members, but membership can range from four to ten. Coming from the same neighbourhood, they know each other well enough to understand the cash flows and requirements of the members' households and have insight into the ability and willingness of members to repay. This model helps financial institutions overcome the difficulties in screening individual borrowers. The borrowers are poor women who have absolutely nothing. They have no credit record, education, or formal employment history. The costs of checking the creditworthiness of these potential clients and servicing their loans would be an astronomical percentage of the tiny amount they would borrow.

Before any group member obtained a loan, the entire group had to undergo a training session, spanning one to two weeks, to learn the bank's strictly enforced rules and procedures and to help members develop their business skills. After the initial training period, each member attended weekly meetings with a bank officer. Up to ten groups of borrowers in one area federated into a "centre" and elected a centre chief and deputy centre chief. Several centres, in turn, formed a branch. Each group formulated and considered loan requests, which were reviewed and approved by the centre chief, bank worker, programme officer, and the bank's branch and zone manager.

All loan applications are discussed transparently at group meetings; transactions between the bank and individual members of each group did not remain confidential. The group scrutinized each member's prospective enterprises and business proposals, ensuring that they were well thought out and, therefore, more likely to make a profit from which the loan recipients could repay the loan. Group members strove to keep business ideas that were not feasible from being approved and to share ideas to make businesses more profitable. Moreover, in forming their groups, members screened out prospective borrowers deemed unlikely to repay a loan. Once the Bank approves a loan, group members monitor how the loans are used. It ensured borrowers were more likely to operate their businesses properly since their peers frequently examined them.

The sequence of loans also sustained peer pressure. Say, for example, that one member of a newly formed group received a loan. The other four members were ineligible for loans until the initial borrower demonstrated regular payment of the weekly instalment. Each JLG thus had an incentive to encourage a delinquent member to make her payments, or it could resort to making the missed payments as a group. Second, loans were not approved for any one member until the accounts of all members were closed. In other words, the group ensured mutual accountability and served as moral or social collateral. By relying on the borrowers themselves to monitor loans and guarantee repayment, the bank could forego close analysis of individual loan applications, lowering the high transaction costs and discouraging individual loans to small businesses. By grouping borrowers, the bank staff could service more loans with fewer contacts required by the bank staff.

Two other factors also contributed to loan repayment success. First, most loans were for shorter periods. Borrowers initially receive a small loan to not overwhelm them with cash. Once the borrower repaid the first loan, subsequent loans could be larger and have a more extended repayment period. This incremental lending technique incentivised the borrower and minimized the risk to the bank. Most countries embraced the Grameen model and became an international model, albeit with tweaks relevant to each country. One weakness of Grameen replications was an emphasis on loans at the cost of fostering savings habits, which was the key ingredient in the original Grameen model. In several countries, this deficiency wrote the obituary of microfinance. When people set goals which are sky-high to the point of silliness, the sensible scoff. They are usually right to do so. Sometimes, it is worth entertaining that even the most startling aspiration might be achievable.

The initial motivation for microfinance was, to a great extent, gender-neutral. It emerged, however, that women entrepreneurs invested the profits from their businesses in ways that had a longer-lasting, more profound impact on the lives of their families and communities. This unassailable truism became a fundamental premise of the microfinance business model and the success of microfinance as a poverty alleviation tool. It also forced the realization that the close knowledge of clients' lives and financial needs—traditionally a hallmark of microfinance—may have become secondary to the push for more significant clients.

The Indian version of microfinance, called "Self Help Group", is quite different from Bangladesh's "Joint Liability Group". The most crucial distinction between the two is that the former emphasises financial literacy, social capital building, empowerment and capacity building of members. These are secondary concerns in the Joint Liability Group model, which focuses more on financial metrics than social ones. The classical avatar of the Grameen model was adapted to Indian culture and social norms, resulting in the evolution of self-help groups. Self-help groups were initially the basic constituent units of the microfinance system in India. Much later, the original Grameen model continued in India but turned into a highly commercial corporate agenda. Still, the Self-Help Group model remained the most authentic indigenous form of microfinance.

The concept of self-help groups

The basis of Self Help Groups existed in rural society before rural planners formulated this concept. A common bond—most commonly caste or sub-caste, community, occupation and place of origin or activity—links affinity groups. Since these groups provide monetary and moral support to individual members in times of difficulty, they are also called "solidarity groups". The agency forming these groups must try to identify them based on their existing natural bonds.

The two models intersected at the point of the belief in extending credit to the unserved and underserved. However, the international Joint Liability Group model and the Indian Self-Help Group model have fundamental divergences in the business models. Whereas joint liability groups are formed in most countries to obtain credit, self-help groups invariably have a savings component that precedes credit. Credit is allowed only after the group matures. While Joint Liability Groups are just credit groups serving as conduits of finance for people experiencing poverty, the Indian Self-Help Group includes capacity-building, awareness-raising, and exposing the poor women to a variety of social, economic and health issues confront them and imparting skills for solving their personal and family problems at the group level. They are also imparted the skills to manage conflicts within the group.

The Self Help Group-led microcredit approach in India first evolved as the Self Help Affinity Groups facilitated by the Mysore Resettlement and Development Agency (MYRADA) in 1985. It was steeped in Indian cultural practices by the National Bank of Agricultural and Rural Development for implementation by commercial banks. The adapted version, which underwent modifications to suit the needs of formal financial laws, started in 1992 as a pilot project and was upgraded to a regular banking program in 1996.

A Self Help Group is a group of a few individuals—usually poor and often women—who pool their savings into a fund they can borrow as and when necessary. Such a group is pu;t I;n the mentorship of a rural, cooperative, or commercial bank where they maintain a group account. For some time in the beginning, the women only save money. They deposit a small sum, ranging from Rs 20 to Rs 50 monthly. After six months, the women are eligible to take small loans. These loans can come from the group savings account or the bank. The group helps determine if the loan is appropriate for each member and serves as a screening point for the bank. Because the liability of the loan is borne collectively by the group, it is in each member's interest to ensure that all other members can repay a loan on time.

Loans are then given out to individual members from these funds upon application at a group meeting. The bank permits withdrawal from the group account based on such resolutions. Such loans, fully funded from the group members' savings, are called 'interloans' and have a short repayment period, usually three to six months. After recording regular loan issuance and repayment for a minimum period of six months, the bank begins to lend to the group as a unit, without collateral, relying on self-monitoring and peer pressure within the group to repay these loans. The maximum loan amount is a multiple (usually 4:1) of the total funds in the group account. Once the group matures and graduates to a business enterprise, the financing is more need-based and is directly linked with the capital needs of the business.

I began my first experiment with self-help groups in the late eighties while managing a small two-person unit in Bina near Nagpur. We were running a small pilot program borrowed from Thailand. It was a wild and risky adventure because state-run banks still had not approved the model. Although my experiment in Bina was not a complete success, I could draw on my learning to refine the model. Warora was to be the first test of this learning curve. Mobilising the villagers, particularly the women, was a tightrope walk of promoting Self self-help groups. Initial spadework consisted of informal visits to our bank's clients, particularly those who were illiterate in finance, to create awareness about the actual role of a banker in the rural economy. My staff would emphasise that a bank loan was a scarce commodity which had to be recycled. The people had such Stone Age notions of banking that many believed bankers had cash printing machines with which they generated as much cash as needed. The bank manager was supposed to own the money in the vault as he held its keys.

Initially, we avoided broaching the subject of SHG. We told the villagers that the purpose of our visit was mainly to know the banking needs of the villagers. We had to ingratiate ourselves with them; they had become used to cheap, subsidised credit under government programmes and would not accept any initiative which would not promise or deliver quick benefits. It was an unfortunate legacy of unimaginative politicians who thrived on the people's gullibility. Money and promises are powerful allurements; on Election Day, when people declined loans because their families were defaulters, they promptly sought help from their political patrons, who encouraged them to boycott loan repayments altogether.

When I began promoting Self Help Groups in Chandrapur district in Maharashtra, the local villagers were suspicious of our intentions.

They could not tolerate our direct interaction with their womenfolk. Their hatred and bitterness manifested in their intemperate language and intimidating tactics. I tried every textbook model to thwart the attempts of these leaders to sabotage my agenda, and I did succeed in weakening their bases and demolishing some of their bastions. Yet the leaders continued to foment trouble, but I remained unfazed. Using discourses, anecdotes and tales from local mythologies, we tried to purge deeply entrenched misperceptions of both banking and bankers. Though the people knew that bankers were much gentler and kinder, more civilised than moneylenders, the hatred they had harboured against moneylenders extended to bankers when they found that, unlike moneylenders, the doors of banks were closed to people experiencing poverty. Our project in Warora appeared to be in limbo as these elements remained intractable. With their strident rhetoric, the local leaders would try to arouse the passion of the villagers against us. We could not bypass the men folk, particularly the hardliners. Only after we built bridges of understanding with a small group of local leaders did we begin forming Self Help Groups and providing loans.

Most of our senior bosses were sitting ducks. They refused to face the reality of the socio-economic dynamics of the rural areas of our country. All too often, they believed these goons, who had been holding us hostages, to be social victims who had suffered years of subjugation in the caste-driven village dynamics. The senior management wasn't keen on poverty alleviation programmes, but the banks were under the compulsion of government diktats to accept them. The senior management saw that these loans were unviable for banks and would directed by politicians to their buddies to obtain them. The history of cooperative banking bore out this fact and was primarily responsible for the failure of cooperative banking in India. To demonstrate a veiled acceptance of the government directive, they issued coded communication without asserting their commitment to these poverty alleviation loans. These loans went against the philosophy of robust banking. Bankers have never been keen on these development programmes because most have eroded the banking system's viability. Clients have misunderstood these developmental loans as government doles.

The women of Warora were the first to hear the overtures of us bank officials. So many fly-by-night savings schemes had burnt their hard-won savings that they had grown cynical of outside agencies flogging savings and insurance policies. Many charlatans selling financial plans did so while juggling other jobs, from driving auto rickshaws to running electric repair shops. These agents sold the raciest products they could and encouraged the villagers to churn policies rather than renew them, avoiding a succession of new policy charges. Some of the women had even the gall to question our integrity.

Bankers' initial discourses on microfinance had set off an avalanche of dismay and protest among the menfolk. We patiently tried to allay their fears and doubts about the new programme. I would break bread with low-caste villagers. To the male folk who thought we were using their women as guinea pigs for our banking experiments, we promised that time would demonstrate that all our efforts aimed to uplift women and the entire village.

The enthusiasm of my team would flag in the face of the politicians' broadsides, the torrents of scolding, and the slovenly postures of village leaders. However, the frequent altercations with villagers steeled us in our efforts, and we developed the confidence to face threats from those with a vested interest in the failure of our programme. Apart from inexhaustible energy, this project needed craft, diplomacy, persuasion and only occasionally, the sternness of rules and laws. It also called for something greater than all these–what I can only call an earnest, transparent sincerity, born not out of years of encountering intrigues and turbulence but the ideals that one brings from one's formative years—the atmosphere in which one grew in one's family and the conditioning that was an almost unconscious part of one's time in school and college.

I found rivalries between leaders were poisonous and based on the principle that if one could not succeed, others had played foul. Each man sought to demonize the other. A war of attrition started between us and the syndicate of village power brokers. It would keep on rotting for weeks. People are only too ready to ascribe motives to you or even run you down. They would jeer us at meetings. One had to develop a thick hide to stand up to the mocking campaign of some villages' rowdy and conversational elements. I would always keep a joke ready to deflect any jeer.

We had to tiptoe through a political minefield. It was a vibrant universe of fast-hatching leaders with diverse stripes and hues. Trying to patch up with these groups is like building relations between a wolf and a sheep. I had to play dumb on several occasions so that leaders didn't get irritated because, on previous occasions, they'd created a big stir in the village the evening after I'd sent them packing out of my office. The burly, moustachioed worthies who stalked me were ferocious and required diplomacy of a high order to pin them in their tracks. The temperature of the political rhetoric kept heating up. Bleeding the banks to aggrandize the wealthy farmers had become a favourite sport of the politicians, who used banks as cash dispensers for populist programmes. A legacy of political interference hobbled most rural branches. The more significant part of the last decade of the twentieth century consumed the banks in cleaning their branches of the avalanche of bad loans they had under which they were groaning. The years of sloppy lending they had left a vast hole in the balance sheets of rural banks.

The success of our initiative

We persevered, and our persuasive approach whittled down the villagers' resistance. It was necessary to purge people's minds of the disease of loan defaults before we could build awareness of our new programme, which used zero tolerance for loan defaults. The default syndrome had mutated into an epidemic which had engulfed entire villages. We had to make clear that loan waivers were not a solution to their financial problems but were, at best, a bandage covering the wound that would continue festering underneath. It set a dangerous precedent, empowering the government to take a heavy hand in all possible matters by passing over the regulatory authorities.

The new programme aimed to build sustainable, self-reliant institutions that would not depend on outside grants. The womenfolk were doubtful, asking us countless questions, the most perplexing being, "Of all places and people, why have you chosen us?" Or also, "Please do not give it to me. Looking at money, I am scared to death; I have never touched money." Some would say, "Give it to my husband because he is the one who handles money." Yet others explained their reluctance by saying, "You know, my mother said when she died, 'My daughter, no matter what happens in life, never borrow from anybody.'" Well, I would try to flatter them by saying there was something special about them that had brought us to them. We tried to convince them there was nothing inherently fearsome or shameful in taking a loan to increase their earning capacities. I worked hammer and tongs to get people interested in the concept. The local leaders urged people to renege on their loans, making delicate local political ecosystems crackle with hate and anger. I judged it best to navigate political shoals without tying myself into ideological knots, but these issues were blunted by the women's coming to believe our intentions were good.

The challenge of establishing even a minimal level of trust with the women of these groups showed itself in all my meetings with female Self Help Groups. My guide, Asha, a passionate and tenacious dynamo who had recently graduated in social sciences and had joined a voluntary agency, emphasized to me throughout that the major challenge of any development initiative was to cultivate the mindset of the villagers. Some women and men took the initiative to mobilize their village to undertake development projects and escape poverty. Regardless, there was a great empathy among the majority that could be the catalyst for a significant change in the livelihoods of the village's entire population.

My field animators would theatrically explain the importance of group solidarity and mutual self-help. "I'll tell you what to do," cut in Asha. She held up a twig in what was perhaps the first lesson they were receiving in the strengths of collective power. "As one person with a complaint, I can be ignored or broken," she said, snapping the twig in two. "Even if there are two of us, we can be ignored, divided or broken," she said, again snapping the twigs. "But if we are more in number, a group together," she held the twigs together and failed to snap them even with a challenging twist, "nothing can break us, and we can get what we want."

The evolution of self-help groups

The first step in building a group is identifying women who can work as a homogenous unit and enjoy each other's trust. The process of group formation can take five to six months. A change in membership is not unusual in the first few meetings. It is necessary at this stage to allow an unrestrained flow of the inner feelings of these women. The purpose of these meetings is to ground the concept of self-help in the minds of these women. In the long run, unresolved conflict will manifest as cleavages that can tear the group apart.

Questions are common in the early stages of the process. At the first meeting in a village called Charurkhati in the Chandrapur district of Maharashtra in 1993, an elderly woman queried: "I am more than 60 years old. Suppose I happen to die next year, what will be the benefit for me from your programme?" Others ask what would happen to unmarried girls' savings should they marry persons outside the village or inquire, "Sir/madam, you are asking us to contribute our money. How much are you contributing for the group? Why should we save if you are not contributing anything?" or "Do you get any commission for this work?"

In any self-help group, once a core set of members collectivises, a leader is identified along with two deputies. All members must accept these three women and will share the duties of running the group and keeping the accounts. The group leader keeps the minutes, the savings and loan register, the weekly register, and the members' passbooks as proper documentation of the activities, especially of the internal lending, which will help the approval process from the bank.

Brainstorming for clarity

Several grievances start erupting at this stage. It is better not to form a group until these conflicts are resolved because the group will always sail in choppy waters. Even small frictions may rock the boat enough to capsize it. As in any new group, the individual with initiative and drive has to shoulder most of the responsibilities in the initial stages. The *sanghatika* (group leader) often protests about her responsibilities, saying things like, "Members may not come to meetings punctually and regularly, so why should I alone be responsible for maintaining the records of the group? All the members should share the work." These members must be tackled and led with courage. The leader must understand that having been chosen to be the leader is indicative of the group's faith in her leadership qualities.

The motto of the Self-Help Group becomes "Savings First—Credit later. Saving is crucial for women to climb out of poverty. They also emphasise saving from sources other than surplus income, such as reductions of essential expenses. In other words, savings must rise, and consumption should be reduced. The Self-Help Group process focuses on building new capabilities for budgeting and managing the cash flow.

The primary goal is for the individual members to become economically independent, acquire basic skills in handling small businesses, and be familiar with local investment avenues.

Collective responsibility and group pressure act as social collateral. The process has three essential steps toward this end: 1. Learn to save. 2. Learn to lend what you have saved. 3. Learn to borrow responsibly. As loans must be repaid, usually within six months to one year, the money will be re-loaned to existing or new borrowers. This cycle of investment and reinvestment multiplies the value of each rupee loaned. The vast majority of the loans go to women because studies have shown that women are more likely to reinvest their earnings in the business for the betterment of their families. As families move above the poverty line, their businesses start building steam. Entire communities stand to benefit from this expansion. Jobs get created, know-how is shared, civic participation increases, and women become valuable members of their families and communities.

Self-help groups are encouraged to practice transparency and accountability. In its vertical relationship, accountability is often perceived f as something citizens seek from power-holders. However, this project focuses on the horizontal, developing women's sense of accountability to themselves and their community. First, transparency has to be instilled through intensive initial training. Community resource people (women who are seasoned, successful members of the Self-Help Groups themselves) train new members about the importance of working together to achieve common goals. New members are aware that their well-being is related to other group members.

Women can be revolutionaries

Traditional wisdom has always held the household as the female domain and the world outside as the male domain. It is more pronounced in the rural areas where women–even though they work in the fields–are inextricably associated with the kitchen, the inside, and the private. "Women were believed to be incapable of understanding what went on outside the domestic walls," writes sociologist MN Shrinivas. However, there is overwhelming evidence that women-run SHGs are the best managed, with women showing a much greater sense of responsibility and commitment to human development objectives such as the health and education of their families. Self Help Groups help inculcate the banking habit in rural women and running them is an excellent lesson in governance, teaching the value of procedural and financial discipline. They broaden the horizons and expand the capabilities of members who must interact with banks, government departments and NGOs. Well-run SHGs are subject to external audits that enforce prudence. Since most SHGs are women's groups, the potential for women's empowerment is enormous. There are reports of SHG office-bearers being elected to *gram panchayats* (village councils) and becoming more effective leaders in panchayat institutions. In a nutshell, it is not merely financial uplift but empowerment that is p achieved in good SHGs.

The collective has to go through phases of 'forming', 'brainstorming', 'norming' and 'performing'. Even if the process is slow, training, retraining and making the group cohesive are necessary. This mechanism can continue to serve the poor and the marginalized on an auto-pilot basis once it stabilizes. Once this happens, people experiencing poverty can take control of their resources and hire professional help to manage them. This transformation does not happen overnight but through a long process of community intervention. It took me almost a year to form and nurture thirty Self Help Groups, but all of them have survived and are now in their eighteenth year. They all have their cash reserves and can service their financial needs conveniently, even if they drop the bank credit line.

The Self Help Group concept has attracted the attention of behavioural scientists trying to leverage social capital to enhance women's self-esteem and develop them into community leaders. A new technique in this area is a design meeting where women undergo various phases of personality development.

Self Help Groups are thus more than a window of financial support for women. They also provide access to information to improve livelihood choices and enhance perspectives. Group members, their families, and community leaders perceive access to information as a critical value of the Self Help Group membership. Members belong to a collective that can negotiate, resolve problems, and ensure a place for them in community life and public spheres.

However, the process is not without concerns. While efforts have focused on the vulnerable, there is evidence that savings groups tend to exclude the most susceptible or impoverished because they are migratory or unable to attend meetings. After all, they are agricultural or casual wage labourers. Several Self Help Groups also report that a few women had left the groups due to their inability to contribute the required savings. While groups are enabled to manage their financial affairs, this leads to another set of dynamics with which groups are now grappling: the dominance of the literate, who are invariably from a better-off section of the community, with others having to depend on their skills and goodwill.

The breakthrough for microfinance

Microfinance has generated considerable enthusiasm, not just in the development community but also at political levels. Inevitably, there was some over-advertising. Microfinance is not a magic solution to propel all its clients out of poverty. However, serious impact studies demonstrate that microfinance benefits poor households. Of course, the microfinance model has had limitations for the past two decades. Most MFIs started as not-for-profit, non-governmental organizations delivering loans. For some time, it seemed that both the development objectives and commercial viability would attract friction. Still, microfinance soon suffered a mission drift, and profit maximization replaced poverty reduction as the main agenda.

One pitfall of the agenda of the new microfinance players who use the JLG model is their belief that credit is the most vital need of the marginalized. They feel that credit can unlock the entrepreneurial spirit, which, as it matures through a process of exposure to market economics, could help in generating indigenous solutions for the problems that have prevented the poor and the marginalized from moving up the economic ladder–issues that include illiteracy, malnourishment, chronic illness and food insecurity. In the name of sustainability, outreach and reliability, the new microfinance is destroying a culture of social trust and a vast reservoir of social capital built by the painstaking effort of a cadre of committed and motivated volunteers who sacrificed personal comfort, social life and many cases, risked their life and career as part of the everyday hazards that go with a rural assignment.

Also, some leading microfinance institutions (MFI) have shifted their focus from building livelihoods to consumer lending, asking how much of the low-income family's purse or wallet they can gain by providing loans and consumer goods. India needs some game-changers in microfinance, not more or bigger loan dispensers fuelled by external funding. These game-changers can learn from SEWA Bank and BASIX and scale up some of the positive lessons of these grassroots organisations.

The international MFI model, as against India's bank-led Self Help Group model, is a different ballgame altogether. The sponsor is a profit-oriented venture capitalist who sees the rural credit market as a fresh business opportunity. The MFI brings excellent professionalism, innovation and technology to its enterprise of venturing to provide loans that banks do not. Yet MFIs form no groups engaged in governance functions, unlike Self Help Groups. Even when they operate through NGOs, MFIs are primarily concerned with lending and recovering what they lend to cohorts of people, at times at very high rates of interest.

While the mainstream microfinance institution model built on the Joint Liability Group methodology turned out to be both unsustainable and detrimental to a large number of poor, the Self Help Group approach has the potential to make a decisive impact on the security and empowerment of the most disadvantaged in the current context of farmers' suicides. It may also be critical in positively influencing banks' profitability in remote rural areas.

I am a diehard supporter of the Self-Help Group movement. Still, I must concede that some microfinance institutions have also done remarkable service in financial inclusion. How do you explain poor women in remote villages without any collateral getting loans of R.1 lakh to acquire plots of land? In a remote town in Wardha, Anu approached me for a loan to construct a house on land she already owned. I tried to convince her to take a small loan and repair her old home, thinking she couldn't repay a larger loan. I was stunned when she showed me her file containing records that she had previously repaid a loan of Rs. 75,000 from a microfinance institution at 24 per cent interest before the scheduled end of the repayment schedule. Where I had hesitated to lend her Rs. 25,000, I sanctioned a loan of Rs. 100,000. I felt satisfied that I had done justice to the poor, hardworking woman with an impeccable financial integrity credential.

I admit that in my new role as a designer of programmes for housing loans for low-income segments, credit histories built up by microfinance institutions are the only authentic guides for the track records of the borrowers. I once believed that banks alone could provide financial inclusion. I now realise that, despite enormous capital, human resources, and technology resources, banks' lack of staff commitment and poor human resource policies have ensured that financial inclusion will remain a vain chimaera for them. Most banks have ramped up their rural banking outfits, but these efforts are mere drops in the bucket.

Few poor households have access to formal insurance against risks such as the death of a family breadwinner, severe or chronic illness, or loss of an asset, including livestock and housing. These shocks are particularly damaging for poor households that can less absorb the financial consequences of such an event. Given the high cost of risk and the limitation of the insurance from informal solidarity networks, one must wonder why people experiencing poverty do not have more access to formal insurance, that is, insurance supplied by an insurance company. Health insurance, insurance against bad weather, and against the death of livestock, which are standard products in the lives of farmers in rich countries, are all but absent in the developing world.

The trajectory of Self-help groups

My hopes for the Self Help Group model for microfinance, which I consider to be the most authentic and women-focused, have been partially fulfilled. More than half of our borrowers have not experienced continuous development. Many made progress only to slip back into poverty. We need to understand why they go on and on taking small loans. Some of the poorest villagers whom I knew as malnourished children have, against the odds, grown into adulthood, married and had children of their own. I marvelled at their endurance and resilience. According to observers, these changes sharply contrast the previously marked absence of women in public spaces and the despair, dependency, and, at times, apathy that defined the Vidarbha region in Maharashtra. These changes have not occurred overnight, and the process has not been simple. Women, eager to share their experiences and accomplishments, unanimously attribute the source of their transformation to their new-found access to 'mahiti' (information) and subsequent growing awareness of and ability to act on their rights. Further, they also assert that they derive their primary strength from their emergence as a collective based on their enhanced economic status. Be it the Self Help Group meetings in Madheli, an informal gathering in Ashi, a discussion with the federation members of Warora or the cluster meeting in Nandra, the presence of women in public spaces and their coming into their voice, accompanied by decision-making and action, is hard to ignore.

The synergy between diverse poverty reduction and empowerment approaches must evolve into a viable paradigm. It is not enough to address just the economic indicators of poverty. While incomes must increase through livelihood interventions, for which credit is essential, determinants of human poverty in health and education requirements require attention. Likewise, social poverty, which manifests in corrosive evils like caste taboos, norms of dowry and adherence to vices such as alcohol and drugs, has to be woven into empowerment programmes.

During nearly three decades of academic work and grassroots involvement as an administrator of financial programmes in local rural development, I have experienced microfinance programmes set up to build enormous returns for investors, which spells the death of the local economy. If local savings are invested through microfinance institutions, that region or locality cannot address poverty and under-development. It is an 'iron' law of microfinance. Focusing on isolated cases of microenterprise success does not add to economic development. Support for microfinance in India is overwhelmingly political and ideological—the economic rationale is absent.

Two decades back, when I first joined the pilot project of NABARD to promote Self Help Groups, I was sceptical about the initiative's success. Several questions kept nagging at me. Would the village women talk to us? Would their husband not dissuade them from meeting us? Given their record of being misled by outsiders, Would they trust us? How would we communicate with these illiterate women? If we fail, should we experiment with them and make them suffer the wrath of local interests?

The connectivity to the villages was atrocious. Bovine trails doubled up as roads, and there were no mobile phones. I still vividly remember several remote villages dimly lit with hurricane lanterns. Poorly paid animators (village women volunteers who double up as social initiators and money collectors} would spend endless painstaking hours imparting financial literacy to poor, illiterate women. The financial institutions were amazed as these Self Help Groups that clocked one hundred per cent repayment rates started emerging at a time when public sector banks were almost groaning under the weight of dud loans. They found it an excellent opportunity to use the model to bolster the quality of their portfolios.

Poor women's struggle for empowerment and participation in India's economic growth has been revolutionary. Surprisingly, the media and public intellectuals, who have been so powerfully and convincingly gunning for transparency at the higher levels, missed the enormous grassroots movement that is reducing the trust deficit and imbuing the grassroots public institutions with greater transparency and more robust governance. For poor women, it is a journey towards the second or the real Freedom, as Mahatma Gandhi said when discussing the unfinished agenda of independence.

Through the Self Help Groups, these women are transforming their lives and communities; the sisterhood is so close-knit and persuasive that women have begun to think of themselves differently. I could see the same eye-popping changes even in the surrounding villages. For example, I burst out laughing when told that women now had so much respect for themselves that they declined to be photographed with politicians in search of publicity, who are themselves disgusted at being rebuffed.

Of late, economists have begun to realise that banking isn't just extending soft loans to people experiencing poverty. More importantly, it is a haven for savings. The primary requirements of low-income households go beyond simple savings vehicles. Many families seek a way to manage their money or cash flow. Still, for these consumers, money management differs from pure long-term savings or credit in that its principal focus is balancing times of cash surplus and cash deficits over a typical salary cycle—for example, 30 days.

Many people get into debt stress at some point in their lives. They scrimp on groceries for a couple of weeks to have the cash for next month's loan payment. Or they miss loan payments because a lingering illness keeps them away from their business. That's *acute* over-indebtedness. While acute debt stress can be severe, some temporary over-indebtedness is a normal part of the ups and downs of life and might not mean that a person has borrowed too much.

Women need holistic exposure

As bankers striving to bring about wholesome development, we must remember that all women, regardless of their marital status, need access to education, good jobs, and support for domestic duties. Both widows and married women deserve freedom from culturally entrenched marital practices that degrade and commodify them, as well as legal protection from their husbands' debts. Although transforming long-held laws, beliefs, and practices may be difficult, it is the only way to keep price tags off women and ensure they have dignity and economic agency. Women are closest to the world's most pressing issues and can be highly instrumental in solving them. In many countries, women are adjusting to large-scale economic changes through community-based grassroots organizing efforts. But can women be expected to use local solutions to clean up and compensate for more significant economic problems without being allowed to influence larger decisions?

The idea that small loans enable millions of poor people to pull themselves up by their bootstraps has captivated liberals and conservatives alike. Yet no one should be lulled by this livelihood finance boom into believing it is a cure-all for global poverty. The problem is that not everyone is ready or able to take on debt. Some people struggling to feed their families require more basic help and financial training.

Low-income persons live in risky environments, vulnerable to numerous perils, including illness, accidental death and disability, loss of property due to theft or fire, agricultural losses and disasters of both natural and manufactured varieties. People experiencing poverty are more vulnerable to many of these risks than the rest of the population, and they are the least able to cope when a crisis does occur. In my experience, fate is likely to provide a greater quota of calamities for people experiencing poverty, who suffer the most on account of the cruel bureaucracy of nature. Poverty and vulnerability reinforce each other in an escalating downward spiral. Exposure to these risks results in substantial financial losses, and vulnerable households also suffer from the ongoing uncertainty about whether and when a loss might occur. Because of this perpetual apprehension, the economically weak are less likely to take advantage of income-generating opportunities that might reduce poverty.

In contrast with many for-profit models, which line the pockets of those aiming to exploit people experiencing poverty, SHG's interest earned on deposits and loans is shared as a bonus among members according to the group's decision. The Self-Help Group is not a static institution; it grows on its members' resources and management skills and their increasing confidence in getting involved in issues and programmes in the public and private spheres. It is a very effective means of empowering the poor women. In this context, empowering implies the personal capacity for action in channelling society to affect the flow of resources and control of the spheres affecting their lives. High expectations have marked few development ideas in recent decades, and microfinance is foremost among them.

Where does the truth lie? Research studies find insubstantial evidence that small loans lift people out of poverty en masse but argue that financial services, like clean water and electricity, are essential to modern life. The practical question is not whether microfinance should continue but how it can play to its strengths, which lie in providing valuable services to millions of poor people in a business-like way.

The crisis in microfinance

Microfinance has come under increasing scrutiny in recent months. Stories of astronomical interest rates driving low-income people deeper into poverty, compounded by tales of malicious moneylenders intimidating borrowers to the point of suicide, have recently come to light in the international press, exposing fundamental flaws in the design of institutional for-profit microfinance. Not only are borrowers often innumerate, illiterate and unfamiliar with interest rate calculations, but they frequently have little or no awareness of local demand for goods and services. Consequently, they often fail to establish successful income-generating ventures and cannot repay their loans. Despite the current criticism, for many years, the enthusiasm for microfinance has left little space for nuance. One lesson is clear: when you set the bar so high, there is a long and likely fall from grace.

Another reason why they get into a debt trap is that, in theory, you should take a microloan to invest in the business. But in practice, many people use microloans for weddings, festivals, or to buy something. A lot of these people don't know how to use debt. Even people in rich countries often don't know how to use debt. They think you can buy anything once you have a credit card. If you get micro-loans, it doesn't necessarily mean you can buy things you couldn't afford before. Indeed, one of those who have thoroughly studied the phenomenon, Thomas Dichter, says that microfinance allows recipients to graduate from poverty to entrepreneurship but tries to publicise the magnified version of the phenomenon. He sketches out the dynamics of microcredit: "It emerges that the clients with the most experience got started using their resources, and though they have not progressed very far--they cannot because the market is just too limited--they have enough turnover to keep buying and selling, and probably would have with or without the microcredit. For them, the loans are often diverted to consumption since they can use the relatively large lump sum of the loan, a luxury they do not come by in their daily turnover." He concludes: "Definitely, microfinance has not done what the majority of microfinance enthusiasts claim it can do--function as capital aimed at increasing the returns to a business activity."

The growth in microfinance coverage is limited to pockets. MFIs across the country tend to congregate in select areas, mainly urban and peri-urban settlements, to have 10-20 microfinance institutions operating within a small geography. It has led to the problem of multiple lending, which has raised the issue of clients' over-indebtedness, default and strong-arm recovery tactics. On occasions, client suicides due to repayment pressures have come to light, but this appears to be more a figment of the imagination of the vernacular press than corroborated by solid evidence on the ground. Hence, multiple lending is a well-known phenomenon, and the sector has continued to exhibit an ostrich-like attitude toward the problem. Despite evidence from across the globe, the shortcomings of the group-based lending product and collection methodology have not been intensively studied, and the lessons have been put into practice.

Hence, the role of private sector microfinance will remain whether in 'for-profit' or 'not-for-profit' formats. However, any business that forgets its clients cannot have a bright future. In the desire to grow at double-digit (and even triple-digit!) rates, the microfinance sector may have forgotten the raison d'etre for its existence – its clients. Adopting a client-responsive approach and ethics-based transparency could take this sector to greater heights.

In some ways, the microfinance seen is not recognisable as the one that was there in the initial days. The sector must change with time. While products and processes can change (hopefully for the better), can the concern for the customer change? MFIs justified their entry on the argument that banks do not finance the poorest and are not empathetic to their requirements. Is the MFI sector better able to deal with poor customers today than the banks? Many MFIs started financing people experiencing poverty, but somewhere, they lost the customer focus and the mission. The goals do not seem to make credit access affordable anymore, nor does it accompany people's livelihoods. It is no more about improving income generation in the hands of the customers. Book value multiples, price-to-earnings ratios and enterprise valuations dominate the discussion. High-interest rates are justified in finding more mainstream funds for further growth.

However, the most significant disadvantage of the MFI model is that it is less participatory and empowering since the "banking" functions and procedures are taken care of entirely by field staff of the MFI, who disburse and collect loans. In the SHG model, millions of poor women deal with the banks and do their own accounting and cash handling. However, some MFIs argue that this is a disadvantage of the SHG programme (because most women do not want to get involved in the banking function) and that it is more efficient to focus on achieving one objective effectively, which in the case of "minimalist MFIs" (the vast majority) is delivering financial services. Also, they point out that given the millions of poor women in SHGs who have been imparted training in bookkeeping and accounting, the training requirements of the MFI model are a little less daunting.

The naysayers may be ready to sound the bugle and shout out, "The king is dead, long live the king", that microfinance may once more redefine itself and, in its new avatar, be a leaner, more modest business with lesser interest rates and moderate profit that yet continue to be profitable. Only time will tell.

* * * * *

4. A LIVELIHOOD OF HER OWN

This month's village self-help group meeting was at Kamal's house; it was her turn by the rotational order. Kamal Mhaski was financially well-placed and could afford to host these meetings; she came from a prominent political family in the village and owned a large parcel of land. In Kamal's house, her elderly father-in-law was the presiding patriarch; his sagging charpoy stood in the corner. He had a stubby, emaciated, sunken-eyed look. The room was lit by by a fluorescent light covered with years of accumulated dirt. The portraits of divinities jostled for space on a worn-out shelf with fading photographs of departed ancestors, all stained by ash scattered from the incense burned daily.

The meeting started with a traditional group song in a husky, melodious expression with a staccato rhythm. Though my Marathi was rusty and the village women's dialect was different from what I was used to, I could discern the song's theme: unity, self-help, trust and the poor banding together to help each other. It was touching and an apt beginning for the group grafted in our minds." Another telling verse described how the poor women drove out a merciless moneylender from their village. The soft, frail voices soared out of the courtyard, chasing away the stillness of the long summer afternoon, and then they trailed off. The women seemed momentarily lost in thought as if they were penitents invoking their lord's mercy and guidance. It was a way of expressing thanks for being given a permanent parole out of the prison of poverty.

A group meeting

It was a delight watching the group meeting. "Sir", someone said, rolling the rs, and then everyone started saying it, laughing. The women conversed together with great animation and all at once. A tiny lissom lady with a sparkling face interjected, "Hullo, what part of the country are you coming from?" This inevitable question came point-blank, with a smile. "I am from Nagpur but have come as a migrant worker to Warora," I said. It was the accepted introduction. A new visitor is a momentary prize. A village gathering will always welcome him more unaffectedly than a city one.

About fifty women filled the tiny room, spilling over and sitting in one another's laps. The floor had been polished with sludge of biogas mixed with cow dung, and the roof was of weathered tiles with grass sprouting from the seams. A few women stifled yawns. Others poked the snoozing companions awake. I asked them what they had learned. How was the Self-Help Group helping them beyond just providing money? The women flushed with pride. They all pulled out their passbooks and the sign in the register column where against their names. In rural India, where literacy often hovered below fifty per cent, and most women received little or no education, these signatures showed the power they felt. Many told me they were the only family members who could achieve this literacy level within their homes. It was ample proof of the success of our literacy campaign in the villages.

I complimented the group leaders and told the members that the number of thumbprints should go down every month so that the village would become eligible for the government award for a hundred per cent literate village. The group leader assured me that in the next three months, they would require ink pads no longer, only pens; there would be no more need for thumbprints. A few months later, when I revisited the group and asked how many women had kept the promise of learning a proper signature, every hand in the room shot up.

A few pleasantries later, the women got down to the crux of the meeting. The group leader called out, "One". On her command, the women stood up in unison, though with a few poorly suppressed sighs; as they did, the air resonated with the sound of dozens of knee joints cracking. There was a pattern of handclaps. Bowing my head, I said hello: "*Namaskar*", meaning "fine." Faces lit up and sparkled. In unison, they responded, "*Namaskar*". One or two began talking to me in Marathi. Any small effort to communicate on my part elicited similar gracious appreciation. They would gleefully lift any Marathi word in an Anglicized accent.

I noticed that nearly half of the women in attendance had their backs partially or fully turned to me, and at least ten were partially veiled. Most were too shy to speak initially, especially since the men, alerted to my presence, had gathered nearby to keep tabs on the proceedings. Some of the women were attending the meeting clandestinely. The women were giggling and whispering to each other throughout, casting nervous glances to see if there were any male folk outside the room observing the meeting through the windows. I told the meeting organizer, Kamal, to ensure that these men no longer loiter. After this, I saw the women's confidence rise a few notches, and we commenced the meeting. Minakshi said softly, "Here, women won't look someone in the eye or talk to someone they don't know. You have to accept it."Minakshi was the only one enrolled in this women's commune.

As the interview went on, and I told them about myself, they began to open up, with many removing their veils and turning to face me. Some of the local grandees at the meeting endorsed my credentials, mentioning that I belonged to a big bank and was a known sympathizer of people experiencing poverty. At this point, I asked the women how they reacted to the presence of moneylenders now that they had access to bank finance. When Kamal assured them my mission was to help rid them of moneylenders, the room erupted with a volcano's blistering lava of rage against the local moneylender community. However, some felt it challenging to avoid the moneylender because of the time and complicated paperwork involved in securing a loan from a bank.

Walking into a women's Self Help Group, one will be amazed at the professionalism and efficiency with which financial transactions are noted, more like those with professional expertise. The women gather each month at the appointed time, usually at the end of a long day labouring in the fields. Each woman arrives, passbook in hand, with the idea for her next loan in her head. Despite the tired faces, the energy in the room is bubbling as the women know they are accomplishing something big, something that will help lead them and their families towards a better future. Tucked somewhere in their saris are rumpled currency notes representing their loan repayments, interest and savings. The women share a community bond—strengthened by these periodical meetings.

Role of group leader

The group leader took charge as she roared for quiet at the top of her voice. Like a crescendo, the stories rose and fell, filling the room with a pervasive energy. Like a seasoned driver, the group leader cleared all these excuses. One woman asked whether saving was necessary to become eligible for loans. Pushpa's voice was new, crisper than the others. She was standing at the back of the crowd. Kamal's face wrinkled, pinkened and seemed to swell slightly. "Hang it all. What do you want to know that for!" she snapped. "Either save or shut up. Bite your tongue, you evil lady. Take your words back!" During the unexpected commotion and venting of pent-up anger, Kamal and I lost the thread of the argument. Pushpa scrunched up her pinched face and launched into an angry speech which flustered Kamal. I had to use all my persuasive skills to restore peace. Kamal then proceeded to upbraid a defaulter who was her neighbour. The lady squirmed when Kamal waggled her finger at her and demanded, "What are you doing with the earnings from your cows?"

"There are so many expenses at my house; I can't cope with the loan", moaned Lata Buradkar.

There came a tart retort, "Why did you eat chicken yesterday? Why did you send your son to a movie? Why are you making plans for your daughter's wedding? My daughter manages with two sets of school dresses. Why did you buy a third set for your daughter?"

As the meeting continued, women, craving gossip, broke into conversation. At Kamal's call to order, the murmuring subsided. Grandmothers, mothers, and aunts rocked restive children on their laps and thumped their foreheads to put them to sleep. The children, conditioned to the numbing jolts, grew groggy, and their eyes became unfocused. A debate about going over the budget had Kamal's mellow voice sharpen into an I-mean-business tone.

"Up-to-date accounts are vital. Even if you spend one rupee, there must be a record. I think this is a genetic obsession with every woman; she must know where every rupee comes from and where every rupee goes," she smirked slyly. She possessed a phenomenal degree of control over every muscle in her face. Some sniggered; some choked, trying to suppress their laughter. She cleared the doubts one by one like a glow-worm lighting misty nooks. Initially, Kamal confided in my ear. One could observe only a ruffle of heads and a babble of affirmatives. However, with time, women started questioning the group on several issues. The meetings had, of late, grown quite interactive.

When one villager asked why she couldn't borrow more money, the answer came straight from Kamal: "It is like when a new bride comes into her husband's home. The mother-in-law won't give her all the keys to the house until she trusts the girl." A wave of understanding rippled through. I made everyone comfortable, asking them to share their doubts and difficulties easily and without fear. "We will sit as long as your doubts remain unclarified. You will not get solutions if you don't share your problems."The women nodded, and whispering started among the small crowd.

There were moments of hilarity as I struggled for the correct vernacular vocabulary. When all the preliminary computing was complete, Neeta Dhote, the village animator representing the local voluntary agency, did a series of crosschecks to ensure the figures and the cash she had collected tallied. (Were she to fall short once she arrived at the office, she would have to make up the difference from her meagre salary.)When that sum came out to Rs. 16,300, the total in the day's collection register, the accounting was over. I turned my attention to the woman sitting in the last row. Throughout the meeting, they remained quiet and did not forward any passbooks or money; this last group was still in its training period.

One group leader stood up and said she had problems tallying the account book after applying interest to the loans. Kamal told her we would straighten out the issues after the meeting. Lalita, the most confident and mature of the lot, raised her hand, but when she saw a senior group leader raising her hand, she immediately brought her own down. When asked to speak, she said she would take her turn after the latter spoke. Suddenly, two older women rose and said the leader was not impartial in dispensing loans, and they felt slighted. Taken aback, Kamal turned to me, rolled her eyes comically and said, "What do you think you would have done in such a situation?" Her first direct question put me in a quandary. Until now, I have mostly been a listener. I told the two women to take up the group's leadership if they could run it better. They withdrew, realizing their blunder.

The proceedings of a group

As I watched Kamal conduct the proceedings, I marvelled at her ability to connect with and explain things to village women. She understood how to reach the women who needed to get the most: illiterate, poor village women. Kamal knew how they thought and lived. Her power and grace seemed to emanate from something she had made contact with, deep within the emotional psyche of her sisterhood. When work was over, I asked the group's treasurer to assist me in reviewing the group's accounts and went through the books more thoroughly than I had during the previous visit. Understanding the group's financial health and how it managed money was necessary. It was a sort of audit in which we could detect financial discrepancies and counsel the group members, particularly the accountant. Lata, dressed in a patterned pink sari, with piercing eyes and a skinny face highlighted by a facial expression that wandered between anger and hilarity, handled the session with great aplomb. She swatted away irrelevant questions with toughness. It was finally my turn to chair the meeting. I regaled the women with amusing experiences with other Self Help Groups to strike a chord with them. I then prodded them to share their own experiences.

Like a musical crescendo and diminuendo, the stories began to rise and fall, filling the room with an energy that was strong and pervasive. Money had started working magic for these women—small, not significant. A borrower who lost her husband inherited a family of seven dependents. Because of famine, she had few remaining means of survival. Yet, through perseverance, she created a web of entrepreneurial activities—from trading in baskets and food grains to animal raising and managing her kiosk—that allowed her to send all the children to school and to clothe and feed them. How did she do this? Through micro-loans, through steady savings, even when saving was difficult, and by buying her way. Most animal-raising loans are for goattery as they do not require any veterinary knowledge or skills. Most villagers also hire a kiosk in the nearby town and sell vegetables grown in their villages. It fetches them a good profit margin.

Painful stories started dribbling out when women got a chance to 'uncrate' their anxieties. Some gut-wrenchingly sad, some viscerally moving, some riotously funny. One older woman began to weep, and the weeping unpicked a deeper vein of grief—such a terrible groan between the whimpers. It was a typical tale of a villager being fleeced by the moneylender and stripped of money and dignity.

Towards the end of the meeting, a woman sneaked into the room and, avoiding looking at us, quietly took place behind an overweight lady who obscured our sight. Kamal glared in rage and hectored the woman. "We all have work to do with the harvest, but this weekly meeting is only one hour. What excuse could you have for being late, tell me. I'm never late to these meetings, ever! I live further away than any of you. Why should I have to round up members and keep bothering myself? Shouldn't you show up voluntarily?"

The reticent village women

Narrowing her eyes and jabbing her finger, Kamal croaked out her favourite argument, "Saving money is not an obligation to the group. It is for the member's welfare. Attending a meeting is not a favour to me. If you are not interested, you are free to leave the group. Members may come, and members may go— but the group shall go on." The offending borrower took it in her stride, staring straight ahead with a blank expression during the outburst. Sounds came from the back row as if a dozen women were choking back their laughter. Suddenly, two women came pelting into the room and stood by the door, wiping the rain from their hair and shaking it off their saris.

Kalpana's brisk description of her group at work struck me as exactly right. She was a matriculate, and the wife of a senior school teacher, and she could gauge the actual usefulness of the SHG for women. According to her, these meetings were not social events or occasions for planning peasant revolution or female emancipation. They had awareness-building meetings, concerned with learning saving habits, getting and repaying loans, keeping proper records of money, learning about better schooling and health for their children, and becoming aware of developments both in the village and elsewhere—the nonsense which the women defined the daily genie of homework in writing her personal account book involved rigorous discipline.

For the thirty years she had worked in the area, Shankuntala was like a saint to the locals. Shakuntala's face always had a calm, resolute expression. When she spoke, it was with cold assertiveness. At Shakuntala's prodding, the villagers went to work with their spades, and before long, wells were dug, and eucalyptus trees were planted as part of the work assigned to them by the village bureaucrats. Shakuntala'sword became a command, and women volunteered to work every Sunday for two years to lay the roads. The wells took months. The pond took a couple of years. But no one complained. Before departing, we told the women they must observe the discipline of punctuality. I emphasized that we had only travelled to this remote village to conduct this meeting, and members should understand the labour and time involved in monitoring just a few groups. The group leader, a sensitive lady, soothed my temper, saying they were aware of the work involved but that the village women had many domestic chores and needed their husbands' permission.

"May I have permission to end the meeting, Sir," Sangita asked in a firm but respectful voice. The sun was just above the curving line of trees on the slope, mellow and tired after a long day's work. As the sunlight thinned and the cold breeze picked up, a farewell *bhajan* was sung in a soulful chorus, emphasizing the solidarity of the group and the importance of thrift. The singing conjured up worlds of lament and forbearance as the babies dug their fists into their sleepy eyes. The plaintive sound of the song mimed the sunset wind.

India's pliant women

The Indian village woman is pliant and adaptable, like the clay the woman potters knead, giving myriad shapes and forms. Bury her, and she will be as steadfast as the earth. Burn her, and she will ride the flames. Women know which emotional button to press. They are not seducers; they are mind experts. There's a brave practicality in the face of the steep nastiness of life, and yes, along with all this, there is also a lot of heart. The women are not lost, just temporarily obscured like stars in mid-afternoon. Perhaps Self Help Groups are those intimate spaces that have enabled rural women to experience that freedom. The confidence these women have gained through training and the solidarity of the Self Help Group allows them to counter criticism at the individual level. "Even if someone opposes me, I can reply with confidence," says Vimalbai, who comes from a Self Help Group and is now the village headman (*sarpanch)*. She only recently experienced false accusations by her male predecessor in an attempt to cover his mismanagement.

The progress of this kind is hard to quantify—and can be obscured in the grand reconstruction of schemes across the country. We can see the strides taken by women in the new cultural patterns. The demure graduates swathed in colourful saris, the sloe-eyed Mangalas and smock-clad elderly girls moving in their ceaseless pursuit of redefining the contours of their life. The Self Help Group model has shown women are creditworthy clients because it debunks and defangs many prejudices and stereotypes that unfairly hold women back, such as the notion that women cannot be the family's primary breadwinners.

As women have gained new skills and knowledge, their self-worth has increased, and they have gained the confidence to take a more vocal stand at the household level. Sunita Ledange explained, "We didn't know anything initially. Before we organized ourselves into a self-help group, we used to believe everything and agree with everything our men told us. We have learned to express our opinions and views, and our men even ask us what we think." Though male family members continue to choose a suitable match for the family's sons, many women report having the final word in decisions on their daughter's marriage partners, a previously unthinkable position.

As Ranibai Meshram and Nirmala Wansinghe put it, their greatest pleasure is that they have won their freedom, at last, from bondage, which was only theirs, which none saw. They fraternize within the village, do not need to seek permission from their tyrant husbands, and caste differences are closed. They even squat and demonstrate at the local BDO's office whenever their grievances remain unheeded. Development practitioners are now pinning their hopes on Self Help Groups to bring about a rural revolution.

Sheela Gulhane remembers a time just two years back when drunken husbands would come to the SHG meetings convened by bank officials and create a stir so that the bank officials couldn't interact with the women. When the women returned home from the meeting, the husbands would vent their spleen upon their spouses. These women have remained married for years to philandering addicts because they feared losing the guardianship of their children.

The influence of commerce

Commerce has a profound ability to make people put aside their differences and interact with each other. "Before the Self Help Group came on the scene, I was zero," Kamla told us as she sat down to finger through her ten-year-old daughter's hair for lice, another daily chore. Her teenage son swept the courtyard beside them. "We were sharecroppers. We could not find food to feed our children or clothes to dress them. Now, we can buy food, lease land and send our children to school. I have repaid Rs. 5,000 for the loan my Self-Help Group gave me. I have money left over from which I want to buy a goat."When asked whether these loans have created indebtedness and consequent stress, the women claim they feel liberated, not subjugated. They have entered a new world; the old world may slowly become extinct.

During one of the visits of the bank staff, the men asked the women to consider their case for being enrolled in Self self-help groups. The timid women murmured their opinions to the ones next to them, and the private information wassilently shared with the leaders like a game of Chinese Whispers. The leaders then spoke on behalf of their groups: the answer was still 'no' because the men were reluctant to save and prone to tinkering away their earnings. Why should they want men to share the fruits of their labour?

"No, but let them have a different group," a woman suggested. "They wouldn't be on the same wavelength," another said. A young, soft-spoken woman said, "There is machismo involved here. When there is not enough income, men are dipping into their savings. The men are not allowing us enough time for meetings. With men joining, the male group meeting will acquire priority." Did their husbands know about their savings? "No!" they responded at once. "If they knew we managed to save," one said, "they would give us no money for the house." Everybody broke into wild laughter.

Lata was a regular figure at our meetings and training programmes held periodically in Charurkhati for the cluster of five villages. She imbibed the values of thrift and hard work assiduously. I joined Lata on the long ride home to her village one morning. As we approached, hordes of curious youngsters swarmed around us. She steered me into her home, a simple cement structure with a tiny shrine built into a wall. She twirled her finger, tinkled her metal bracelets and gestured to her mother. Her mother daubed my forehead with purple rice. As the whole family squeezed inside, Lata lopped the top off a fresh coconut, popped in a straw and offered it to me. After I had finished and handed over the rind, she hacked it with a scythe and gathered the cotton-white cream in a steel bowl. She was keen that I tasted it and consumed the entire bowl.

When it was time for me to leave, she wished me *namaste*, then grabbed my hand and squeezed it tightly. She said in a barely audible whisper, "I am grateful to you for introducing me to this programme... Now, I am on my third loan—Rs. 20,000. My husband does not take even a rupee from my shop. He pays for our food and clothing from his shop while I have bought things for the house—tape, TV; I have paid to get my son trained as a carpenter in Nagpur; I have bought my husband a wheelchair from Chandrapur to manage himself. I am not interested in raising cows or anything. I am busy enough with my shop."

The journey of empowerment

I was stirred as I listened to the stories of these tenacious women. They have sophisticated credit algorithms: "Does the woman own a buffalo? Some chickens? Does she have a toilet in her home? What kind of roofing material does her home have? Does she bring a shawl to the village meeting? Does she come barefoot to the meeting, or does she wear slippers? Do her children come to the school properly washed and dressed?"

If you go to Charurkhati today, you will find that life in the village is quite different from what it was a few years ago. It is not substantially richer because there is still drought, and no industry saves rain-fed agriculture, but the overall quality of life is better. There's a bank, a school, biogas plants; farmers drive around on motorcycles. Women leave the house and work on village improvement projects such as sanitation and vegetable gardens. They have started small businesses. The fields are heavy with grain. People eat more nutritious foods, use toilets instead of the woods, and wash their hands and bodies with the clean water now piped into their backyard. They know how to prevent the diseases that kill poor people. They use mosquito nets and repellents to ward off mosquitoes. They know they must boil water for drinking to protect the family from water-borne diseases. Even more remarkable is the social transformation that the movement has wrought. No one drinks. Only a handful smoke.

There hasn't been a crime here in years. Even the practice of untouchability has weakened. Dalits suffer far less discrimination than before, as do women and girls. The village is brisk and prosperous. Signs of rural modernity abound. As Muhammad Yunus himself says, "When a destitute mother starts earning an income, her dreams of success invariably centre on her children. A woman's second priority is the household. She wants to buy utensils, build a stronger roof, or find a bed for herself and her family. A man has an entirely different set of priorities. When a destitute father earns extra income, he focuses more on himself. Thus, money entering a household through a woman brings more benefits to the family." (*Banker to the Poor).*

Women producers lack the contacts to reach better markets. A small grower of tomatoes has to sell her produce at the village level to traders at half the price that she could command in the city. An embroiderer has to sell her exquisite fabric to a trader at one-tenth the price it finally fetches in the larger venues. A small salt producer cannot hire a railway car to reach the wholesale market and has to dispose of her salt at a fraction of the actual price. The handloom weaver buys scarce yarn at double the price that a factory pays.

Similarly, for capital, a small vendor borrows 15 per cent per month from the moneylender, while banks lend to businesses at the same rate per year. A marginal farmer mortgages her land—and all rights to produce on it—during a lean year, as she cannot access cheaper sources of credit. Seeds are borrowed during the sowing season and returned with 250 per cent interest at harvest.

My encounter with loans

The first loan I sanctioned to a village woman gave me a unique experience. Women entrepreneurs will shy away from loans, having witnessed the shame women in their village suffered at the hands of moneylenders. Villagers would dissuade me; saying a woman would hand the money over to her husband, who would fritter it away. Our staff said, "Let us forget about this project because we cannot compel them if their husbands have reservations. Why are you forcing them to use these loans if they are unwilling?"

I emphasized to my staff that it is not their voice when these women say no. The voice of their history and the way the feudal leaders exploited them took away all their confidence. One day, after we coax off the crust of fear that grew around them, one or two of them take a loan, and others feel encouraged to follow suit. Nevertheless, it took me six years to bring about that increase in awareness and ambition.

There is an internal wrestle in the mind of the borrower. She quakes, fumbles, sleeps poorly,

and frets. She agrees with great hesitation. She was tossing and turning sleepless nights, debating whether she should go through with it. One nagging thought keeps arising: "What will become of my parents if I cannot repay the loan? My mother has toiled so hard to guard her reputation." The woman has created problems for the family already just by being a girl, being a woman. She doesn't want to make more by borrowing what she cannot repay. Her friends encourage her in the morning because they have all decided to go through with it, and if she drops out, everything collapses. "Don't worry, we all will support each other; we have to take a chance; otherwise, our fate will never change," counsels a fellow member.

Godavari Uikey was a fifty-two-year-old illiterate woman who was a member of one of the oldest groups in the village. Still, since the group did not have a credit line with the bank, her loan application could not be entertained. Because of the drought, she had few remaining means of survival. Married at 18, she had three children, all daughters, and she was the sole breadwinner. She had an alcoholic husband whose habit she funded out of her wages and who beat her if she answered back. Godavari's life consisted of cooking meals, caring for her children and staying quiet. Constantly required to ask her husband's permission to leave the house, and these requests usually denied, she described herself back then, in a breathy, weak-lunged voice, as "sad and alone", with a body work-hunched and wiry. Her neighbours confided that she was a tear factory even on good days. While struggling to survive on her family's meagre income, she did not think she had the authority to tell her husband to stop spending thirty per cent of their earnings on liquor. Fear of poverty and respect for society kept her locked in a bad marriage, as did the prospect of losing custody of their children. The glassy stare in her eyes revealed some of the despair.

One day, Godavari's neighbour, Vimal Dahule, told her about the programme that helped women pool their savings—sometimes as little as Rs. 20 a month—and then provide loans to each other. Defying her husband and leaving the house without permission, Godavari and some women in her community went to learn more about the programme. They decided to start their own village savings and loan group. Godavari was excited about what the bank and its manager might mean for them. Still, her husband tried to dispel what he considered her silly notions that any bank would help them."I don't want to have anything to do with the bank," he said at first, with a dismissive toss of his hands to his wife who convinced her that she should not be taken for a ride by a charlatan banker.

When I first proffered the loan, Godavari stuttered with fright and her honest face crumpled in despair. Clenching and unclenching her fists, she drank a full glass of water from a battered aluminium jug. I assured her that if she made a serious attempt at properly investing the loan and failed to generate a surplus, we would not divest her of her bare belongings in the way of a moneylender. Godavari scratched her head, did quick mental math and decided to give the loan a try. There was nothing to lose. When I placed the envelope in her astonished hands, her eyes grew large and lambent, and she darted at the chequebook lying on the table and then back at me. She signed the receipt in a hurried, untidy scrawl.

She screamed in delight as she saw what was inside the envelope. She trembled. Tears rolled down her cheeks. With our help and the combined resources of her new business partners, Godavari bought a cow for around Rs. 4,000, which continues to produce daily dividends—more than three pints of milk she sells to the upper-caste landowners in the neighbouring village. Recently, the cow gave birth to a calf. Godavari was already engaged in dairying as a wage labour, and her vision of an independent enterprise had been realised,

The experience reinforced our belief: you can't just give a woman a loan and then send her on her way—you must accompany her as she struggles to escape poverty. Godavari's business took off quickly, and she began earning enough income to provide for her family, send her daughters to school, and pay for her husband's medical bills. She gained some of the respect she deserved from her husband, who allowed her more freedom and even began to help her with her business ventures. Her community now sees Godavari as a 'husband-tamer' and a savvy businesswoman. Since joining the programme, Godavari has inspired other women in her community. It is a prime example of how economic security can provide the right aid for women and their children and even positively affect marriages.

Though illiterate, her skills in financial arithmetic are phenomenal. She and the thirty other women of the village Self Help Group even managed to chase the local liquor shop out of their village. They walk about proudly in their uniforms—identical saris they bought from the money they pooled from their precious savings. Contrast them with their appearance just a few years ago—a group in discoloured rags. She remembers standing for hours at the local water pump—which she could not touch—waiting for a higher caste woman to take pity on her and fill her bucket. She was so poor she washed her hair with mud and owned a single sari. When she laundered it, she had to stay in the river until it dried. She says, "When I started, I had no support from anyone, no education, no money. I was like a stone with no soul. When I joined the Self-Help Group, it gave me shape and life. I learned courage and boldness. I became a human being." An infectious smile seemed to have dug a permanent home in her face. Other women in this village got tiny loans to invest in miniature businesses.

A savvy woman

None had made better use of the cash than Renuka Mahalle, a wise, flinty young mother who put her profits from four loans into cows, goats, land, a sturdy house and private tutors for her daughter. "I can make money out of anything," she boasted in her wheezy voice, a flower-shaped gold stud glinting in her nose. Her house had small fire pits were lit by twigs that emitted flames and embers for cooking sorghum flatbread. A brown cow lay contentedly in the shade. When the dynamic Renuka got her first loan, for Rs. 5000, she already had Rs.2000 saved from working as a cook and raising chickens, the family trade. She invested her savings in a cow she sold for Rs. 10,000. Her next Rs. 10,000 she invested in a thresher machine. It takes care of her farming requirements, and she rents it out when it is not in use at her farm. The villagers are also happy they don't have to hire someone from outside.

Sushila's story tumbled out in a gruff voice. Despite a poor home, she had a wonderful childhood and dreamt of lending enthusiasm to the new house. An abusive husband shattered her dreams of a peaceful family life into a hundred tales of suffering. She worked twelve hours daily, six days a week. She held up her chafed hands as evidence, and we squatted by the fires, hearing the notes of the hounds dying out in the countryside, watching a small temple, shaded by a hallowed *pipal* tree, slowly filling up with worshippers.

When she was starving, her neighbours helped as best they could, she recalls, but the woman who helped most was her friend, who brought her to the Self-Help Group. She had to save a certain amount before qualifying for a loan—as do all members—so she took in laundry to supplement her tenant farming. Her bruised dream of happiness and prosperity slowly started healing. We had brought back some of the gloss of her dream.

When Laxmi, in a depleted village in Chandrapur, had first held Rs. 500 in her hands, they had trembled. Money gave strength to her hands and changed her life, as did thirty other women in the village who tilled a patch of soybean that glowed like emerald and scorched their bare feet. Laxmi's eyes filled with tears while telling us that, as a widow, she couldn't provide her four children with enough to eat. Today, although finances are tight, Laxmi and her family are getting back on their feet. "I've always wanted a better life but didn't know what to do, but now I have this mushroom-growing skill and can support my family. Why didn't you people come three years earlier?" she asks playfully.

The local panchayat leader, Ashabai, comes from a five-hundred-person village. "My village has no lights, no water, and no road. The women got together because of the *bishi* (an Indian *ROSCA*, Rotating Savings and Credit Association)." Ashabai was a woman of sterner stuff, and despite being alone, she maintained her patience, which would often run out. Exposure to the groups has honed her patience and built resilience. Initially, she attended the meeting with her husband in tow. A few months back, the husband left. Since then, Asha has been on her own. She knows she will be debarred from the group if the husband continues to accompany her and if she remains dependent on him. One of the cardinal goals of group membership is that women must be encouraged to gather enough self-confidence to no longer need male chaperones. Speaking about her experience on stage, she could mumble and stumble only a few sentences. Today, she is a refined, confident public speaker.

Rekha Asutkar, who now is an organizer for her saving group, used to reside in a tiny, rickety.

Her house could no longer withstand the fury of the monsoon. She was in a dilemma whether to invest her meagre savings in business or to construct a small, sturdy room. When the bank agreed to give her a loan to start a business, she built a pucca house and used the bank loan to set up a grocery store. She has a decent home and a small but flourishing grocery shop today. She proudly proclaims that Self Help Group women have become celebrities in Andhra Pradesh. She is confident that the day is not too far when a woman from Warora will grace the cover page of a women's magazine. The women snap pictures of various celebrations in their group as a matter of record for posterity.

Vimalbai was a fiercely independent woman endowed with the gift of logic and love for mainstream participation. Her rasping voice and stern demeanour marked her out for a leadership role. She wanted to understand and break all notions of male exclusiveness in local political decision-making. Her husband was a drunkard who used to beat her. She invited us into her hut, where it was dim and cool. She lit up the small *chulha* (stove) to brew tea and recounted how membership in the Self-Help Group helped her rebuild her confidence and life.

Manda had already taken out a loan to construct a house and was not eligible for a business loan, which she desperately needed. She was a reputed tailor in the village, but her sewing machine had broken beyond repair. Because of the drought, she had few remaining means of survival. She raised half the amount and took the rest from the moneylender. During one of my visits to her house, I saw a strange creature at her doorstep. Manda opened her steel almirah and took out a bag containing loose notes. She was stealthily counting them, trying to avoid my gaze. I could sense it was all about a moneylender's loan. I took out my wallet and gave her Rs. 1,000 with an assurance that I would assist her further if she shunned moneylenders. Manda resisted, saying my money was equally hard-earned, but took it hesitatingly, saying she would repay the whole amount as early as possible. I told her that I was not worried about getting back, and my anxiety was the continued dependence of the women on moneylenders.

Each of these women began with not a scintilla of hope. "I had nothing, nobody," said Mina, who worked as a maid for payment in rice after her husband abandoned her. "I was scared to become a member of the group. I was too poor to repay a loan. But now that I'm getting goats at reasonably priced loans, I'm interested."

"The village men would flare up at me if they found me talking to the male staff of the bank," recalls Savitri with a giggle. She remembers the *pradhan* (headman) asking her, 'Why were you talking to the bank staff alone?'I told him, 'I am talking to you alone right now. Is that any different?'He sputtered for a while, but that shut him up."

Bayabai still lives in a windowless hut, sleeps on a mat on the floor, and cooks outside over a twig fire, but the programme has made her rich in other ways. When it's dark inside the shack, she strikes a match, lights a kerosene lantern, and turns the flame up by twiddling the metal hoop at its side. An amber glow seeps through the dingy glass panels, a dull, flickering light, and shadows spill across the room."When I came to Charurkhati, I was like a stone with no soul," said Bayabai. "People would sneeringly comment, "See her, the dirty skin and bones. Is she a woman or a muddy stick?"The bankers gave me shape and life, courage and boldness. I became a human being." Her face had worn out, but her eyes were purposefully alight.

Attests Sanjay Modak, the *upsarpanch* (deputy headman), the strongman of the village: "It is only when the *mahila mandals* (women clubs) emerged that life changed in our village. Our women would not even sit, let alone talk with us. They tell us what to eat and how to function better in the fields. My mother's position in society depended on how many children she had. Her children consumed her energy. She had no time to think of the village or other women. My wife now works more outside than in the home. She not only runs her home but also helps other women run theirs. Our women now question and know their worth."

A Self Help Group also offers its members housing loans. It provides them with valuable items at cost price: seedlings and seeds for the vegetable garden, alum to purify drinking water, iodized salt to combat goitre. Bank employees hold workshops to educate borrowers, who have established village elementary schools, paying for them through their contributions. Many eat more nutritious food than before and now plan their families. Tellingly, the dowry custom is under siege.

We trained some women as village health workers. The quality these women had was not the mechanical ability to store information but to recognize needs, relate to them and communicate what they had learnt. Beginning in the benign area of health, the women slowly gained confidence and moved on to other social areas. They started asking for change from the bus conductor, demanded the presence of a school teacher and expected proper services from local village officials". The women's hands have now blossomed into fists," says Suvarnarekha Patil an NGO activist in the vanguard of the Self Help Group movement. "From birth, a woman is doomed in these parts. She is cursed and deprived—first of a mother's love, then of a husband's love. She is not married to a man but to his whole family. The only way she proves herself is by bearing children. They lend her prestige and become her security. A woman may have five daughters and one son. If you ask her how many children she has, she says one. She does not count the girls. That has begun to change."

Why does this focus on women?

The woman is the centre of these initiatives because she is the fulcrum of the village poverty economy. From the early dawn, the woman is up and around, working about the house, caring for the family and catering to her husband's whims. Millions of such women are also wage-earners, working all day on the farm. Back home in the evening, it is back to cooking and more chores. Yet these women match their male folk, nay surpass them, in everything—hard work, initiative, patience and adjustment. At the lower end of the economic strata, women have husbands who only drink and help produce children. However, the women still work from dusk to dawn, assisting their families, including a drinking allowance to errant husbands. While the village woman cooks, she may breastfeed one child and watch over three others. If she fails in any of these tasks or performs them too slowly, her husband often feels it is his prerogative to beat her. And yet, invariably, she considers her husband a god. The women are constantly on their toes at the well at dawn, in the hearth at dark, ploughing, sowing, harvesting, threshing, milling. As Muhammad Yunus himself says, "When a destitute mother starts earning an income, her dreams of success invariably centre around her children. A woman's second priority is the household. She wants to buy utensils, build a stronger roof, or find a bed for herself and her family. A man has an entirely different set of priorities. When a destitute father earns extra income, he focuses more on himself. Thus, money entering a household through a woman brings more benefits to the family."

Consequently, the vast majority of microloans go to women because experience has shown that women are more likely to reinvest their earnings in the business for the betterment of their families. As families cross the poverty line and micro-businesses expand, entire communities will stand to benefit. Jobs become available, know-how is shared, civic participation increases, and women are valuable members of their families and communities.

Women traditionally face more significant access barriers to formal banking services than even the poorest men and are thus also credit-constrained to a greater extent than men. In the developing world, women are not recognised as credit-worthy since they do not hold formal sector jobs or titles in their houses. Interestingly, women's lower opportunities, if they do not hold formal sector jobs, make them more likely to pay the high-interest rates required for sustainable microfinance.

Second, experience has shown that repayment is higher among female borrowers, primarily due to their more conservative investments and lower moral hazard risk. Since moral hazard seems to be the constraining factor in outreach to low-income households, women might be the more attractive clients. While adverse selection might be more problematic among women, the joint-liability technique helps control this risk.

Last but not least, one of the often articulated rationales for supporting livelihood finance and targeting women through Self Help Groups is that these groups are a compelling entry point for empowering women. Given an opportunity to fight hunger and poverty, a poor woman becomes a better fighter than a poor man. It has been our experience that poor women have an intense drive to move up; they are hardworking, concerned about their human dignity, concerned about their children's present and future, and willing to make personal sacrifices for the well-being of their children. For a woman to be empowered, she needs access to the material, human, and social resources necessary to make strategic choices in her life. Not only have women been historically disadvantaged in access to material resources like credit, property and money, but they have also been excluded from social resources like education. By putting financial resources in the hands of women, banks help level the playing field and promote gender equality. I was awed by the resilience and strength of the women I met. Given a chance to improve their lives through economic activity, they showed a remarkable ability to grasp the nuances of business. They disproved the myth that villagers are trapped in the sloth of poverty. Gandhiji's words always inspired me in *Harijan:*

"In the case of the Indian villagers, an age-old culture is hidden under an encrustment of crudeness. Take away the encrustation, remove his chronic poverty and illiteracy, and you have the finest specimen of what a cultured, cultivated, free citizen should be."

But even as the self-help philosophy grew and the movement spread, the slow response from banks showed that large swathes of women remained unserved. At one of my meetings, I discovered that none of the poverty-stricken women who attended had ever dared to apply for a microloan. One woman's pierced nose was empty because she had already sold her gold stud for money. Another's nine-year-old son pedalled a rickshaw for Rs 20 a day to keep the family fed. But they eagerly joined our new programme—and were pleased to see their goats multiply. They were still so poor that their bodies seemed little more than collections of bones beneath worn saris, but their new assets offered hope.

My farewell from Warora

By the time I left Warora for my new assignment elsewhere, the roots of the self-help movement had penetrated the nooks and corners of Warora's hinterland. The momentum was too vivid to wear off immediately. During one of my recent visits, I found that women had hollowed the male-dominated power grid in villages. Like termites, they had mined out the male bastions.

I remember there was a woman who started with a mud hut. When I returned after three years on a personal holiday, she had a three-room house with a cement floor, and the goats were kept in the hut where she had stayed before. When her group of women first came for loans, they sat hunched, looking down into their laps. They would take the small pile of pastel and white notes they got as part of a loan and fold it into a hairpin behind their ears. They were looking so frightened because, they said, they were afraid they couldn't pay it back. One of them was so dizzy that she wanted to know the name of the person who had recommended her for the loan. Some of them even suggested taking only a part of the loan. For the remaining, they said they would consult their husbands and then come back. Two or three years later, these women were running businesses and often involved in politics in their village. Does everyone succeed? No—but it is the same in the investment business. You don't want to take a lot of risk? Buy some hens. The less risk-averse borrowers will pool their loans, buy a baby water buffalo, and rent it to men for farming. And then some blow right past livestock and build a brick factory.

As individuals, women are insecure and indecisive, but when serried into groups, they blossom into creative efflorescence. I visited a village a month away from the rainy season. The villagers were getting their fields ready. Equipped with agricultural tools, the trained women measured the fields and estimated the quantities of needed fertilizers, insecticides and weed killers. Others observed and got trained on the job. "Our objective is to master all basic agricultural techniques perfectly," said Sunanda, a dynamic new farmer. Accounts were recorded meticulously, and the cash value of all borrowed inputs was noted and accounted later. Each shareholder had an individual account, and the borrower informed and attested the loans taken.

"This way, we are sure not to find ourselves with inflated bills after the harvests," Sunanda added, adding, "We make it a matter of principle to pay back the money lent to us to the last penny. We do not want to discourage those who trusted us." The village men were unanimous in their admiration. "We have been surprised by their rigorous management and the output of their fields," they remarked. In their determination to become self-reliant, the women had collected savings, which, complemented by a small government loan, was to help them set up a bore well equipped with a pump. It would irrigate seedlings before the first rains fell and augment the village's water supply. Taking advantage of this, the women could sell their harvest in the market before the other farmers at better prices. As they said, these earnings would "help improve the menus at home, help purchase medicines and clothes for the family." This year, part of the profit created a ten-hectare vegetable garden, which produced tomatoes, cabbages, onions, lettuce, and potatoes. Some of it was used locally. The rest were sold at the weekly markets. Despite the success of their enterprise, women still have several hurdles to overcome, not least the traditional prejudices against women's independence. For instance, most organisations giving agricultural loans prefer to give them to men as the leader of the women farmers confided, "Till now, we didn't even have our plough to work. We had to borrow it from the men. Sometimes, we had to postpone the dates of ploughing." The women had, therefore, decided that the profits from the next harvest of the vegetable garden would be used to buy ploughs. In the meantime, they did the work with their hands.

Rupali was so excited that she could barely stop talking about her experiences. "I used to be so ignorant—I barely stepped out of my house—but now I know where the BDO sits and where the Collector's Office is. If the village *sarpanch* (headman)does not listen to our problems, I do not hesitate to go straight to the higher officials to lodge my protest." Her confidence stems from her involvement with the literacy programme operating in her village for over five years. The women explain how they discovered their inner strength through participation in the Self Help Groups. It is no longer possible for anybody to short-change them by paying them lower wages. "Now we are armed with information. We know the minimum wage and demand it without hesitation," says Malabai. Earlier, the sarpanch would bring in cheap labour from neighbouring villages to work on government projects. "This is illegal. We fought against it and battled it to ensure the work was allocated to the villagers, and they were paid regular wages for their labour ." The real benefits, the women say, cannot be measured in rupees—a lesson for anyone who believes that people with low incomes are motivated simply by material needs and not the desire for respect, community and recognition. The fellowship they share with their sisters is vital to the entire programme. The Self Help Groups have become astringent for soaking up their members' pain.

If you visit Warora today, you will find that life is far different from what it was a few years ago. Not substantially wealthier, no—there is still drought, no industry, only rain-dependent agriculture—but better. Warora's villages have clean water; many have pipes carrying that water to a pump in every backyard. Most houses have soak pits, and a simple and cheap drainage system was set up outside every house to clean standing wastewater; they are moving on to toilets. In an area nearly barren of trees, Warora's villages have planted millions. The government's afforestation plans, supported by dollops of aid, have given a fillip to the greening of barren lands and helped restore the environment's health. There are several incidental benefits, such as better rainfall patterns, improved quality of soils, and food security. Dalits are less oppressed, and upper-caste women are free to leave the confines of their homes. Women are better educated and more interested in educating their girls. The fact that most credit is used for consumption and not for income-generation purposes is not necessarily an indictment of development finance. Consumption can go overboard if the loans finance a lavish wedding or other ceremony. But much micro-borrowing goes into paying school fees because the borrower can't afford the lump sum fees, paying for medical services, etc. Offering timely credit to a poor woman whose son needs medical attention is an essential benefit in terms of the created livelihood.

The most significant drain on a villager's finances is a health problem. Also, every day of sickness means the loss of a day's wages. Villagers must get timely medical care so ill health doesn't compel them to skip labour. Studies show that the effect of micro-credit is not only income enhancing but, more importantly, income smoothing, enabling the purchase of goods or services otherwise unaffordable. Self Help Groups have formed federations, leveraged their finances and influence, and even delivered insurance, ambulance services, and other commercial and government services. The loss of income due to sickness, the incapacitation of a borrower or a family member, and the high cost of health treatment are detrimental to individuals and families in the developing world. Therefore, it is not surprising that illness and death of family members are among the most common reasons why livelihood finance participants remain mired in poverty, default on their loans and drop out of a livelihood finance programme.it is a strong reason institutions think of providing micro-insurance to women of Self Help Groups. My personal experience is that villagers can themselves set up, administer and manage an insurance fund pooled out of their monthly savings; the school teacher or the postmaster could serve as ombudspersons.

Suppose you want to see the credibility of poor women borrowers. In that case, you must visit villages in the suicide-prone Yavatmal district of Maharashtra, where banks had to plough dud agricultural loans like a mountain of rotten potatoes. My experiences during the last few months in Yavatmal have made these convictions indelible. I led a credit camp for my company and engaged in housing finance through Self Help Groups in the interior tribal villages in Kelapur block. I was sad at the plight of a family whose tin roof had blown away. I offered a Rs. 5,000 loan to the women. To my great surprise, she refused, saying she could not repay it. I tried to convince her to accept it and to get my company's interest rate further reduced, but she remained unmoved. Her daughter, observing our interaction, told me that the mother would never take a loan, as the last time she took one, she was already under great moral stress and had to donate blood at least twice at the nearest hospital to meet her loan instalment commitment.

In Sakhra, deep into the forest belt infested by tigers and other wildlife, lies an island of incredible honesty. In a village called Nagezari, almost twenty kilometres deep in that belt, a group of twenty tribal women told me that they had repaid the bank loan despite assurances from political leaders that the government had waived the loans. They went to the bank office to ask the manager if the loans had been waived since they had the impression that the loans of all village borrowers were waived. He told them this was incorrect and the loans of agriculturists alone could be waived.

Sakhra is a unique example of totally illiterate backward women ensuring the rights the law has guaranteed them under their being forest tribals and also the protection under the laws for displaced people. Sakhra is a resettlement village where villagers uprooted by a development project have been rehabilitated in a forest. Seventy households led by Anusaya, lovingly called Amma, have fought independently. They demonstrated before the local administration for days to get a barely motorable road constructed. Each family owns six acres of irrigated land, at least a pair of bullocks, two cows and a few goats. Six enterprising young boys own premium brand motorcycles. A few weeks back, a tiger had mauled a resident beyond recognition.

Now, the villagers have set up bamboo fences around the courtyards of their houses. Ammai was a wonderful host and served a sumptuous meal to our entire group. I offered a token donation for village welfare after we had a splendid dinner at her place. Ammai was up in arms. "Feeding guests is a fulfilment of God's obligation. How dare you do that? If I visit your house, will you charge me for hospitality?" I became embarrassed when I realized that as we grow prosperous, our hearts grow narrower. These women are now star clients who can make the best of financial intuitions blush. For example, after support from her husband in establishing a cluster incubator in the village of Khairgaon, Ranibainow manages the hatchery on her own. Another incubator, belonging to Manisha Meshram, is now the family's most important source of income, as her husband is too old to work. This economic dependence, she says, has altered her family's internal structure, with particular implications for decision-making. Her two sons, who also contribute to the family's portfolio, now come to her to debate relevant issues and make joint decisions.

Four women in Maya's group in Bina village in Nagpur district had used their loan capital to buy the expensive thread needed for weaving fishing nets. Before joining the bank, they wove nets on a contract for others, arrangements under which they earned next to nothing for their efforts. Manda, the only tribal in the group, invested Rs. 5,000 in a grocery store she ran from her home. When her group was set up six years back, the four original members wanted no room for Manda until the branch manager told them sternly, "The bank was established for people like Manda, the dirt poor. If you do not take her, there will be no group here."

However large or small their income gains, poor women find empowerment through access to livelihood loans. According to the World Bank, for instance, livelihood finance empowers women by giving them more control over household assets and resources, more autonomy and decision-making power, and greater access to participation in public life. This defence of microcredit—particularly livelihood finance—stands or falls with individual success stories featuring women using their loans to start some small-scale enterprise, perhaps renting a stall in the local market or buying a sewing machine to assemble piece goods. There is no doubt that, when they succeed, women and their families are better off than they were before they became micro-debtors and have solved numerous community problems through grassroots measures. They have created ways for other women and themselves to earn a living, especially when traditional agriculture, mining and factory jobs are no longer available.

Leaders of these projects recognize that income alone is not enough to alleviate poverty, so they often pair skills training with education, particularly in primary and financial literacy, and give women information about their legal rights and social issues, including protection against violence and exploitation. Women farmers face various obstacles, including a lack of access to information technology, agricultural training, financial services, and support networks like co-operatives or trade unions. Without these services, women cannot develop resilience to withstand political, economic, social or environmental upheaval and remain dependent on their male family members. However, despite the structural problems and widespread despair, female entrepreneurs such as Godavari Uikey are finding creative ways to carve out a place for themselves in the marketplace, boosting the economy and their confidence and independence. Today, Godavari has repaid the first loan and gotten another, doubled her merchandise, and gained a new sense of freedom as the family breadwinner. Poor people show inspirational courage and the ability to transform the little the deck has dealt them into livelihoods for their families and communities. They already have skills, are politically conscious, and know the need to educate their children and care for their health. However, their lack of income makes using the skills they have impossible. Providing investment capital for additional income generation can unlock the capacity of poor people to solve many, if not all, of the manifestations of poverty that affect their lives.

I recently decided that it would be a good moment to go back to the villages in Maharashtra to find out what local people had to say about our twenty years of work among them. I uncovered memories of the early days of the social mobilization work. After over a decade and a half of it, I wondered what the villagers would say. Would there be the same story of initial enthusiasm and hope worn down by a string of disappointments as the fate of the social actions programme before me? Did villages still suffer much poverty? Where were all these empowered women and their successful microenterprises? I was interested in these questions because I had detected a new mood at the corporate offices of banks and microfinance institutions: a growing sense that another change in direction was immediately needed. On a walk through the quiet lanes in October, past herds of snoozing water buffalo and carts pulled by teams of oxen in Nandra, Swati pointed to the village hand pump she had gotten fixed. She showed off the new brick lanes, electrical poles, and street lights installed on her watch and checked on the progress of a new community.

I found that the villagers had now put a premium on educating girls. It was in contrast to the trail of unkempt, unwashed children who would circle me during my stay in the village. I overheard a group of children in school singing a series of what sounded like nursery rhymes. On closer listening, they became catchphrases from popular television commercials. The women's bright clothes were flashy symbols of their newfound prosperity; some had jazzed up their houses. Irrigation previously had consisted of asking the gods for the rainbow. I now found sprinklers spouting rainbow streams of water into the fields. In one village, a new deep well replaced the inadequate shallow one. A large pond had been dug to catch rainwater and provide for aquaculture. Irrigation stretched from the pond to fields planted with grains, quick-growing rice and potatoes. There was watershed management to stop erosion of the steep slopes. A light shone in the villagers' eyes when they talked about the transformation of their village economy. Hope had begun coursing through communities once shackled by fatalism and low expectations. It is an essential step for a world where people live on less than an American dollar a day. Women who were previously shy and withdrawn are stepping out of the confines of their homes to acquire an identity of their own. They have learnt the art of adequately presenting themselves in the assembly of men, whittling down emotion to its barest expression. Over the years, most of the one million women elected at the panchayat level came from the Self Help Groups. The women are not asking for handouts. They are simply asking for an opportunity. People experiencing poverty probably have a more significant say over their lives than at any other time in history. Though not dramatic, not a headline grabber, the change is a slow and quiet transformation underway in even the most far-flung villages. Almost everywhere I went, I found local campaigns to share essential resources like land and water, to build democratic school boards, trading co-operatives and credit movements, and to make the government accountable at the highest and lowest levels. These are the small revolutions that are changing the world. But the revolution is not yet complete. Now is the time to move beyond livelihood finance to create broader economic opportunities for women, situating them as central and pivotal players in the 'macroeconomy'. Only then will we bring our revolution full circle. In the words and expressions of these unlettered people, I found the bliss and flavour of quotidian wisdom worn humbly and lightly. In the lives of these tenacious women, I found the story not of a country's doom but a story of a country's will to survive.

It may not be a revolution, but at the very least, it is.

* * * * *

5. WHERE PEOPLE PLAN THEIR DESTINIES

Nandra village in Chandrapur district of Maharashtra has access to the nearest motorable road by a three-kilometre stretch of dust that masquerades as a road. During the rains, this path would be a treacherous swamp. Someone intent on finding new passages across the bush might drive through, on the red and rutted track that is the only thoroughfare, without pause. But a stranded traveller, perhaps someone whose motorcycle has broken down among herds of cattle and thickets of thorn, might stop here and glimpse, for a moment, lives remote from the towns. With fewer than one hundred residents,Nandra's tender children outnumbered adults and appeared like wandering poultry.

It was scorched, so there were long stretches of dusty roads, yellowed brush and withered and knotty trees. The earth in some areas was a deep red colour, rich in iron. Tiny villages dotted the landscape, and rutted dirt roads snaked into the odd copse of trees. We finally arrived at the town where I was to implement on an intensive scale the lessons I had gleaned from my earlier experiences as a development banker. The focus was to be a development strategy owned and driven by the local people. After my limited exposure to development banking programmes in my earlier assignments, I believe those toiling at the bottom of the pyramid need all the levers they can get.

Bottom-up approach

The 'bottom-up' approach is about living and working with people experiencing poverty, humbly listening to them to gain their confidence and trust. It could not be manipulated with money or achieved by urban development assumptions onto existing rural practices, which may destroy workable structures. New ideas should be our lifeblood. We must first understand their economy at a granular level and, most importantly, thoroughly understand their local culture. That approach is a welcome contrast to the grandiose foreign aid schemes that do more harm than good. Experiences show that governments too often derail the money intended to help people experiencing poverty to pad the pockets of civil servants instead. Mired in bureaucracy and corruption, the benefits of the development rarely reached those most needed.

The bottom-up approach means that local actors participate in decision-making about the strategy and in selecting the priorities that require persuasion in their local area. Experience has shown that the bottom-up approach should not be considered an alternative to top down approaches from national and regional authorities but rather as a combination and interaction with them to achieve better overall results.

Rural policies following this approach should be designed and implemented in the way best adapted to the needs of the communities they serve. One way to ensure this is to invite local stakeholders to take the lead and participate. The involvement of regional actors includes the population at large, economic and social interest groups and representative public and private institutions. Capacity building is an essential component of the bottom-up approach, involving:

Awareness raising, training, participation and mobilisation of the local population to identify the strengths and weakness of the area (analysis); Establish clear criteria for selection at a local level for appropriate actions (projects) to deliver the strategy. The regional leaders aided us in involving different interest groups in drawing up a local development strategy.

Participatory approach

Participation should not be limited to the initial phase. Still, it should extend throughout the implementation process, contributing to the strategy, the accomplishment of the selected projects, stocktaking, and learning for the future. There are also important issues of transparency which need to be addressed in the mobilisation and consultation procedures to reach a consensus through dialogue and negotiation among participating actors.

Too often, how outside aid displaces or discourages local resource contributions, resulting in total aid that is zero-sum or, worse, negative-sum. The constant presence of poverty and despair on your doorstep imparts an oppressive sense of guilt and frustration to life here, which no amount of benevolent paternalism ever entirely removes. When poor communities think at the human level, all their goals are interconnected. However, the goals suit donors and governments under the top-down model without a global grassroots movement partnering with the communities. Rural development involves the integration of its subsystems into an organic whole.

The buzzwords *empowerment, participation, partnership, ownership, transparency* and *accountability* all imply changes in power and relationships. Still, these are contradicted, especially in aid by top-down standardised demands and the mindset that goes with 'delivery' Reputed consultancy firms now use the "curveball" technique during training to put consultants in situations where they need to think fast and solve problems on the fly. The aim is to see how they respond and whether they can think on their feet. Modern education means that younger consultants are better prepared for this than more senior staff because students today are encouraged to discuss and question rather than just being told what to think.

It is now almost an item of faith with me that the poor act rationally, however straitened their circumstances. If their undertakings are too small, or their efforts too thinly spread, to be efficient, it is not because they have miscalculated but because the markets for land, credit or insurance have failed them. Good management of even the most minor asset can be crucial to poor people who live in precarious conditions, threatened by lack of income, shelter and food. Importing expensive, unworkable ideas, equipment and consultants from the North destroys communities' capacity to help themselves. Any goal-driven from the top by international donors and governments, not accountable to the communities served, and without financial transparency is doomed to fail.

Although imported programmes have the benefit of supplying 'pre-tested' models, they are inherently risky because they may not take root in the local culture when transplanted. Home-grown models have greater chances of success. The hundreds of millions of households that constitute the rural poor are a potential source of great wealth and creativity. Under present institutional, cultural, and policy conditions, they must first seek their survival. Their poverty deprives them and the rest of us of the more excellent value they could produce under more conducive circumstances. The people who pioneered the world's most successful development programmes recognized this potential and always sought to evoke it. The results have been miraculous.

The poor must be given a platform

We need to bring in the poor to the conversation. Interventions that consider the end user almost always have better success rates than top-down decision-making. However, many social enterprises are still not talking enough to their poor customers to find out what they want. Too often, policymakers have no idea what their end beneficiaries need. I hope that the expanding use of technology across all segments of society will help create platforms for exchanging ideas so that people can better express their needs.

The poor are yet to find their voice, even as the media (for that matter, the entire establishment) have become the megaphones of the prospering classes. The preference for growth over social justice, indeed the argument that economic growth is the road to social justice, is advocated over and above increased spending and is required for accelerated growth to translate into inclusive growth. The answer, I fervently believe, lies in inclusive governance. In the absence of Inclusive governance, the people at the grassroots, the intended beneficiaries of poverty alleviation programmes, are left abjectly dependent on a bureaucratic delivery mechanism over which they have no effective control. The alternative system would be participatory development, where the people can build their future through elected representatives responsible to the local community and responsive to their needs.

Not only is responsive bureaucratic administration almost a contradiction in terms, but the Indian experience of the last six decades would appear to confirm that bureaucratic delivery mechanisms absorb a disproportionately high share of the earmarked expenditure: up to 85 paise in the rupee, said Rajiv Gandhi; perhaps 85 paise says the Planning Commission in a recent evaluation; not relatively so high, says the Prime Minister. We can leave it to experts to argue how many angels can dance on the head of a pin; for our purposes, it is enough to note that the delivery mechanism itself absorbs 75% to 85% of expenditure on poverty alleviation schemes. No wonder outcomes are so derisory. A; a large number of schemes are directed at the same set of beneficiaries through mutually insulated administrative silos set up government with the intent of jealously guarding their respective fiefdoms. Thereby, the convergence of schemes at the delivery point becomes virtually impossible, thus depriving beneficiaries of the multiplier effect if they use their locally elected leaders and have the authority to plan and implement the utilisation of these resources in keeping with their respective priorities. So far, I am on well-trodden ground. However, the argument for a systemic reordering of the delivery mechanism to shift from bureaucratic delivery to participatory development runs much more profound.

The limitations of experts

The failure in practice of so many typical professional solutions points to examining the perceptions and priorities of professionals—those standard, non-poor, urban-based and numerate members of elites who define poverty and how to tackle it. The other is to examine the perceptions and priorities of people experiencing poverty themselves. Neither has received much attention in anti-poverty discussions. Most professionals—politicians, bureaucrats, scientists, academics and bankers—have plunged into debate and action in the middle without questioning what has brought us there, what we see and believe, or what others see and feel. We have had neither time nor incentive to examine ourselves and our predispositions, nor people experiencing poverty and theirs. In contrast with everyday professional practice, our starting point here is different: it is to stand back and analyse the divergent views of deprivation and priorities held by these two groups—professionals and poor people themselves.

Top managers, academics and consultants live on a planet of their own—in a total disconnect with the average citizen—dominated by summits, conclaves and conferences – each one considered an important saloon for designing some unique and path-breaking solutions. The same big names adorn the podiums, speaking about lofty aspirations and oversized ambitions, preening and drooling the same figures, the exact weary phrases reverberating the halls. The same residents chewing on the same cud amidst the usual fanfare that marks such events as the latter-day emperors—presidents, prime ministers, plutocrats, puppets, dictators, heads of scientific bodies and development organizations and barons of finance parade in their pinstripe suits, labour in their ivory towers and ride in their jets as poor people continue to suffer the pangs of poverty. The glitz of advertisements, posters, brochures, campaigns, publicity material and fancy talks overflows with verbiage and rhetorical grandeur that give an impression that a mountain is going into labour. And what we get at the end is just a mouse. The speakers exult in long-winded commentaries without savouring life itself. They are like someone who stands on the bank of a river, taking it as his ultimate destination, while the poet plunges into deep waters, for isn't that the only way to taste the flavour of the water midstream? We live in an age when noisy posturing substitutes for reasoned debate too often, and brash opinion trumps hard facts. The thread of the argument usually disappears in a blizzard of gee-whiz statistics, acronyms, and catchphrases in interviews with eminent folks of all kinds. Yet overuse renders the words used to describe them—inclusive growth, environmental sustainability, poverty eradication – meaningless. They will quibble over how to fix responsibility, fight over words in long documents, challenge evidence presented as proof of the crisis, and negotiate percentages and deadlines for reducing poverty levels.

During my assignments in rural India, I witnessed how seemingly simple knowledge can significantly impact farming communities. I have been puzzled ever since why information-driven initiatives have not flourished. Many of the Self Help Groups I worked with struggled to come together to save Rs. 20 per month, never mind becoming the catalysts of change in their communities. Their struggle was not due to a lack of ability but merely a lack of willingness. My boss has emphasized this point many times. Still, I did not honestly believe him until I witnessed the construction of a community well and the installation of a hand pump, the money for which came as voluntary contributions from women. Without any external assistance or prompting, the villagers convened and decided to take up the challenge.

At the site, there was a high level of organization. The monitoring was on how much each family had contributed and worked. Men and women were working diligently together, hauling stones up the hill. The entire project was finished in a month. And yet this was the same village whose SHGs could not manage to meet together once a month to save Rs. 20. If only they could be convinced that building the foundations for development, such as constructing water-harvesting structures or investing in good breed animals for future dairy profits, was of equal importance to that of building the community well, then rapid changes in the livelihoods of the people could happen.

The project was a watershed. It showed us the potential for collective action that lay beneath the villagers' passive exterior and paved the way for the building of the village centre. Villagers worked together, stitching banners, painting posters, erecting flagstaffs on the roofs, and stringing wires across the street for the reception of government officials who came to visit. They marvelled at this voluntary initiative of the local community. It was a significant lesson for them.

I saw villages that enjoyed a dramatic increase in crop yield and incomes after agricultural scientists advised farmers on watershed techniques—a fancy term for digging ditches so good that soil is conserved. While it will not solve India's deep-rooted agriculture problems, better information can significantly boost food production and rural incomes. Although there is much discussion in public forums about involving stakeholders in the appropriate development of the society in which the poor live, poor people rarely get the opportunity to develop their agenda and vision or set terms for the involvement of outsiders. The participatory paradigm illustrates that people participate in plans and programs we—outsiders—have designed. Not only is there little opportunity for them to articulate their ideas, but there is also seldom an institutional space where their ingenuity and creativity in solving their problems can be recognized, respected and rewarded. It resembles the situation of the proverbial cart placed before the horse. Any such project requires meticulous planning and careful implementation, involving complete and accurate information on all the essential variables, including socio-cultural, environmental, and economic aspects.

Our perception of superior wisdom

One of the things that can happen as you go into a community to serve it is a subtle dehumanization of the people there. It's not intentional, but it happens, especially when you roll into a village with formulated projects. There is a difference between being invited into town to live and learn where you can help with the endogenous development process already underway and arriving with ready-made solutions to problems you haven't yet encountered but assume (or hope) exist. It's as if you've got a hammer and are looking for nails. This approach shifts the people in your new community from the subject to the object of development. If the inhabitants have not yet given you their trust and shown you the social topography of the community, the people may even seem like obstacles! You think, "If it weren't for these damn people and their baffling behaviour, I'd have had these women's projects finished long ago!"

Tackling poverty requires an approach that starts with the people themselves and encourages initiative, creativity, and drive from below, which must be at the core of any transformation of their lives to be lasting and enduring. I had the privilege of watching the village women acquire a sense of dignity once they had the tools for self-sufficiency. And I learned, maybe most importantly, to listen with my heart and not just my head. Are poor clients last on the long list of our objectives?

Villagers no longer trust the elite. In this, their instincts are correct. The *gram panchayat* (village council) members are also handicapped. On their backs ride the brokers of power and influence, who dispense patronage to convert a mass movement into a feudal oligarchy. They are self-perpetuating cliques who thrive by invoking the slogans of caste and religion and by enmeshing the living body of the panchayat in their net of avarice. For such persons, the masses do not count. The lifestyles of such persons, their thinking—or lack of it—their self-aggrandisement, corrupt ways, linkages with the vested interests in society, and sanctimonious posturing are wholly incompatible with work among the people. They are reducing the panchayat organisation to a shell from which the spirit of service and sacrifice loses relevance.

The panchayat leaders block officials, and the local elite shows no sensitivity to the poor people's problems during their visits to villages. They strut arrogantly, treating others like *prajas* (subjects), which anyone of consequence of India usually does. It requires a temperament honed in the company of individuals steeped in noble values to endow oneself with charm, grace and the ability to mix easily with all ranks. The villagers consistently speak to visitors scathingly of the snobberies of the elite.

That paradoxical nature of India is a cliché, which has worn its usage rather well due to the truth embedded in it. The paradox is rooted in the attempted imposition of a modern democratic ethos on an entrenched feudal culture, which articulates itself in various ways. The dominance of a feudal mindset in India resulted from centuries of Brahmanism, which privileges birth over all other attainments, thus preventing the maturing of democracy in the country. Political choices are made not based on merit but on family or other primordial ties. Affirmative action programmes are now aggressively realigning the caste calculus. No one wishes to harm powerful interest groups.

It is, however, not to diminish the role of professional outsiders who have successfully entered into the conditions and outlooks of rural people to fashion programmes from the inside out, so to speak, by showing deep respect for the capabilities of the people whose lives they hope to improve and being persistent as well as patient (being impatiently patient, one might say). We must try to relate to our clients as people, not as some mathematical abstraction or algebraic alphabet.

What is now needed is for development managers to work with people at the lowest level of the economic ladder rather than dealing with them as statistics in a file. We need people with discerning minds and receptive hearts.

The determinants of poverty reduction are policy instruments that benefit the dominant political power coalition but also benefit poverty reduction. If a set of instruments harms the interests of the dominant alliance, it will not succeed, even if it is known to eliminate poverty. Advocacy for poverty reduction must mean advocating for instruments that we know will lead to this outcome and for a realignment of the dominant coalition to orient it to the interests of people experiencing poverty. Specifically, this means that we should advocate for the empowerment of the poor so that they can indeed challenge the dominant interests and shift alliances in a way that will make possible policies and interventions for poverty reduction.

Regarding policy matters, there is a vital concern at the senior levels of banks for reforming the rural credit delivery system and making it more effective. It is because of the heightened interest in self-help groups among top executives who have participated in seminars or workshops organised by foundations, universities, and the government. Seminars are also used for business purposes, where the institutions sponsoring the show showcase their achievements. These seminars resonate with buzzwords and end in copious policy statements. Participants arrange discussions and workshops over glitzy parties at expensive hotels. I had a quick eye for vanity and would perceive the frequent contradictions between how people talked and the realities of the situation.

Nevertheless, most banks' successful development finance programmes are driven more by individuals than institutions. The difference is that it accounts for the level of commitment. Most senior managers are thrifty in praising juniors. The time has come when we must institutionalize the best practices by recognising individuals who have innovated them. Recognition indicates an organization's endorsement and appreciation of an individual's work. It brings it to the notice of those who can replicate it with necessary modifications based on the local culture.

Any debate about the economic policy for low-income people is usually tortuous, long-winded and insular. Without poverty eradicated, there will not be anti-poverty programmes from which funds are siphoned for private use. Without laws, there will not be opportunities to extort side payments for their violations. A vast number of papers are required to complete even a small piece of work, which then meander through several sections before they can yield fruitful action. To cut through the fog, we have to lend our ear to the voice of the people who are the stakeholders. We need innovative solutions that can consider the peculiarities of the people at the bottom of the pyramid. Social innovation occurs at multiple levels, driven by a passion to make a difference.

Financial institutions have recently focussed on scaled-down versions of their conventional products. They realised very late that rural society has peculiarities and requires exclusive products appropriate to its needs. The poor have different requirements than the urban clients; hence, research will have to be conducted on financial versus consumer products to see the feasibility of the product—for example, documentation. Electricity and telephone bills are readily available in cities, but villagers often do not have those amenities. Power breakdowns plague some villages, and so have solar-powered or battery-powered refrigerators. A monthly saving scheme is suitable for city dwellers, but villagers will love a daily collection scheme because constraints prevent them from accumulating money over a month.

Thinking about novel uses of existing products, such as mobile phones, is another source of solutions. The mobile phone is part of various business processes, with poor farmers accessing commodity prices and providing vital health information to rural families to pay for water. Since the majority of these farmers are women, this means not only overcoming decades of neglect of smallholder farmers in general but also overturning generations of entrenched gender inequality, during which women have had less access to the essential elements of farming: land ownership, seed and fertilizer, capital and credit, education and training.

My experience working with poor women emphasises that work is their foremost priority. Most poor women in villages are intelligent, hard-working and have nerves of titanium. They know that if they do not work, their families will not eat. All self-employment—sewing, delivering small items, making handicrafts—could be facilitated with a small amount of capital for a sewing machine, a bicycle, or tools. The availability of decent loans is far more vital to them than shaving a few points off the interest rates of those loans.

Over years of wandering the villages, I have revised much of the wisdom I have received about our rural priorities. We must see the reality of poverty and vulnerability through the eyes of a particular individual, typically a woman, and understand how that person strives to overcome it. This way, we can get a feel for her daily worries and needs and develop solutions that are relevant to her needs.

Involvement of the poor

It's crucial to help people shift their thinking so they believe they can do the job. Role models matter more than words. Mentors are more important than formal training. To that end, we must introduce bank clients to people like themselves who are succeeding in the kind of environment in which they will need to succeed. The tacit knowledge that senior executives have accumulated over the years must be passed on face-to-face, revealing culture in action.

Consider, for example, the remoteness of our professional lives as bankers from our villages. In the town, each successive generation is born into the rigidity of caste; each generation must bear the avarice of the moneylender and the merchant and the random cruelty of nature: floods, famines and pestilence. And yet, the majority survive and adapt. In other words, there is some collective wisdom in the villages for which the professional's knowledge is not a substitute. It is why the divide between the professionals and the villages is so severe; now, if we go to the villages, it is to study and do good for them—but not become *of* them.

Don't volunteer for work where you 'educate' the community about its problems, in which you generate plans and then get 'buy-in' from the community, and in which the priority is the development product (latrines, health centre, church building) rather than the people, for which you bring in the capacity rather than help build it within the community. This kind of 'help' will likely stunt development because it creates dependency, conflict and feelings of helplessness. If you are already inside such an organization, do what you can to help colleagues realize that development is an ongoing, endogenous process. It cannot simply lurch along, dependent on outsiders arriving with solutions and resources.

Instead of mapping problems from needs through external solutions, help the community identify its values and map them through local resources to develop a vision and action plan. We need the kind of intervention that gets people experiencing poverty over a bump in the road, not the kind that builds the road, provides the car, petrol and driver, buckles the seatbelts and pays the tolls.

I have encountered many small organizations that handle all their international consultancy work in-house. They could easily have given contracts to the swelling band of consultants growing up as microfinance has expanded worldwide, but they chose not to. Instead, they send their staff so what the world sees of these organizations is not polished international jet-setters but men of modest backgrounds and basic English language skills, lacking fluency in the latest microfinance theories but single-mindedly committed to getting on with the job and happy to work long hours as long as they can find somewhere to sleep soundly and cook food. Having come up through the ranks, they are used to being reposted from branch to branch throughout the entire network of the bank.

Writing good memoranda and reports and speaking well in meetings with important people are often rewarded, and the lowest value lies in hearing the poor. Some senior staff regard immersions as frivolous voyeurism and feel personally threatened by them. More activity, aid, projects, and coordination mean more office time and less field time. The virtual reality in which its authors live, full of action plans, road maps and fact sheets, is frightening—only intellectual activists who have no idea how to reach the impoverished need that. Seniors must immerse themselves periodically in the lives of people experiencing poverty they serve to grasp the reality.

What is required is sympathetic but hard-headed leadership operating from various institutional bases (government agencies, NGOs, banks). It should make common cause with rural people, learning with and from them how to make desired and sustainable improvements in the customers' conditions of life. NGOs that carry out developmental work must work within programmes specified by planners in far-removed developmental agencies and donor institutions. Creative plans that run counter to the conventional wisdom at the core of most programmes seldom qualify for funding. Thus, project proposals reflect these far-removed planners' requirements regarding methodology and outcomes. Demonstrating compliance on paper is more important than getting the job done. As a result, recipients of developmental funds spend significant time preparing reports that will find approval from the planners to qualify for continued funding and spend less time worrying about what benefits the poor.

I feel that approaches to rural development that respect rural people's inherent capabilities, intelligence and responsibility and systematically build on their experience have a reasonable chance of significantly improving those people's lives. The real challenge for development practitioners is finding tools aligned with local capabilities. If, therefore, nearly fifty years later, it has been found necessary to re-emphasise the need to ensure that social justice accompanies economic growth, it is not because we were not conscious of that need from the start but because we only now have come to realise that, however high its rate, economic growth does not automatically generate a proportionate rise in financial status.

Participatory research implies a process in which local people articulate their views and knowledge. It is they who describe and analyse their situation and problems. Although the level of control may vary, they are in charge of the process. Action is an essential part of the research process. People get together and discuss possible solutions to the problems they have made visible and think of actions to take. Participatory research can, therefore, be empowering. Empowerment, however, cannot be uncritically assumed to result from participatory research.

As a development journalist, I always travelled with a camera. I had a morning college curriculum and spent evenings working with a newspaper. Photojournalism was a specialized field, and I had developed enough expertise to get bylines for my pictures. This skill further helped me ingratiate myself with the villagers during my rural assignment. Whether digging the bed of an irrigation canal, repairing a road at the height of summer, or transplanting rice seedlings in the wind and rain of July, all enthusiastically posed for me.

One of the basic requirements of a bank account is a photograph. Every individual was required to submit three copies of a picture to open a bank account. I found this requirement the biggest bottleneck for villagers, particularly women. They would incur not only the expense of the studio photograph itself but that of travelling not once but twice, often ten kilometres, to the town in which the studio lay, first to have the photograph taken, then back to collect the pictures after the three days it took to process and print the photographs. Dairy farmers were in a worse plight. When an animal died, the insurance company required a close-up photo of the dead animal in a pose that displayed the insurance tag latched to the earlobe. Sometimes, the borrower would surrender his claim if he could not shell out the required amount for the photograph.

Colour photography had just been introduced in India and was a great novelty. Previously, colour photo rolls had to be sent to Mumbai for printing, but a lab had recently opened in Nagpur, offering a substantial inaugural discount to attract customers. The printing process had a technique that produced four passport-size prints on a single postcard-sized sheet. The cost was, therefore, kept to the barest minimum. We retained three copies for the bank's use and returned the extra copy to the customer as a complimentary souvenir. My staff also visited the farms to photograph dead animals for insurance claims; this token service won us a lot of laurels. The bank already had a provision in its operations manual for reimbursement of the expenses of such photographs. We used this provision to purchase photo rolls and defray the costs of the processing lab.

The failure of urban assumptions

The reality of village life as experienced by the poor living on the margin of existence often differs from the assumptions made by the administrators, who do not have a deeper perspective of life at the ground level and whose understanding comes from secondary sources. Past biases and prejudice may also colour these assumptions. It is difficult for us to understand the fears, the hesitancy, the pain and the labour with which the poor live, which separates the project from its implementation, or what is easy or difficult for the rural poor.

As Robert Chambers has pointed out, the rich, the powerful, and the urban-based professionals are at the core of the development process, while the poor, the weak and the rural people are at the peripheries, leading to a systematic bias regarding rural poverty. Any attempt at economic reform or better governance cannot succeed without addressing the needs of the poor. Gandhi advised policymakers: 'Recall the face of the poorest and the weakest man whom you may have seen, and ask yourself if the step you contemplate is going to be of any use to him.'

Then there is the new phenomenon of rural development tourism—brief visits which may be part of a CSR initiative of corporate houses that plant saplings in a few villages and then spend a fortune to run massive banner lines to continue their commitment to Rural India. Roadside tarmac meetings with the more influential people in rural areas, asking the predetermined questions. Car convoys with the entourage zoom through a crowd of villagers overawed by the grand peacockry. Vehicles are a classic expense because donor agencies love having cars that can dazzle people and draw attention. These projects require grassroots workers who can stay a few days at the centre and get complete insights into the villagers' problems and needs.

The aid structure often involves top-down decisions, incredible bureaucracy and paperwork. Most development practitioners will tend to agree that aid personnel normally interact little with the project beneficiaries and are more interested in the documentation of the partner agency than confirming whether it is practising what it has documented. Lack of time eliminates the open-ended question; fact-checking is impossible, and prudent, hopeful, or otherwise self-serving lies become accepted as truth. Refugees in a rural camp said of government officials,

"They come, and they sign the book, and they go", and "They only talk to the buildings. We must crane our necks in the caustic heat to see them, forget about talking with them." "They slouch in grimy plastic chairs under a nearby tree. Or else they plop themselves down where they can and start beavering away."

The visitor sets out late, delayed by last-minute business, by subordinates or superiors anxious for decisions, by breakfast delayed at his wife's eagerness to pack some sandwiches for the husband lest he might have to take a nibble of the unhygienic outside food; there could be a last-minute cable or telephone call from an upcountry colleague. Delays might come from mechanical or administrative problems with vehicles or urban traffic jams. Even if the way is not lost, and there is enough fuel and no breakdowns, the programme usually slips behind schedule. The visitor is ensconced in the luxury of the Land Rover, seeking a temporary escape from the rigours of an imposed rural visit through music on headphones.

As the entourage arrives, accompanied by a haversack of sandwiches and soda-water bottles, there is a gala welcome, a tribal dance by girls, women in traditional attire daubing vermilion on the foreheads of the temporary gods, dignitaries warming hands on flickers of holy fire, local notables (headmen, chairpersons of village committees, village accountants, progressive farmers) waiting obsequiously for a *darshan* (view) of the dignitaries. Whatever their private feelings, the people had been taught to give their children an early bath and dress them in their best clothes. The school teachers have been helping the girls rehearse the welcome dance for the dignitary. All are mouthing slogans that will portray the visitor as a great saviour.

Buntings are hung; the villagers remain awake overnight, cleaning the entire village. Girls had got up early to deck their front yards with colourful *rangoli* (ornate patterns drawn with coloured chalk powder). As the dignitary's car zooms in, you have the village official in his pinstripe suit chasing the car with impeccable etiquette to be the one privileged to open the door and usher the visitor into a new world.

They nervously respond in ways which they hope will bring benefits and avoid penalties. As the day wears on and heats, the visitor becomes less inquisitive, asks fewer questions and is finally glad, exhausted and bemused to retire to the rest house, the host official's residence or back to an urban home or hotel. Before returning, he asks his deputy to write remarks in the Visitors Book using the most fulsome adjectives, and he mechanically signs off without bothering to read the statements. Villagers suggest they have prepared a special meal for the dignitary, putting their culinary skills to the best use. A few offer packs of custard apples and exotic local varieties of vegetables, which the driver manages safekeeping. After the dignitary's departure, the village returns to normal, no longer wearing its unique face. These people have no time for piffling sentimentality when they have to return to their everyday struggles.

For government staff, there are similar pressures and patterns. On the first appointment, the inexperienced technical or administrative officers have to work in the poorer, geographically more remote, and politically less significant areas. Those who are less able, less noticed, or less influential remain in those outposts longer, if not permanently. The more able and visible, and those who ingratiate themselves to bosses or have friends in headquarters, are soon transferred to more accessible or prosperous rural areas or to urban peripheral regions, which continue to be rural areas, thanks to certain inept yardsticks set by government authorities. With the promotion, contact with rural areas, especially the more remote districts, recedes.

Suppose a severe error occurs or a powerful politician is offended. In that case, the officer may earn a 'penal posting' to serve out punishment time in some place with poor facilities—a remote area, hot and healthy, inadequately connected to the nearest town, without proper infrastructure, distant from the capital—in short, a place where poorer people live. The pull of urban life will remain: children's education, medical treatment for the family, chances of promotion, pleasant company, consumer goods, cinemas, libraries, hospitals, and power, all drawing bureaucrats away from rural areas and towards the major urban and administrative centres.

Once established in offices in the capital or regional or provincial headquarters, bureaucrats and bankers quickly become over-committed in terms of their time unless they are idle, incompetent, or exceptionally able and well-supported. They have meetings, committees, sub-committees, memoranda, reports, programme notes and urgent papers; vendors trying to get their air conditioners, furniture, computers, taxi and travel booking services organisation-approved; going daily through the dossier of newspaper cuttings, staff recruitment, training programmes for staff, workshops for themselves; finalising tour itineraries with personal secretaries, discussing weekend recreation plans with liaison staff, disciplinary enquiries, and far too many investment experts with alluring investment options and opportunities. There are times of the year, during the budget cycle, performance review, preparing and approving business plans, and supervising proper juxtaposition of figures on the spreadsheet when they cannot contemplate leaving their desks. The emphasis on agricultural and rural development creates work, further restricting them in their offices.

If the head of the department or organisation is inactive, he may be relatively free. But the more he tries to drive his goals and introduce new management techniques that he picks up from the occasional seminars that are part of his professional circuit, the busier is our official. Post-seminar and – workshop organisation consumes further precious time: business cards sorted, emails sent to important participants with brief but pithy sentences praising their ideas, and acknowledging with appreciation emails from participants who have similarly eulogised him.

By then, it will be time for the next seminar. The same formalities undergo repetition. The subject experts in the organisation prepare registration, travel and hotel bookings, and short background papers. The circuit continues, and the networking process keeps sprawling, spawning a planet. The more paperwork is involved, the more coordination and integration set in. Consequently, the more reports have to be written and read, the more inter-departmental coordination and liaison committees grow.

The more critical these committees become, the more members they have, the longer their meetings take, and the longer their minutes grow. The demands of aid agencies are a final straw, requiring data, justifications, reports, evaluations, visits by missions, and meetings with ministers. Each member is on so many committees that it is hard to ensure that he at least marks his attendance even though he may be mentally occupied with the agenda of another meeting. The staff must process data, find logical conclusions, and marshall arguments to support their assumptions. A whole battery of staff is immersed in designing flip charts and preparing PowerPoint presentations, embellishing them with illustrations, graphs and tables and drafting executive summaries of committee reports. The grip of the urban offices, capital traps, and elite activities has tightened for government, aid agencies, and NGO staff alike: more and more emails, meetings, negotiations, and reports, with often limited staff. Participation has risen in the pandemic of incestuous workshops, many of them about poverty, consuming even more precious time.

When poor communities think at the human level, all their goals are interconnected. However, the goals have been categorised into project mode to suit donors and governments under the internationally conceived top-down model, absent a global grass-roots movement with the communities as equal partners. Where possible, I think it's much better to support local groups rather than international organizations, as the locals cost much less than foreigners and usually have a much better idea of what people need. Outside aid prevents people from searching for solutions while corrupting and undermining local institutions and creating a self-perpetuating lobby of aid agencies.

The urge to reduce the poor to a set of clichés has been with us for as long as there has been poverty. The poor appear in social theory as much as in literature, by turns lazy or enterprising, noble or thievish, angry or passive, helpless or self-sufficient. Even journalists who feign such deep interest in the lives of the poor struggle to get even a single fact straight. When people talk about fighting poverty, they talk about making agriculture more productive, educating girls, passing laws to prohibit discrimination, building roads, fighting traditional superstitions about health, and equalizing trade balance between countries. There are endless solutions because poverty is endlessly complicated.

The poverty industry

The international poverty industry is worth tens of billions of US dollars annually. It's bursting with experts and consultants. There is a surfeit of studies, reports, books, PhD grants, loans, and consultancies. Rural development is now becoming an old-fashioned cause. Rural reform has become the policy bandwagon everybody is clambering on, and every progressive politician across the country wants a piece of the rural development pie. The new bandwagon implies rural reform, a new way of developing the villages, changing their mindset from a charity-oriented approach to an opportunity-oriented one. To bring a new novelty to their appellation, writers and journalists have added the new professional label of 'activist'. This double-barrelled appellation is a lethal combination, with the country's judicial system also becoming an important stakeholder. The political leaders, too, have their share of acrobatics in the development 'circus', with minions projecting themselves as missionaries leading the crusade to redeem the wretched.

Indian development finance experts have come into their own, and, after mystics and godmen, they occupy a good position in the global space. Poverty does not catch their attention, but poverty stalks their arguments in a metaphorical guise; what it refers to remains vague. The language used to describe people experiencing poverty is the purplest of late Victorian prose. In contrast, poverty lies in the simple expedient of citing the observations of British administrators about the conditions of the Indian poor: terms that people make any sense of. Figures are tabled, graphed out, charted, and used to compare India with other countries, but not Indians with Indians.

I recall when my idealism for the Bhoodan movement was fierce enough to close my eyes to the difficulties of rural reforms. I realize now that the greatness of a rural reformer lies not in ideology but in natural human qualities that can inspire faith and enthusiasm in people.

The important thing is not the number of years you've worked in the field or your educational background—what is important is whether you have the necessary commitment to transform the lives of the poor. To create a cadre of visionary rural programme leaders, organizations must send people out, whether from a local college or an elite institution, a college graduate or an MBA, to discover India and spend time in villages to better understand rural culture and the ecosystem. You have to be an anthropologist first and a financial manager second.

During my engagement with NGOs, I found them very possessive of their staff and clients. To consider people experiencing poverty as a permanent source of income is outright commercialization, which strongly militates against the primary mission of civil society—ensuring that people don't remain pawns in the hands of their leaders. It has lost much of its credibility by trying to keep the stakeholders it represents as captives and hostages; it holds a moral responsibility to develop the capabilities of people experiencing poverty to become the sole arbiters of their destiny.

Today, without any legal definition, a voluntary organization comprises a wide range of civil society and interest groups, called Non-Governmental Organizations (NGOs) and non-profit associations. The people associated with them are generally human rights or social activists, academics, intellectuals, celebrities, high-profile journalists, think-tank hirelings, retired bureaucrats, jurists, lawyers, environmentalists, etc. They espouse a range of cultural, political, economic, security and philanthropic considerations.

Regarding resources and expertise, some NGOs are sometimes as strong, if not stronger, than some smaller sovereign states and international bodies. They can breed new ideas, advocate protests, mobilise support within and across borders, provide goods and services, and shape, implement and enforce national and international commitments. Their vast network, crossing territorial boundaries, offers the civil society groups an unprecedented reach and extent of influence. Some NGO leaders have influenced the government's decision-making process from within by being part of government delegations.

The hazards of development work

The members of civil society must understand the significant personal risks and hazards that those in positions of authority have to face. They must remember that loans are given out of public deposits, not out-of-state money, representing the hard-earned precious savings of people experiencing poverty. Bankers are the custodians of this money, and civil society members are responsible for educating the people about the sanctity of loan repayments. Then there are cases where officials lose their promotions and even sometimes their jobs when forced by deceitful borrowers into actions which are later labelled negligent acts by the institutions. The civil society space has begun to be dominated by groups with questionable credentials. Civil society activists must undergo competency tests from independent authorities to qualify as legitimate activists. The government is equally clever in patronizing those groups owing allegiance to its ideology. Civil society should show the same zeal and commitment to cleaning its own house the way it wants to clean the stables of the establishments.

Despite positive contributions, NGOs have not been involved in developmental undertakings to create significant employment and comprehensive income generation through sustainable businesses. It is attributable to their lack of good managerial skills and the organizational structure necessary to take up business ventures. Further, donor funds go to narrowly defined projects. Consequently, NGOs are best suited to support projects funded by governments and international agencies or limited initiatives approved by private donors.

The less professional NGOs carry out developmental work in the field according to the specifications given by donors. New ideas seldom qualify for any funding. Thus, project proposals reflect the requirements set by donors according to their planned methodology and outcomes. A mere demonstration of compliance on paper trumps getting the job done effectively. As a result, recipients of developmental funds spend significant time preparing reports for the planners to qualify for continued funding rather than conceding the projects they want to seek, which can attract donors.

Civil society has failed Bharat, not India, compromising the very spirit of volunteerism. They do not know what sacrifice means. They have not set an example of simplicity, compassion, humility, or courage (as Hemingway defined it, 'grace under pressure'). Civil society has no role models to offer. We see greed and materialism surrounding us; nothing sets civil society apart. The only sign of success is how much money you make or how big your business is.

Rural poverty alleviation is not a matter of resources; it's about designing policies that will work on the ground. We create something while sitting in government offices with some experts, but we never try it out. We never admit failure. We never suggest returning to NREGA, taking what worked, and dumping what didn't. Skill development for wage employment is perhaps most crucial to the long-term alleviation of poverty. However, much thought must given to proper training. It should focus on learning by doing rather than in the classroom. A range of entrepreneurs in construction, textiles, leather, gems and jewellery, and so on will have to be brought in, and candidates will need to work as apprentices. A better approach to eliminate poverty, however, would be to make the environment conducive to increased flow of credit to the poor, leaving micro-level credit management to financial institutions and transferring the subsidy from the individual level to the community level for human capital formation of people experiencing poverty and developing physical valuable infrastructure to them.

There is growing evidence and recognition that serving poor people requires intentional outreach to those living below a nation's poverty line. However, matching intent with action requires a strong commitment from business management to improve poor people's lives through better incentives, leadership, communication, and culture. It also requires effective use of information systems—electronic or manual methods of promptly collecting, analysing and acting on information.

I often wondered why it was that when there were so many government programmes for the welfare of the rural poor, poverty was still so endemic. Either the nets were not cast adequately wide to cover most beneficiaries, or too many holes were blown into it. But money. What is the point of putting more water into a bucket that is already leaking badly? The problem is not a lack of funds. It is a lack of accountability for those who spend it. Even the government feels that 85% of development spending does not reach low-income people, either sponged up by the 'delivery mechanism'—the consultants, advisers, their equipment or studies—or pocketed outright. It has become a touchstone for all government programmes and is a permanent feature in development literature.

The siphoning of aid

In many cases, Western aid is running down bureaucratic ratholes. Fortunately, civil societies are training local leaders to serve as watchdogs using the audacious Right to Information Act. The aim is not to directly blame or indict per se—bare-knuckled confrontation would alienate the government—but to remind public servants that someone is watching them and that the negligent will be named and shamed.

A critical success factor is creating organisational capabilities at the local level that can mobilise and manage resources effectively to benefit the many intended recipients. We need plans, systems, mutual accountability and financing mechanisms. And even before we have all of that apparatus in place—what I call the economic plumbing—we must first understand more concretely what such a strategy means to the beneficiaries. Capacity building at the village level is crucial to making them aware of the entire development process, including the aid structure, so they can monitor and oversee it effectively.

In a small project, everyone can participate in decision-making. Practical advantages of participation for project effectiveness and sustainability weigh heavily in favour of the same: participation can reduce waste of project resources and lead to recurrent cost recovery.

Most importantly, it gives people a stake in the project resources and thus makes them willing to support it. The negatives of participation are that it is difficult, time-consuming, and tricky; it can permit elites or freeloaders to get more than their share; it can stir up conflicts that society and culture have traditionally been able to keep under wraps; it can alienate governments; and so on.

The success will depend on the charisma and the personal commitment of the project leader who inspires the team and lets their creative aquifers charge back to life. Although there is much discussion in public forums about the appropriate development of the society in which the poor live, poor people rarely get the opportunity to develop their agenda or set terms for the involvement of outsiders. The participatory paradigm illustrates that poor people participate in plans and programmes we—outsiders—have designed. Not only is there little opportunity for them to articulate their ideas, but there is also seldom an institutional space where their ingenuity and creativity in solving their problems can be recognized, respected and rewarded.

Financial development through public participation enables individuals to maximise their potential and represents a tool for expanding financial democracy. We have made historic strides toward consolidating political democracy and revolutionizing governance in India's rural hinterland, but the democratization of means and opportunities has not accompanied these. Financial democracy is fundamental for achieving greater inclusiveness, improving social cohesion, and generating broad-based growth. It is, therefore, crucial for economic dynamism and political stability; the lack of financial democracy prevents people from gaining access to resources that would enable them to make the most of their opportunities!

Proper development involves a transformation of the state of a human being. However, such a transformation must have those affected's active involvement and participation. Proper development transforms groups without destroying their culture, traditions, environment, livelihood and social patterns, which must be protected because they are central to the very life of the people. The forests around them provide food, medicine, and livelihood, a sustainable solution to the triple whammy of food security, healthcare and employment, which the state is ill-equipped to address. Proper development shouldn't translate into development, as seen by the elite. They are essential to those whose lives need support.

The diversity of the development landscape

A development strategy that has been successful in one village may not necessarily give the same results in a neighbouring town. Hence, planners are increasingly emphasizing area-specific plans. Transplanting cultures has been a favourite idea of armchair development experts, but time has shown that nothing could be as damaging as the imposition of an alien culture. Each society, however nascent, has a social and cultural apparatus that regulates and balances the divergent traits and traditions. I have always believed in Paul Devitt's famous words: "The poor are often inconspicuous, inarticulate and unorganised. Their voices may be unheard at public meetings in communities where it is customary for only the big men to put in their views. It is rare to find a body or institution that adequately represents the poor in a certain community or area."

Land, water, forests, and environmental reforms will be ineffective if they don't give space to the voices of those affected by the reforms. These communities comprise eighty-five per cent of the country's population. Yet, none find even half a per cent's space in these seminars and conferences, particularly when we are deliberating programmes targeted towards women.

Participatory development moves away from externally led interventions. It aims to facilitate action and social change led and shaped by the so-called 'beneficiaries' themselves. It emerged as an alternative to the top-down development approaches of the 1950s and '60s.

Participatory development has now adopted a more pragmatic approach, which results in a broad spectrum of methods used, most of which are less ideological than their original Freirean roots. Participatory projects can also differ from one another in their nature and objectives; there is no easy single answer to how to implement them, but looking at what pitfalls to avoid can be a place to start.

Techniques of participatory approaches

The early nineties saw the introduction of a sound participatory paradigm initiated by Robert Chambers, known as Participatory Rural Appraisal (PRA). It involved all the stakeholders of a development programme in the entire decision-making process. It caught on when microfinance gained vogue and affected the villagers' ability to identify prospective borrowers, learn about loan activities, and learn about loan amounts. Participatory Rural Appraisal is an approach to analysing local problems and formulating tentative solutions with local stakeholders. It uses various visualisation methods for group-based analysis to deal with spatial and temporal aspects of social and environmental issues. It mainly deals with a community-level scale of analysis but is increasingly being used to help deal with higher-level systemic problems.

The techniques are typically used in the field to gather qualitative data, often to complement quantitative data derived from traffic counts and origin and destination data. We must begin with the people who know most about their livelihood systems. This approach must value and develop the recipients' knowledge and skills and put the means to achieve self-development into their hands. It will require reshaping current practices and thinking associated with development assistance. In short, it will require the adoption of a new paradigm.

This emerging participatory development paradigm suggests two perspectives: involving local people in the selection, design, planning and implementation of programmes and projects that will affect them, thus ensuring that local perception, attitudes, values and knowledge are taken into account as fully as possible; and to make more continuous and comprehensive feedback an integral part of all development activities.

Poverty is not just a lack of income; hence, there is a need to identify categories of wealth relevant to the specific village or locality, e.g., animal ownership, type of house, family size, farm size, and other criteria. Wealth ranking enables villagers to rank households in the community according to economic and other 'well-being' categories. It helps identify target group members for projects, specifically the poorest sections of society. It also subdivides larger groups for further PRA discussions. Differences in wealth and well-being affect people's perceptions and coping strategies. It is essential to understand this before further appraisal or planning. This type of ranking discusses the relative positions of households in a community and points to local indicators of wealth and well-being.

Another essential technique complementary to PRA is resource mapping. The women can learn rudimentary planning skills to map the resources in their settlements and initiate a discussion on increasing their access to resources. For the first time, they used rangoli (powdered chalk of diverse colours), chalk, and pens to draw maps of the village on the temple platform, on the wall of the Gram Panchayat building, or under a tree. They sketched a map of their settlement, featuring houses, infrastructure, roads, boundaries, and survey-specific services, such as drinking water sources and assessment of schools and health centres. The map can help the community identify the features they want to eliminate or add in five years. They then draw a map of the future settlement comprising elements they wish to see in the community and spell out steps they must take to achieve this. They estimate the time and resources needed and identify the people who will be responsible for each of the steps. Whether attending a dialogue with the block officials or in training, they can articulate the village problems and assess what is further required. They then use this as a record to monitor and track whether the earlier development objectives have achieved their goals.

It is possible to distinguish three distinct objectives of self-education: development, local governance, and empowerment. The first enables women to identify their survival needs, map available resources to address them, decide upon an appropriate strategy through participatory planning, acquire requisite skills (masonry or keeping accounts), mobilize community resources and collaborate. The second concern is the skills required for local governance, which allows for more significant and fruitful interaction with local political structures and, ultimately, a more inclusive vision of social development. The third is about the strength women derive from being members of collectives, which allows them to be more assertive in dealing with issues and have an expanded coverage (geographical and issue-wise).

A decade ago, many in the development community acted with the best intentions but without the best evidence. If households lack clean water—help build wells; if people suffer ill health—health services; if the poor lack capital to start businesses, give them credit. But the reality is complicated. Water can be contaminated, people don't always use their local clinic, and savings or insurance may be better than credit. In theory, low-income people are in the best position to know what their communities need and demand accountability from their governments.

The problem with the villages in Central India, where I spent most of my career in rural banking, was that the people were known for following their instincts; they followed each other. There was no leader in the bunch; there were scores of them. They followed each other into oblivion. The womenfolk would huddle behind curtains, giggling shyly at us, content to fade into the background, letting their husbands speak for them, or they would blink a coded language to fellow women with their eyelids.

I saw my role as that of the initiator. I was a catalyst for change and the one who 'intervened for change'. In other words, the perception was that of myself as the leader, insomuch as the group action traced back to a set of actions for which I was responsible. It may have been an idea or a set of ideas. I gradually began to understand that perceptions and ideas exist differently in people's minds. What is needed is the time, space and opportunity to put them into action.

All around me, I saw development programmes failing because they did not consider the politics of the ground reality. An effort for deep-rooted social change needed to derive its strength from the people it intended to benefit. I worked in rural projects for nearly three decades, and throughout this time, I was disappointed by how the government, banks and development agencies approached rural development. Their traditional approach failed to build the capacity of the people. They undertook projects that kept funds flowing but failed to consult the affected villages. The projects weren't collaborations with the people, resulting in a lack of sustainability. Most importantly, the people were not empowered or valued enough to learn and think for themselves in finding solutions. Instead, they were instructed and subsequently followed directions like servants.

Tackling poverty requires a fundamentally different approach: one that starts with people themselves and encourages initiative, creativity, and drive from below, which must be at the core of any transformation of their lives to be lasting. If people get the support they need to make crucial decisions in their communities and build their democracies, they can do the rest themselves. In doing so, they will move their communities out of poverty and take the world with them. Change must come from within: communities must make decisions regarding their future. We have to promote participatory approaches that address the specific needs of each community, as well as increased education.

The bit-push thinking brushes over one of the underlying problems of aid, that it is fungible—that monies set aside for one purpose and then diverted to another; they can be invested in agendas that can be worthless, if not detrimental, to growth. Proponents of aid have acknowledged that unconstrained aid risks being consumed, rather than invested, going into private pockets instead of the public purse. When this happens, as it so often does, no real punishments or sanctions are ever imposed. So, more grants can mean more graft.

Outsiders cannot impose economic development and social change. They go to the individuals pursuing opportunities for self-realization. People considering giving aid should be open-minded and listen to those working in the field and facing day-to-day challenges. That respect opens many doors. Lasting change comes about so slowly that you may not notice it until people resist being taken care of—they need options to fulfil their potential. If we can inspire people worldwide to reconsider what it means to be poor, we will have made a real impact. We have a real chance to end poverty when we design solutions that recognize people experiencing poverty as clients or customers and not as passive recipients of charity. And I believe we can do that in our generation. I learnt very early the importance of empathy—not one that comes from a place of superiority, but one born from a profound humility and sympathy.

If the primary focus is ending poverty, we must establish partnerships between communities so that they learn practical knowledge and skills from one another. Importing unworkable ideas, equipment, and consultants destroys the capacity of communities to help themselves. That model encourages colossal falsification of figures, excessive hiring of private consultants and contractors, conflicts of interest and a massive patronage system. The development community seems constantly and restlessly searching for a singular approach that will 'solve' poverty. The fundamental flaw with this system is that each new approach fails to break out of the underlying technocratic and specialized paradigm in development work. I have found armchair and ivory-towered development experts apt to unveil new buzzwords every few years, only to toss them aside. I have also seen how creative risks and an innovative spirit can revive development work.

Reflections of Prof Shrinivas

In his reflections on fieldwork, the doyen of Indian anthropologists, Professor M.N. Shrinivas, described successful ethnography as passing through several stages. An anthropologist is 'once-born' when he initially goes to the fields, thrust from familiar surroundings into a world he knows little about. He is 'twice-born' when, after living for some time among his tribe, he can see things from their viewpoint. To those anthropologists fortunate enough to experience it, this second birth is akin to a Buddhist urge of consciousness, for which years of study or mere linguistic facility do not prepare one. All of a sudden, one sees everything from the native's point of view, be it festivals, fertility rites or the fear of death. A banker or a development expert is no less an anthropologist than a sociologist: he is a financial or a development anthropologist.

There was a need to find a research method that would give power to the powerless and make people the subject, not the object of research. The methodologies employed by the anthropologists marked a radical departure from the research methodologies of the social sciences and the mathematical objective systems of the physical sciences. These methodologies provided 'windows' that took people's words and ideas at face value. As participant observers, the anthropologist, the social activist and the development worker lived together with communities and chronicled their felt needs, priorities, art and worldviews. It marked the beginning of the practice of a participatory alternative to conventional research. An intellectual ferment permeated academe during the 1960s, questioning the ivory tower stance of development research and how their results turned out on the ground,

Take a lesson from this field experience. Laxman was an impoverished, landless agricultural labourer living in a Chandrapur village. A well-meaning official decreed that Laxman take a subsidised loan to buy a rope-making machine. Laxman, afraid he might be unable to repay the loan, tried to resist this offer but was forced to take it by then. The rope-making machine turned out to be defective, and while the bank officials promised to send someone to repair it, this never happened. Unable to fix the machine, Laxman sold it for a relatively small sum and bought seven goats with the proceeds. One year later, six of the goats had died. Laxman no;w had just a tiny goat and a debt more extensive than his annual income. We must ensure that development programmes are relevant to the beneficiary and are sustainable to the local economy.

When programmes viewed their clients as beneficiaries, they tended to see them as relatively passive people and to picture microenterprise finance as a money transfer from rich to poor. In such a context, decisions about what type of help to provide were made based on what programme designers thought would benefit the beneficiaries. At the same time, such programmes spent a great deal of effort deciding which beneficiary groups most deserved assistance and how to target them. The new microenterprise finance programmes consider clients as customers they wish to serve. Policies need to suit their relevant context. We need to try them, fail, redesign, and succeed. Think of policy as a live object, a domain where all stakeholders can engage. Talk to customers because they understand what they want and what their life is like. Every time we make policies, we forget that the customers have ambitions and aspirations. They are not zombies.

The ingratitude of the poor

When foreign dollar investors make millions off the backs of people experiencing poverty, the poor are liable to display a decided lack of gratitude. This global issue should be addressed by scaling back, going local, giving borrowers ownership of the loan process, and generally being much less ambitious regarding growth rates. Full-service banks should grow organically out of local communities, then have venture-capital funds making a colossal splash and implode.

The idea is to use local wisdom before we involve expertise from outside. Encourage private initiative without commercializing education. Give private initiative more responsibility, more space, and more freedom. As things stand now, the formal system alone cannot answer the challenge of rural education. It destroys initiative and creativity. Tackling poverty requires a fundamentally different approach: one that encourages initiative, creativity, and drive from below, which must be at the core of any transformation of their lives that is to be lasting.

The failure of so many development interventions over the past half century can be partly due to their lack of rootedness in the society they should have changed. Development interventions must engage with people's identities and values, whether individuals, communities, organizations or institutions, to catalyse fundamental change. Capacity-building has to be grafted onto pre-existing foundational values rather than importing another's base. Experience suggests that a participatory process helps ensure more active engagement by local people, greater local ownership, and increased reliability and quality assurance. It also helps overcome ethical issues around such processes, including agreeing on its scale and scope, who is involved, and who has access to the data.

The key to strengthening the sustainability of livelihood strategies lies in empowering the primary stakeholders or users. Additionally, it is necessary to provide them with the ability to link with state, market or civil society participants. These linkages provide access to assets critical to strengthening poor people's livelihoods. Access to holdings through participatory management does not simply mean access to the use of resources but also the capacity to act, negotiate, debate and make decisions. Participatory methods, creatively evolved and carefully facilitated, have opened up aspects of life that are too private, sensitive, or dangerous to allow public analysis.

An early example was wealth or well-being ranking, in which community members first draw a social map showing all households, then list these on cards, and then sort them into piles according to degrees of wealth or, more usually, some concept of well-being. Middle-class urban professionals often regard this as either impossible or unethical, supposing it will be demeaning for those who are worse off. These fears have proved unfounded.

Although the data is sparse, many anti-poverty schemes don't appear to have a beneficiary orientation. The beneficiary perspective, that is, the scheme seen from the point of view of the beneficiary, the rural poor, is missing. Targets, commands, exhortations and threats come from above. From the periphery and bottom comes a weaker filtered information flow, which placates and misleads. In meetings, subordinates are upbraided and given orders and praises from visitors. A few prominent villagers meet the guests, and to them are parroted sentences that can sound musical to the ears of visitors.

Inundated by the demands of high-profile visitors, the managers set up public relations units. When visitors come, a fluent guide follows a standard route and routine. The same set of people are welcomed t with folded hands, and in the case of village dignitaries, there is a handshake. The same buildings are visited and appreciated; the same polite praise is handwritten by an official and signed by the visiting boss in the Visitors Book. Questions lose their way in statistics; hand-outs inhibit doubts. Inquisitive visitors depart, loaded with research papers, technical evaluations, and annual reports that they will probably never read, with a sense of guilt at the unworthy scepticism which promoted their probing questions and impressed by the charisma of the exceptional leader or manager who created it. They write their journey reports, evaluations and articles based on these impressions.

Partnership of all stakeholders

Participatory development stands for partnership, built upon the basis of dialogue among the various actors. All stakeholders set the agenda during this time, and local views and indigenous knowledge are deliberately sought and respected. It implies negotiation rather than the dominance of an externally set project agenda. Thus, people become actors instead of beneficiaries. Participation is concerned with the organized efforts to increase control over resources and regulative institutions in given social situations on the part of groups and movements of those hitherto excluded from such control. Participation in decision-making and evaluation helps stress control and, by implication, power issues. Participation is a process of empowerment of the deprived and the excluded. This view recognises political and economic power differences among social groups and classes. Participation in this sense necessitates the creation of organizations for the poor that are democratic, independent, and self-reliant.

For rural communities, participation is a way to identify and implement priority rural development activities through better use of existing resources. To do this, communities analyse constraints and resources available, identify and agree upon priority problems, develop action plans to address the priority problems, implement the action plans, and pressure the service providers and development organizations to provide the necessary assistance. Communities also identify what incremental resources are needed and organize themselves to mobilise them. Moreover, villagers influence how the development organizations and service providers manage their work within the village. Through their strengthened organizations, villages can more strongly voice their satisfaction or dissatisfaction with the services received and indicate how the participation of all concerned can improve services.

Villagers have so many problems that they can't handle all of them with their meagre existing resources. How can the team of facilitators avoid creating unrealistic expectations when asking villages to identify their priority problems? It is essential to highlight the difference between consultations of villagers on the use of external resources and discussions on the better use of existing resources.

* * * * *

6. MY ODYSSEY WITH DAIRY FARMERS

When the sun is still a brown moon in the early morning, a lovely landscape stretches along both sides of the highway from Nagpur to Chandrapur, two important towns in India's central province, Maharashtra. The overcast sky softens the landscape, and flimsy wisps of clouds drape the shoulders of hills like gauze scarves. Much before this blurred silhouette of the morning starts its lazy climb, the broken leaves start billowing like the wings of exotic butterflies. Outside the thatched huts, men sleep sprawled on the ground, their faces covered with torn sheets to shut out the sun. The dawn coming out of the cusp of the hills pinkens the eastern sky and makes the Wardha River as lustrous as silk. Even as the men snore, the women are up, the bronze pots on their heads glinting in the sun as they trudge across the barren fields. The tinkling of their anklets lingers in the rhythmic sound of a nearby hand pump. A woman squats by a fire at the edge of a muddy path, preparing breakfast. As the morning meal is ready, smoke drifts somnolently over the countryside. We are in Ashi, a village in the Chandrapur district of Maharashtra, which I intended to serve as an epicentre for dairy programmes for marginal farmers in the area. In this village, I would have my first brush with dairy farming in India.

The morning bus to Ashi will take you past dry fields of jowar wheat and other seasonal crops. A two-kilometre stretch of freshly laid glittering asphalt separates the fields from the main road. This tarred road stands out like a fresh scar on the red soil. The road is eminently motorable, giving no tell-tale signs of the backwardness of the village. The roadmakers seemed to have been in a hurry; however, as the road ended, it was incomplete and a mile from the town. A rickety wooden shack stands at the entrance to the village. On my first visit to the city, I had tea there that was so cold, so stewed, and so thin that you had to be a tea addict to get through it all; the cafe shop had an owner so absent-minded that he poured salt into the tea instead of sugar.

When we left the narrow strip of asphalt, we began bumping alarmingly over a cart track, with bamboo and tree branches scraping the sides of our vehicle, until we suddenly saw green fields of thick, lush millet, with a row of simple huts down one side of the cultivated area; beyond was dense jungle. My colleagues gazed at the crops with visible emotion. It was the first time it underwent tillage, yielding high productivity. The cycle of sowing and reaping has always been like a creed. The mystery of life is all around us—right here, for anyone with eyes or a heart to feel.

The central laneway was lined on each side by thick mud walls with hundreds of dung patties, a mix of manure and straw, slapped on to dry in the warm winter sun. Once the dung cakes were dry, the village women stored them in mounds, which they sealed with more mud, giving them the appearance of anthills, to serve as family woodpiles. We followed a narrow cobbled path beyond one of the big new water pumps, around the water hyacinth-covered swamp and past two women bickering about a broken wall between their huts.

One of the oldest traditional occupations of humankind is herding and grazing cattle. Providing cows to the poor was one of the most common programmes I pursued to equip villagers with a business they could manage while at the same time meeting the nutritional needs of the family. I kept this learning in mind when I travelled to a village as a bank manager for my first assignment. I believed the best way I could help the poor villagers was by helping them with loans for purchasing livestock. I dreamt of beginning my career on the romantic note of providing goats or poultry so the poor could swiftly pull themselves out of poverty. I believed a goattery or dairy was a much more accessible source of income than training a low-income family to set up a small business, as the female of the family could conveniently manage it.

Livelihoodod through livestock

Goats and cows are sturdier than paper money. Friends and relatives can't ask for small pieces of them. If you own a cow, it yields milk, it can plough the fields, and it produces dung that is also a fuel or fertilizer. Goats also have economic value, as they cost little to maintain and breed fast. They can be slaughtered and turned into saleable meat or eaten in a pinch. The same is true of ducks and chickens, which are valuable for their eggs and meat. If the business profited, the borrower could graduate to a buffalo. Dairy animals' end product is the same whether you own an expensive imported breed or an inexpensive native: cheese, yoghurt and butter. Cows are the main draught animals of India; their manure is the fuel that cooks Indian food, and their milk is an essential part of the Indian diet.

Financing cattle is a routine business strategy in rural banking, as it benefits the local economy by generating income and providing employment. Rural poor, with no agricultural land or small landholdings, can manage both a goattery and a small-scale dairy. The simplest way of assisting people experiencing poverty in this regard would be to lend them Rs 4000 to buy a cow that will yield four litres of milk during the lactating period and then dry up. We can work out a nearly uninterrupted flow of income for the dairy farmer if we provide a second cow to provide milk till the first cow calves again. The recipient of the loan will have an income sufficient only slightly to improve the quality of his daily meals but not enough to permit saving.

Goat rearing for tribals

Although goat-herding is one of the world's oldest economic professions, it turns out that goat-herding is a little more complicated than it appears. First, the average life expectancy of a goat is around ten years. It means you will lose about ten per cent of a herd to old age annually. Secondly, although goats typically give birth twice a year to one or two kids with each gestation, the viability rate is around seventy-five per cent, such that each goat will only net an average of 2 kids per year. The kids are worth about fifty per cent of the mother goat's price. So conservatively, by the end of the year, you have a hundred per cent return: the doe, worth Rs 2000, and two kids, worth Rs 1000 each. Even if you took out the cost of capital at twelve per cent of the loan, you're making a seventy per cent return on invested capital.

Goats had intrigued me for years–their intelligence, their seeming disdain of human dominion. I once trailed a herd of goats in India through the sandy dunes of Rajasthan. The goats marched single file, hoofs clicking cobbles, while scooters and trucks squeezed past. At each narrow curve, another goat broke from the parade and turned into a home where a member of the household–a child or a woman–held open a wooden door and greeted the returning goat with a palmful of salt. The goats had returned from the desert to be milked and bedded with their family at night. In the morning, they'd gather again with the herder. I'd never seen such an excellent arrangement before–goats and humans living side by side–but it was one of the most ancient relationships between mammals.

They balanced on my back legs to reach hanging boughs or used my chest for a leg-up. I knocked apples off limbs with a long stick, and they chased them down and fought one another for the fruit. A goat's anus would open like the aperture of a camera and produce perfectly round pellets, one by one. The dog ate these pellets; we couldn't convince her that the goats' faeces were not a treat.

Every herd develops a hierarchy of its own, an acceptance of its members, even those at the bottom of the order. Goats establish rank by jousting, rearing up on hind legs and crashing down horn-to-horn or head-to-head. Usually, the contests are playful, but sometimes, a doe will bite or use her horns to slash or ram an inferior with bruising force. Outsiders to the herd often crash harshly.

Back home, I remained stirred by the memories of seeing these poor goats' tragic fate at the hands of other marauding animals. I was present one day at the veterinary clinic close to my office when a client of ours, an older man, a wrinkled farmer, walked into the dispensary. He held a bleeding goat in his arms. The goat had been bitten on the neck by a dog. The farmer pleaded with the doctor for help. The doctor administered an injection, but he said the goat would die. I heard the older man tell someone that the goat was all he had–no land, children, or other livestock.

Goats were to be my priority, followed by cows. It was a popular and easy way for villagers to make money: you could buy a goat and take it to the agricultural fields, where it would graze while you worked, as a goat would eat just about anything. You could then breed the goat and sell its kids when you needed money. To me, it appeared to be a simple but magical formula. I even wondered why banks, government, and development agencies needed highly qualified bankers and veterinary staff to handle such a simple task. Perhaps even a villager with some basic level of literacy would do a more efficient job than we bankers who couldn't distinguish between a Jersey and a Holstein or the average milk yield of a local breed. Only later did I find that the wily villagers had turned goat financing into a notorious farce. Thanks to this, it took a lot of time for bankers to eliminate the aversion they had developed for goat financing.

Goat-rearing was the top priority in the programmes meant for combating poverty. Those eligible for finance would buy and tend a flock; the surplus goats are usually sold f during festival time. All the bank's village units distributed many such loans. Past loan ledgers showed that the number of goats financed often exceeded the village's population, but what happened to the increasing population, which has now shrunk, can only be explained by the sale of goats.

The first livestock loan camp

My first exclusive loan camp for goats provided the first clue. The government had already issued a notification for purchasing goats from cattle auction markets located out of the district area. The purpose was to promote interbreeding that could improve the strains. However, we suggested that we continue purchasing animals locally for some time. The local administration accepted our request, and a camp took place in the village with great fanfare.

Two days after the camp opened, an older woman entered my office. She was sobbing inconsolably, her eyes red, tears streaming down her cheeks. I asked my lady peon to offer her a chair and fetch a glass of water. As the woman settled down and the sobs grew weaker, I wondered what tragedy had befallen her. "Aajibai, (old mother), why are you so grieved? Has any tragedy befallen you or your family? We are here to stand by you." She seemed to be unrelenting. "Sir, thank you for your good words. My problem is that I have lost two of my healthiest goats in just one day." I asked her to explain the entire issue adequately.

She calmed down, assumed a stern expression and started speaking. "I think the entire system of financing and insuring cattle is wrong. It would help if you had properly verified the goats and ascertained their true owners," she said.

"But what is wrong in the present system?" I asked.

"Wrong?" she burped as she raised her decibels. "This has been happening for years. We have been complaining for long, but nobody wants to believe us."

A veteran borrower watching the drama suddenly interjected as he found the woman beating about the bush and me instead of grasping the problem by the horns. He explained that some of the notorious borrowers of the village would borrow goats from the villagers for a day. In return, they would promise Rs. 10 per goat and return the goat by the evening. These borrowers bring these goats to the camps and get their earlobes tagged on the strength of which the money is released. If the owners resist, they convince them these tags are necessary to ward off evil influences. I now understood the entire operation, but it was still unclear how the lady was affected.

The daughter of the woman who accompanied her stepped into the conversation. "Sir, the tags used for the goats were rusted, poisoning them to death. We want the bank to pay us the cost of those animals to compensate for the loss." It was my first encounter with the netherworld of goat finance. I later learned it was an old routine practice that had imparted notoriety to the government's goattery programme.

In another case, we financed a borrower to purchase a flock. We knew the borrower already had one goat in this case, but she wanted to increase her business. The week after we gave the woman her loan, we returned to check whether she'd bought a new goat. It is one of the cardinal lending principles: checking on borrowers to ensure they use loans for their stated purpose is good. Otherwise, the money too often goes for household expenses or other non-income-generating purchases. We call the process the technical phrase verification of assets. Suresh and I drove to the village and met the woman at her house. "I bought the goat!" she said brightly. "Here it is!" With a flourish, she gestured to a skinny brown goat standing nearby.

"Great," I said and smiled at the woman. It was the beginning of a goat revolution we had so passionately planned. I didn't quite realise that this embryonic revolution had the seeds of one of the most rampant malpractices that plagued the goat economy.

"Wait!" said Suresh. "This is not a new goat. It is the one we saw last week. It's the same colour, with the same markings." I looked at Suresh, amazed. How many goats had we seen, and in how many villages? And he remembered that this goat was the same one he'd seen a week ago. How could he tell? I felt Suresh was unnecessarily trying to micromanage things to impress me.

"No, it's not the old goat!" the women protested. "I just bought it! The one you saw last week was black."

But Suresh stood firm. "We're not stupid," he told the woman. "This is the same goat we saw last week."

I felt abused, standing in a dusty village in the middle of nowhere, arguing with a woman over the colour of a goat. Was this what I'd spent all these years preparing to do? But we knew we had to clarify from the beginning that we wouldn't bend the rules for anyone. If we were going to establish a culture of accountability, we had to be firm. Suresh wouldn't back down, and the woman finally confessed. Yes, she admitted, this was the old goat. She intended to use the loan to buy a silk sari. "You can't use it for that," Suresh told her. "Buying a sari doesn't generate any income, so you'll be no closer to getting out of poverty that way. Either buy a new goat or give us back the loan money."

My experience has shown that most loans fail because bankers do not ensure borrowers purchase the financed asset. For instance, if a loan is for a grinding machine and the borrowers buy a television, there will be no return on the investment, and the borrowers will not be able to repay the loan properly. Thus, ensuring the proper end-use of funds is essential to banking.

During my association with dairy programmes as part of my assignment as manager of a village branch of a bank, I found that the extension departments of the government have an innate obsession with exotic breeds of cattle as against the native or local variety. My disillusionment with most state-driven dairy programmes was mainly because of the inadequacy of skills and knowledge of people experiencing poverty in handling exotic varieties; mortality can rip a massive hole in the precious savings of the farmers. The climate may not suit the cattle, and the farmers cannot afford the luxuries and amenities needed to provide for the vulnerable exotic breeds. These breeds are helpful for larger farmers who can offer luxurious parlours to house them and have a sufficient buffer of assets to cope with contingencies. In poverty alleviation programmes, most beneficiaries are the poor who do not have adequate savings to meet the expenses of proper veterinary care. It may be a coincidence that the development programmes have a more significant fascination for cows when other alternatives could work better. For instance, goattery doesn't require any complex veterinary care. A single goat could help tide a financial emergency while the business remained intact.

An affair with livestock finance

My initial exuberance and enthusiasm suffered early jolts, and I soon realized that financing cattle was not a simple apprentice's job. My notions of dairy finance being the simplest of all types of finance were based on my naivety and lack of exposure to rural realities. I later realized it was the diciest finance in which nature's hand had a more significant role than our financial and agricultural skills. As long as the cows keep gushing out gallons of milk, yoghurt, and cream, padding their wallets with cash, and the gravy train keeps chugging, it is a happy romance for the dairy farmers. The problem starts when the cattle start falling ill. An ailment, if left unattended, may lead to mortality, resulting in a heavy loss for the poor household.

My plans soon vaporized as illnesses wiped out the livestock like a baboon plague. I slowly started moderating my enthusiasm. In one of my assignments, I found that several of these decimating waves were man-induced and had nothing to do with nature. My knowledge of cows was rudimentary. We knew the cow was a highly revered animal for

Indians and had several healing properties. The dung was of great utility to villagers who used it for making fuel briquettes.

In a city, cow's milk was a rare commodity and much more expensive than buffalo milk, which was a preferable choice. Only when my grandma had to prepare medicines, or somebody was recuperating from a long illness would cow's milk be needed. We had to persuade the local milkman to help us with half a litre daily. Grandma would tell us how to distinguish cow's milk from buffalo's. Cow's milk was thinner and slightly yellowish, and buffalo's was thick and dense. However, since cow's milk was so scarce and in demand, milkmen often tried to dilute buffalo milk with water and dye it with an edible yellow colourant to pass it off as cow's milk. The only way of being sure that it was genuine cow milk that we had was the reputation and credibility of the milkman and possibly getting the cow milked in our presence. I learned to keep a keen eye on the milkman to make sure he didn't, via a well-concealed tube, water down the milk.

A cow (or any animal, for that matter, but let us stick to the cow) has many relationships. It is related to the farmer who has bought it. It is associated with the farmer's wife, who feeds and milks it. It is related to the farmer's child taking it to graze. It is associated with the local doctor who cares for it in sickness, the land on which it grazes and the pond from which it drinks. The productivity of this cow depends upon the quality of all these relationships. Therefore, a cow cannot be seen in isolation but in the context of its environment. A healthy cow in an unhealthy environment is of no use to anyone.

I found that the best intentions could produce negative results if they have faulty assumptions. It is valid for animal husbandry programmes as much as for other programmes. Somebody (let us say the veterinarians, bankers, or farmers from high-rainfall, well-developed areas) tells us that giving good, crossbred cows to farmers in our area will improve their economic status. But will it?

The combat with veterinarians

I found that veterinary services in villages are inferior, and veterinary doctors behave like sharks, trying to fleece the poor even to treat common ailments. The much-touted insurance of livestock is quite cumbersome. Techniques for increasing the quantity of milk were but one part of a vast repertoire of practices in which dairy farmers must be thoroughly grounded. They must also have a thorough exposure to traditional veterinary practices.

I worked out a strategy to outsmart the despotic local veterinarians' guild. With the help of a few veterinary friends from college, I developed a small veterinary kit for common ailments, and we designed a simple chart indicating the ailment and the medicine for fixing it. The village woman who was a peon in my office served as a barefoot veterinary doctor. We included medication capsules and tablets of the lowest dose. A single tablet was enough for a cock or hen; a goat required two, a cow three, a bullock four and a buffalo five. The strategy worked very well, and the mortality rate fell drastically. My bosses agreed to absorb the medicines in the monthly overhead costs. Drug companies supplied medicines at concessional rates and generously provided us with charts and other product material, which we disseminated to cattle owners. It was a novel initiative highly appreciated by visiting dignitaries from development agencies who would enthusiastically share it with other organizations. Several newspapers gave positive coverage for the innovation.

My initiative drew many protests from veterinarians who lost their businesses as we relied on the government's veterinary infrastructure. They banded together to start a smear campaign against me, alleging that I had become an agent of multinational drug companies whose medicines I was promoting in exchange for fat commissions. They also started advising people that the medication was harmful to animals, attributing some of the regular ailments of the cattle to the effects of these medicines. "Will you ever accept medicines without consulting a doctor? How do you know whether the drug is benefiting or harming the body?" they would ask the superstitious villagers. I knew they represented an institutional lobby which could block my innovative efforts, but my dogged persistence thwarted their attempts to sabotage this initiative. The local block development officer tried to unnerve me by saying that anonymous complaints against me were pouring into his office, and he could no longer postpone action. I knew these tactics would discourage me from disturbing the status quo in development programmes. I had to straighten these fellows out, although they had a fair idea of what we were up to by now. Critics scoffed at my notion of getting much traction from the initiative, but I persevered. To my good fortune, most of the borrowers were quite happy and came out openly supporting me.

This unique idea won me a lot of goodwill and popular support even though we initially faced many protests. The veterinarian guild was incensed. I had pitched the doctors back into their lairs. They couldn't swallow such bravado from a puny manager pretending to have the gall to confront the giants. They tried every sort of trick and stratagem to entrap me. Despite the smear campaign, some sensible people lauded my initiative and debunked the veterinarians' charges, labelling them as greedy merchants. Seeing that the main stakeholders–the borrowers–vehemently protested the veterinarians' stance was gratifying. Rural programme managers must remember that innovation and creativity have always met with obstinate resistance from those who gutlessly follow a path someone else blazed for them. Rhetoric is cheap; action is always demanding.

The cattle suppliers have a powerful cartel fully blessed by the veterinary doctors and government development staff. Unlike medical professionals, veterinarians' filial feelings for each other are intense. Still, when it comes to treating animals, they are hard-hearted and careless because the mortality of an animal doesn't suck them into the legal hydra of consumer protection.

The Animal Husbandry Department was following a faulty mechanism for releasing payments to suppliers: it was to remit the loan sanctioned by the bank to the veterinary department at the district headquarters. The department then released the total amount (bank finance + capital subsidy) to the supplier after the delivery of the animals. Since the government officials promised full cooperation and the villagers also appeared enthusiastic, I decided to implement the project on a larger scale. The district veterinary lobby had overhyped the benefits available to dairy farmers under the scheme, and there was a scramble to include names. The most attractive feature of the scheme was a subsidy component of fifty per cent, irrespective of the families' income level.

As a bank manager handling livestock, I accompanied the farmers in negotiating the purchase of dairy animals. I could have delegated the task to my junior officer, but I felt that I should make personal efforts to negotiate a fair deal for them. The farmers, too, were apprehensive, as this was the first time they had purchased exotic varieties, and they were keen that I should join them. The government Animal Husbandry Officer fixed up transactions with a cattle supplier from Bihar who had settled in Wardha. We travelled together by jeep. I would have customarily checked into a hotel, but the farmers insisted I be present throughout the dealings. I could comfortably undertake night halts in villages, and accommodating their request was not a big challenge.

We visited Wardha, where the famous cow supplier, Musa Sheth, the wholesale livestock dealer, had his barn. Inside the stables, three hundred cows stood flank to flank, and behind the stables, fringed by manure, was the pool where dairyman washed themselves, their cows, and the milk containers.

The dairy cows smelled the whole night. All farm animals do, of course, but these particularly pungent Jerseys had just come in from the rain. They were huddled in open stalls, swishing their tails, chewing on hay bales, and remarking on the terrible weather with a series of disappointed moos. Musa Sheth chatted with the farmhands, inspected the milk storage tank, and laughed when a curious cow followed him around the barn. The cows mooed *ooaaw, ooaaw*.

The benefits of jersey cows

The Jersey cow is small, amiable, and very pretty, with delicate, deer-like limbs, enviably long-lashed eyes, caramel colouring, and sometimes embellished with cream or dusky markings. Farmers and breeders laud the Jersey's capacious udder, impressive fodder conversion into milk, and ability to calve quickly. The rest of us marvel at the extraordinary richness of Jersey milk, like liquid silk to drink and cream that churns to deep golden butter. The exceptional composition of her milk and her tolerance of poor pastures and hot climates proved unbeatable in world markets.

The cows underwent a ritual bath, after which the teat cups were put on. A pulsating vacuum drew the milk into a receiver by piping it into the farm milk tank. Musa Sheth ordered his servant to boil the milk and serve it to us with a glass each as we sat and discussed common issues about milk dairies. Musa Sheth was rueful about the government's apathy: the shrinking of the grazing land and frequent droughts had compelled farmers to rely more on market fodder, spurring higher milk prices. "It is our life, and we invest a lot of emotion, energy, and money into developing a cow herd, "he said. "When we have to liquidate, it is not an easy thing to do. It is heart-wrenching sometimes, but it is part of the business. Cattle have been streaming into auction yards across the country in recent weeks as grazing land burns up in the sun, ponds and streams evaporate and prices for feed corn rise. With land, these days, commanding heady prices, as financial investors snap it up to plant high-value crops like corn and owners put more into conservation easements, finding land cheap enough to raise forage for cattle is hard."

Like Musa Sheth, most ranchers focus on their animals' lineage and weight. "The glitz and glamour are in the genetics," he said. "The value we see in what we sell is in the calf. Ranchers breed calves, raising them on pasture and hay for six to nine months until they separate from their mothers and are sold to stockers. Stockers pasture the cows and fatten them before selling them to feedlots. "

Our cattle supplier's house was small, and we decided to sleep close to the spacious courtyard, redolent with the fragrance of jasmine. We shared the cowshed with the bawling calves and the wafts of cow dung that kept producing an acrid tang and doused the resonant effect of jasmine. Our host opened the windows to freshen the air and rushed flies from the stable. Shooing them away, we stretched out. It was a mildly chilly night, and I kept myself swaddling in a thick blanket. I had the luxury of a comfortable cot, and the farmers slept on the t carpet. The farmers had had an enormous meal and farted painfully through the night.

The tension of cattle purchase

My mind was tense with all sorts of worries. All the borrowers were illiterate and very poor decision-makers and had entrusted the responsibility of the entire transaction to my judgment. While there, a fistfight broke out among the farmers, and I had to restore order.

We were planning to buy at least a dozen cows. If the planning went well, the scheme would improve the lives of the dairy farmers of Ashi. Controlling the primary and collateral damage would mean an uncertain and painful job if the planning failed. There was already bickering among the farmers, from tongue-lashing to abusive outbursts, as each tried to project himself as a dairy wizard. I had to remove the blanket and get out of bed to restore order. I raised my voice and asked the farmers to concentrate on sleep so everyone could rise early for the morning ritual of milking the cows.

A flood of questions kept me tossing. The average milk yield of two days–at least twice daily–calculates a cow's milk output. For every one litre of milk, the cost was Rs. 1000. Thus, a cow having a yield of eight litres was priced at Rs. 8000. After jerking awake several times, I dozed off into a fitful sleep around midnight, but the bustle of activity aroused me early.

My hosts didn't want to wake me up at that odd hour. They knew I was exhausted, and a lot of work lay ahead of me for the coming day, including finalising transactions and working out logistics for transporting animals. I was jousted out of sleep by the sort of violent effort with which one wrenches one's head away from the pillow in a nightmare. After a bath, I decided to have a stroll to purge my mind of confusion about negotiations for the purchase of the cattle. A haze of smoke drifted somnolently over the countryside as we relished the morning meal. Then the sounds of the rural dawn came like a jarring note to the ear—coughing and wheezing, raucous clearing of throats and nostrils, spilling water and brushing of teeth, the clang of utensils, the sputtering of taps, the slurping of hot tea. For the older village men, there is nothing like a deep chestful of bidi smoke to quell a morning cough.

Stepping into the gentle sunshine of a spring morning, I heard the lowing of snowy white cows impatient for milking to ease their udders. Musa Sheth had already organized the buckets and was gently caressing the cows. I could see how dearly he loved them. I was sure that after the cows reached the villages, the yield would dip by a litre because none of the borrowers would extend such fond care to the animals—Musa Sheth' greased his palms with vegetable oil, which the cows licked with relish.

After getting up, Musa Sheth would first quaff a goblet of cow's urine. He believed it was a great rejuvenator. One of the aides brought a tray of steel tumblers with steaming tea made out of milk from the cow tethered in front of us. It was the best way to start the day. With the occasional massages, careful milking twice a day, and the spacious living quarters of the cow community, the farm was the bovine equivalent of a five-star hotel.

Musa Sheth and his aides sang a lovely pastoral tune as they went about the task of milking:

Oh, the maid who
Minds the dairy
Is a barnyard dignitary
And her rule is arbitrary
Where the brown-eyed bossies browse
Every day, she has to putter,
And at twilight, out
She'll flutter with her pail
To mil the cows!

The milking ritual

The calves sequestered away from their mothers, and he and his aides began milking the cows. He was wrapped tightly in a brightly washed loincloth raised to the knee as he squatted in a hunch, positioning the pail to collect the milk. Musa Seth and his friends milked the cows so enthusiastically that I feared the calves might lose their quota. Musa Seth put my mind at ease. "We milk only three and leave the fourth for the calves. They never complain." He dipped his forefinger in a small milk pool and lifted it in the air. The white blob clung to his fingertip; not a drop rolled down. It spoke of the quality of the milk.

I asked some of our borrowers to participate in the milking ritual so that they could assess the quality of the animal. I was unhappy with the poor pace at which they milked the cows. It appeared they were the best candidates for animal welfare awards, too gentle and kind to squeeze out even the surplus milk. Musa Sheth placed three buckets on the table when our farmers were halfway through the first cow. Peeved at the excellent performance of Musa Sheth, they started making unnecessary complaints about the cows, blaming them for being uncooperative with strangers. They asked me to reject these cows as they were sickly.

Musa Sheth pushed the farmer aside, took the bucket from his hand, and sat below the udder. The bucket was firm between his two legs, and jets of milk started streaming into the bucket. It looked as if milk was almost on the point of bursting through the udders as Musa Sheth's lubricating hands hastened the flow. It proved that milkmen who practice dairy as a hereditary vocation turn milk into gold.

Anthropologists tell us that indigenous people practising their traditional vocation inherit practices handed down through generations and apply them successfully in their vocations. Modern dairy farmers with large mechanised farms with professional support are a different case, but small farmers cannot afford these facilities. The milk was thick and creamy; I had never seen such a dense cream. When I asked Musa Sheth why such good quality milk was unavailable in cities, he picked up a wicker basket and showed me the fodder he was feeding these cows. He told me that he always ensured high-quality animal nutrition; this was the secret of his cows' milk quality. Musa Sheth said that he was pained that villagers were grazing these exotic cows on country grass and heaping so much cruelty on them. "They don't deserve these cows," he railed.

His comment provoked an angry response from the villagers, who contended that a luxurious gruel was out of the question for the cattle when they could not adequately feed their families. I tried to reason with the dairy farmers that if the milk quality were good, they would get better rates, which could help them purchase superior-quality fodder.

We spent two days and two nights identifying the animals, measuring the milk output and then negotiating the price depending on the milk yield. We purchased animals worth Rs. 4.5 lacs. On the evening of the third day, the veterinary officer latched the insurance tags onto the earlobes of the cattle. The cattle were loaded, and we saw them off. The borrowers and my junior colleague accompanied the animals while I went by jeep to Warora, the block headquarters for Ashi village.

The tragedies in cattle finance

Back home, I was caught in a round of malaria and was in great pain. When I resumed office, my table had many files awaiting my clearance during my agonizing odyssey with cows and their old and new masters. I decided to visit these borrowers in their villages on a Sunday, but the farmers appeared to have messed up everything. By evening, our cup of woes was brimming over.

Rekha Teltumbde, who had purchased a pair of cows, walked to my cabin with moistened eyes. "Both my cows disappeared during the night. I had no experience handling this strange breed; you should have given me the local variety," she wailed. She brought the local councilman who launched a long, condescending discourse, "Poor people have to unnecessarily suffer because the banks do not understand their needs correctly." I told the councilman that government experts designed the scheme, and there were different schemes for different borrowers. I tried to calm Rekha, assuring her that I would try my best to seek a solution and requested her to meet me after two days. Rekha tossed a polythene pouch on my table, asking me to relieve her of the loan. "I would prefer to put up a grocery shop; at least I would not have this headache of keeping a watch on the buffaloes".

Before departing, the councilman insisted I give a written guarantee absolving Rekha of the debt. I bluntly told them that it was public money and I had no power to forgive the debt. They should meet the Animal Husbandry Officer, whose office was just across the road, opposite the bank, if they needed further clarification. Fifteen minutes after they had left, my telephone buzzed; it was the Animal Husbandry Officer. To my shock, he sang the borrowers' tune: "When the cattle are lost, the borrower cannot repay the loan." The next time your department talks of targets for financing livestock, I will lodge a written protest," I railed as my high-pitched voice trailed off into the main hall. I demanded a written communication about his views so I could discuss the issue at the monthly meeting of bankers, NGOs, insurance companies, development officers, and the state government, and I slammed the phone down.

We held a staff meeting where everyone suggested adopting a tough stance. "Too much compassion is bad. It can backfire on us," chimed in my farm credit assistant. "If the government staff was so casual as to misguide borrowers, we might have to spend most of our time fending off accusations from local leaders who are always keen to tap the discontented voices." interjected another colleague, a senior and wizened man.

We were yet to face the problem when Mangla walked in with a photograph of the buffalo who died during transportation. "Sir, you had advised me that whenever an animal dies, a picture with the tag latched to the earlobe. Too many animals were jostling o;n ac;unt o;f cramped space in the mini-truck; it must have died because of suffocation." She tossed a polythene pouch containing the detached ear lobes of the cattle on my table. Each buffalo costs Rs 10,000. I telephoned Musa Seth and narrated the incident, sharing the tight situation with him. A gentle and understanding human being, he discerned my plight from my plaintive tone. "Please don't worry. We will help you in every possible way. I have handled this sort of customer for years. I will send you two buffaloes to compensate for the borrowers' loss." I assured him I would compensate for the loss in the next round of purchases, but he suggested I wait for two days, saying the buffaloes would be found or returned on their own.

Two days later, I received a call from Musa Seth informing me that both the buffalos had reached his farm. To this day, I still believe that Musa Seth must have gifted me the buffalos to redeem me and strengthen my trust in him. Although the event astonished me, Musa Seth was not the least surprised. He said it was a routine affair, and he knew of cattle which could nose their way back over distances of almost three hundred kilometres.

The buffalos were transported back to Warora and transferred to a new borrower in Ashi. Rekha signed the transfer deed and settled for an auto trolley in exchange for the buffalos. I sent an excoriating letter to the District Collector, vehemently pleading for a thorough inquiry. The same week, I received a telephone call from my boss in Nagpur asking me why I was creating unnecessary problems for the bank. He advised me that entering into an altercation with the government could harm the bank's business. I resisted the provocation and gently replied that there appeared to be no immediate threat to the rising business graph at the branch. He was a little uneasy with my answer and advised me that as long as I was representing my bank, I should keep my emotions in check and focus on the organisation's interests. The message was clear: I should not regard others' egos as unhealthy, even if I had a healthy ego. If I ruffled the feathers of my peers in government, the government bosses would settle scores with us. I knew the only solution lay in brokering a peace deal.

The solution to Rekha's problem was not the end of my woes. Vandana Dhawas, a farmer from Mohbala who had purchased Jersey cows, confronted me the next day in my office. She had not yet found sufficient customers for her milk, which had soured in the summer heat, putting her at heavy losses. She had come with a small canister containing the foul-smelling milk. "Sir, you should have given me a refrigerator before you gave me these cows. How can I repay your loan now? I want to return these cows." We sought the help of one of our customers, the leading sweet mart of Warora, and they agreed to buy bulk quantities from Vandana daily. These experiences opened my eyes to the vast issues involved with helping people experiencing poverty, particularly when you don't have the support of various linkages to make the business deliver. On paper, the dairy programme appeared beautiful, but in practice, I found myself sinking deeper and deeper into problems.

The hazards of cattle insurance

The most unnerving part of cattle finance is the handling of cattle insurance. If a manager doesn't handle it shrewdly, he can get trapped in shady practices. The problem becomes complex if the cattle die before the insurance formalities. Theoretically, such a situation should not arise because the animal's financing and insurance are supposed to be simultaneous. But the field worker knows that there are umpteen times when, during the purchase, the loan amount is paid earlier, and the cattle remain uninsured for days,anad sometimes weeks.

The date, time and venue of purchase of the transaction have to be fixed in advance by the Animal Husbandry Officer, and there are occasions when the Animal Husbandry Officer fails to turn up at the market. Since the borrower and the bank's field officer have already agreed on the purchase price, and the loan amount has to be released, the deal must be over before the market closes. If the cattle die before being insured, it may mean a long and unending ordeal for the banker as the borrower may disown the liability for repayment of the loan. The manager must then undergo the excruciating rigmarole of enquiries, explanations and reprimands. The insurance company has a haven under its ubiquitous template: "no tag, no claim".

The owner thinks that the animal is insured and that the animal's death relieves him of responsibility for repaying the loan. I have encountered cases where the borrowers have avoided treating the animals during sickness, hoping the ailment would hasten the animals' death and relieve them of the loan's repayment burden.

I want to recount a case where a particular insurance company had run out of stocks of tags and my horrifying ordeal of searching for genuine help for the poor beneficiaries. Since the animals were being financed d under the government's veterinary programme, all the formalities needed to be over before the close of the financial year, March, or the government funds earmarked for any development programmes would lapse. With time already running out and chances of the consignment of tags reaching in time looked difficult, The bankers and block development administration decided to complete the financing and purchase, leaving thc tagging to finish later. To my good fortune, no animal died during the intervening period; otherwise, it would have meant a few more sleepless nights and another journey through a dangerous blind alley. Outsiders would be amazed that bad debts from failing to realise insurance claims form a significant portion of overdue loans under animal husbandry programmes.

The formalities for lodging a claim with the insurance company are cumbersome, time-consuming and entail costs which a small borrower may not be able to meet: a photograph of the dead animal positioned such that the ear with the insurance tag is visible, a *panchakarma* (statement attested by five witnesses), a post-mortem report from the government's Animal Husbandry Officer, and so on. The owner knocks the ear and dumps the foul-smelling, decaying morsel at the bank branch. Even if the manager has the necessary forms to claim the insured sum and is willing to assist in completing the insurance formalities, the borrower often has the gall to say he has nothing to do with the paperwork once he/she doesn't have any loan liability.

If a cooperative and sympathetic manager decides to take care of the formality (in most cases, he is compelled to, despite his aversion because recovery of the bank loan is at stake), he could handle only a few instances. The insurance companies are no saints; they are there to do charity. They can't keep paying claims and losing profits. They, too, have understood the clever tricks of villagers the hard way. They have devised methods to filter claims to the minimum.

One such method may have been issuing plastic instead of brass tags, ostensibly as a cost-cutting measure. Still, it worked in the insurance company's favour but was detrimental to the poor farmers. When the cattle grazed in the thick underbrush, the plastic tags often snapped off when the animal scraped through bushes. Getting a new tag latched was as tricky as getting a new insurance cover done.

The nearest insurance company branch to villages financed by our bank was Chandrapur, almost sixty kilometres away. The borrower would, therefore, apply to the bank branch known to him. The bank forwarded the claim to the insurance company, whose representative came at his convenience, as retagging was not new. Hence, he was not entitled to any commission. This whole process would take ten to fifteen days.

Meanwhile, the insurance company had no liability if the animal died before the completion of insurance or the tag had fallen off. All insurance policies carried a terse fine-print message: "*No Tag — No Claim*". And then you have the arcane asterisk in an obscure corner of the insurance policy indicating the ghastly omnibus phrase "*Conditions Apply*". I feel this clause is a licence to the company to treat each complaint as it likes. Moreover, for a post-of the animal, which is an essential requirement for securing the insurance claim, the borrower must spend days chasing the veterinarian, who often insists on an unofficial fee for which the banker must give the borrower a temporary overdraft.

A bewildering array of forms had to be filled with too many details when making an insurance claim or filling in subsidy claims. Rural bankers and veterinarians must know technical Marathi vocabulary, especially the jargon and phraseology used in government notifications. I remember visiting the local *panchayat* office; I was utterly confused by the maze of unruly papers. One of the men, his face softening with an embarrassed grin, matched my linguistic attempt in Marathi with a few trial words of English. The grin spread around the table. Finally, we identified the correct form, which we filled out when the section chief appeared. We told him what had happened, and he offered his profuse apologies and inadequate English. Escorting us to our car, he said, "I hope, please, that you will try to be understanding."

Insurance is one of rural India's biggest markets, but cattle insurance poses high risks to insurers depending on the region. They are arranging for an agent to underwrite the cattle's lives and prove the cattle's deaths when making a claim, which entails extraordinary cost and effort. Insurance companies issue master policies to reduce the cost of underwriting, and banks, cooperative societies, and state government departments usually take such policies. However, the insurance companies have not been happy with the ease with which villagers manipulated e proof and certification offered for the death of animals.

After the first lot of policyholders universally claimed to have lost their cattle, the insurance companies decreed to place a claim. The owner would need to show the ear of the dead cow. The result was a robust market in cows' ears: any cow that died, insured or not, would have its ear cut off and sold to those who had insured a cow so the farmer could claim the insurance and keep the cow.

A recent breakthrough is insurance against drought: pay-outs are monitored and overseen by satellite images, which show how much grazing lands in the region have deteriorated and how many herders they lost due to this development. Tracking forage cover–rather than the number of dead animals–circumvents claims for animals whose death was due to disease or neglect rather than drought. Previously, insuring livestock for pastoralists has proved near impossible due to the difficulty of verifying the death of animals over a vast and remote area.

Ashi had acquired the reputation of a model village, and I decided to try the programme here.

The veterinary officer at the local block headquarters insisted that the cattle had to be procured from a market outside the district where the borrower resided. It was a precondition to ensure that farmers could not purchase the cattle for their local friends. It entailed higher costs. Moreover, we had to deal with suppliers with whom we were unfamiliar. In contrast, not only did the local markets offer an abundant variety of local breeds, but as these livestock suppliers were familiar to us, we preferred them. We were conversant with the local trade practices. The specified supplier was Kishor Thakur, a tautly-muscled macho man who resembled a Mughal warrior with a splendid manly moustache and menacing glare. The bank manager usually does not get involved with the veterinary doctor's choice, but I hesitated to deal with this particular supplier. Even the villagers endorsed my opinion and felt uncomfortable in dealing with him.

I tried to convince the Animal Husbandry Officer of the need to negotiate with other suppliers to safeguard the interests of the farmers. It irritated him: I had encroached on his turf and chipped at his authority. I recalled how possessive his tribe could be. It was clear from the bloated unofficial fees built into the transactions involving the purchase of animals and, after that, settlement of insurance claims in case of the animal's death. I had to cave into their pressures. However, I kept the campaign going by writing letters to their bosses informing them of these abusive practices. I did not have the faintest suspicion that this decision would later trigger a chain of problems and finally snowball into a severe personal and professional crisis for me.

One evening, I was alone in my office when I heard a pattern of cowboy boots and a western belt clanking with every step. I could see the silhouette against the wall. Kishor, radiating pure animal anger, was negotiating with the security guard at the entry gate. He had poorly shaved that morning, and the tiny patches of stubble lay under his throat just above where the polo-neck collar touched his skin. The ends of his moustache twisted to a dagger's tip, standing clean away from the cheeks. He reached for them every few minutes and gave them a slow, hard twist. Spittle flecked his betel–reddened lips as if they were bleeding. He wore a tight black shirt and hair spiky with gel. Kishor wore several rings on his fingers, each set with a different stone. He was a man of pancake makeup, hair dye, and aviator sunglasses.

He swept into my office. After confusion over where everyone would sit, Kishor selected a chair on the far side of the room, with his back to the wall. With a sweep of his large hand, he instructed his underling to take the chair to his right. I retained enough composure to offer him tea and ask what had brought him here at this weird hour. He downed the tea in a single swallow and swirled the dregs around in the glass. He let his aide open the conversation, but when he found his aide fumbling, he took over. He said that the government's Animal Husbandry Department had still not released the payment and that he was going through a financial crisis. He wanted the payment or the animal to be returned. I told him I had already remitted it to the government and politely told him he should follow it up with the government department. I explained my difficulties and pleaded with Kishor to understand that I was an employee bound by specific rules. Still, he insisted that the staff at the branch had told him that I could sanction a temporary overdraft that would be closed on release of payment by the government. "You can't give excuses. Your staff has fully briefed me. They have even told me that you have released an amount in a similar case to a cattle supplier." I reiterated my stance, but he left my room in a huff. I felt relieved, not knowing that I would reencounter him.

The drama of the previous evening was still brewing in my mind when I arrived at the office the following day, only to find Kishor reappeared there. He said that the Animal Husbandry department had not received the necessary grant, and there was no possibility of any payment materialising shortly. Kishor insisted fo;r a temporary loan for the intervening period. At first, he was calm, but then, on impulse, he became hoarse with anger. The words hit me as if someone had punched my heart. I snivelled and flinched backwards in my seat. I asked Kishor to meet me during office hours and promised to do something. After he left, I rested my head against a stack of files.

He returned that afternoon accompanied by the government's veterinary officer. I decided to sanction an overdraft, hoping the bank account would be closed when the department released the payment. I was sucked into the passion of the moment and didn't read the undercurrents of the racket which operated in the veterinary transactions.

My action in helping Kishor proved to be my undoing and set me on a long and painful journey of vigilant enquiries by my employers, leading to mental suffering for my family. The veterinary department released Kishor's money without our knowledge, and the only remedy was to recover the overdraft amount lost because of the veterinary department's connivance.

Encounter with cattle finance

I remember our visit to Mumbai's Aarey Milk Colony, accompanied by two village elders (including the local village headman, or *sarpanch*), the government veterinary doctor and our field officer. The Colony is one of India's prominent emblems, on a par with Anand of India's

White Revolution. We stayed at the New Zealand hostel, established by donors from New Zealand, a pioneering country in dairying. I was tired after a long journey and preferred to rest, so I skipped dinner and had a slice of toasted bread with buttermilk. The next day was Sunday, and we had to stay indoors as there was some trouble outside, and the area was under police patrol. We came out of our rooms only for lunch and dinner.

At the lunch table, we met officials from other centres. The initial pleasantries were over, and we all got involved in an animated discussion. Some of the veterans who were regular visitors spoke bitterly of their experience but admitted that there was little they could do with the system. I sought their advice on my banker's responsibility in the transaction. They said accountability would naturally rest with us since we had sanctioned the loan amount. Still, they suggested a few simple tests to independently verify the quality of the animal. Examine the animal's eyeballs and make it stand or sit three or four times to determine its agility and gait. The appetite and the rate of belching give an idea of intestinal health, which is the most critical aspect of cattle's well-being. During negotiation, we should keep reminding the suppliers that we were disappointed with the quality of the animals and that we could have bought much superior quality anywhere else. We should still think twice. He said that the sting in the message straightaway knocks twenty per cent off the price and puts the seller on the defence.

The next day, we visited the *tabelas* (cattle camps). I had expected something cheerful, maybe with dancing and music, but I saw no festivities. The atmosphere was serious, even tense; it reminded me less of a fair than the stock market floor. It appeared as if the country's buffaloes had converged for an annual convention. Men, carrying or counting bundles of pink thousand-rupee notes, shouted and shoved their way into deals, occasionally getting into heated arguments that hovered at the edge of violence. Cattle brokers, called *brokers*, go from farm to farm buying buffaloes just before they calve and send them by train to the market where city dairymen buy them. The *brokers* and the dairymen consider the newborn calves expendable, and one can see dead calves piled high outside the stables.

The entire area stank. I was surprised at the insensitivity of my new friends' olfactory organs. All of them moved around without the slightest trace of disdain. Their noses didn't seem to register even the slightest whiff of the stench that wafted through the sky. Soon, the sky was hailing mosquitoes. The eagles were also working a frightful racket around us. My nose kept registering so many odours that I felt I would have to be driven straight to a hospital to pump out poisonous gases from my lungs. The scene from the Bhopal tragedy started crossing my mind.

By evening, I emerged from the scrum, dishevelled, glassy-eyed and soaked in sweat, and wearing mismatched sandals packed with grime and cow pee. The moist heat was intense enough to steam up my glasses. I was so exhausted that I could not negotiate even a single transaction. The mad cattle bog equally overawed my villagers. My shirt was drenched in sweat, which trickled down my face and neck. I later discovered that somebody had picked my watch adorned my wrist since I joined my bank. During the afternoon, they had fetched me a few greasy snacks daubed with lots of chilli powder, wrapped in a torn newspaper. I immediately signalled an emphatic no, as my mind would constantly hallucinate explosive gunpowder when I saw the flaming red ochre powder resembling the diffused particles of an angry sun.

The veterinary doctor waited impatiently, accompanied by a ferocious-looking man with an outrageous moustache and whiskery cauliflower ears. I could see wrinkles of suppressed rage on his face. He couldn't express his displeasure to me, but he told the farmers to give up the village slack as long as we were in Mumbai. He then asked them to settle the transactions with the broker, the man beside him, whom he introduced as a renowned authority from Haryana on buffalos. He could tell by looking at a buffalo how much milk it would yield. The farmers looked at me, expecting me to lead the negotiations. I clarified that I would not spare anybody if the procedure were faulty. I told the doctor bluntly that I wouldn't hesitate to complain to the government. The frowning faces of the doctor and the buffalo master relaxed, the creases on the faces dissolved, and their tone became conciliatory.

The buffalo master took the initiative to break the stalemate and said he was open to further discounts as he was keen to get a foothold in Chandrapur, the district from which our farmers hailed. "Rs 8000 for each buffalo, transportation cost to be borne by the borrowers." The farmers shook their heads and raised their eyes upwards to show how puzzled they were.

Finally, after a telephone discussion with the Dairy Commissioner at Chandrapur, we finalised the deal. The vendor would also provide one month's fodder free along with the buffalo. Two giant vehicles with massive wagons carrying these exotic cattle arrived in Warora. The doctor and the farmers escorted the cattle. I boarded the night train. There were no mobile phones then, and there were no means through which I could remain in touch with the buffalos, their new owners, or the doctor. The buffaloes arrived forty-eight hours later, to much excitement in Ashi. In Warora, people saw these huge vehicles for the first time. The two well-built Sardars who drove them were pretty upbeat and still fit enough to commence their return journey immediately.

At this juncture, I realized that every dairy loan must have a component for veterinary care, and the government can chip in with a fodder allowance to be paid to the farmers till the cattle calve. Before taking this risky step, I sent urgent messages to the veterinary staff, but no help appeared to be forthcoming. The only way out of the predicament was to sanction overdrafts. It was a minor liberty I was taking with the rules, but my auditors could very well label it as a significant transgression because it was a scheme to be designed by the government.

A few days later, while reviewing the minutes of the monthly review meeting, I was astonished to find an obscure remark mentioning that the District Collector had lauded the veterinary officers for their zeal and commitment to achieving the target for the supply of dry buffaloes. There was no reference to the travails and agony the bank staff had undergone. I felt deeply hurt that the government had such a myopic view of rural development programmes, feeling that the government staff must be under the impression that we were naïve. When we coolly analysed the programme processes, we realised we were victims of an agenda. I wrote a powerful letter to the Dairy Commissioner, pointing out that the poor tribals had suffered under the guise of a programme ostensibly designed for their welfare.

The term "rehabilitation and relief" has become a much-abused term in relief manuals and has been used as a smokescreen to camouflage corrupt practices. I cannot but marvel at the title that P. Sainath, the well-known rural affairs editor, gave to his excellent book *Everybody Loves a Good Drought.* Natural calamities like drought and floods lead to inundation of relief material and provide fantastic opportunities for the self-aggrandizement of the relief staff.

My complaints evoked a snigger from the lower veterinary bureaucracy, and my letters created a flutter in the veterinary department, and an inquiry took place. I later learned that the dairy officials visited Ashi and got a signed undertaking from the borrowers, stating that the dairy department had extended its full cooperation and the scheme had failed owing to the borrowers' negligence. I don't know whether it was the borrowers or the local *sarpanch* who took brides for the consent.

Risks in financing cattle

A significant risk is financing livestock, mainly with weak veterinary infrastructure. Large numbers of milch animals are often bought for beneficiaries simultaneously in cattle fairs, pushing their price. The difference in the price and quality of financed assets over their market price, along with the costs of time, out-of-pocket expenses and payments to intermediaries, is estimated to raise the transaction costs to the borrower by an estimated twenty per cent. It takes a discerning eye to know when to sell a cow, such as in the early stages of an outbreak of bovine disease.

The real villains who sabotaged the development agenda of the banks were the staff of the local development administration. The veterinary doctors made life miserable for banks, insurance companies and people experiencing poverty. At the time of purchase, these doctors would charge exorbitant fees for certifying the animal's health and then again charge the cattle owner an equally hefty fee for endorsing the insurance claim when the cattle died. The veterinary doctors' certification about the quality of the animal and the suitability of the price is ten per cent of the loan value. When the animal dies, you have to shell out another ten to fifteen per cent for the so-called post-mortem, which is a written recording of the cause of death as reported by the borrower. I used to envy these doctors, whose fees were higher than even the best cardiac surgeons in the country. The insurance procedures are complicated, and veterinary doctors create further problems by insisting on complex conditions. The veterinary doctors have their cartel, which aligns with the cartel of suppliers. A bank manager cannot break this cycle to explore better markets and broader choices for the borrowers.

I became aware of the messy procedure much too late. I found that whenever a poor farmer thought of availing himself of any assistance from the government, he had to brace himself for the usual struggle with a venal and slothful bureaucracy. The so-called purchase committee for purchasing livestock under the government's development programmes is a big sham, and the veterinary doctor indulges in outright manipulation. If the borrower or manager doesn't accede to his diktat –there is no other way to describe his dictatorial role–he has to face severe outright non-cooperation from the veterinary staff. In case of the animal's death, the borrower cannot think of even a faint possibility of claiming his insurance.

I remember a young, hard-working boy whom I financed to purchase a unit of two buffaloes so that he could have his own independent business. The extra income gave the boy the luxury of visiting the nearby township and befriending youth from elite families. In the process, he got involved with a girl with whom he eloped. The panicked family, which used to sing my praises earlier, suddenly started charging me for spoiling the boy with the loan. The boy's mother would wail that the family had lost their peace after their son got the loan. After the boy left, there was no one to look after the buffaloes, and the mother flatly told me that she and her husband were not in a position to take care of them and that they would not be able to pay the loan instalments any longer. I spent an almost sleepless night wrestling with this typical problem.

My colleague, who had only watched the situation until now, found it necessary to intervene. He made short shrift of the *sarpanch,* who softened his stance. I then pleaded with the woman to engage a labourer and manage the dairy by herself for the time being. I promised to lend her any support she needed, like arranging for veterinary care and stocks of fodder to help her in the calamity that had befallen her. It eased her trauma. I also asked my clerk to explain the financial transactions and how she could manage her loan account without any hassles. The shy housewife turned out to be a very efficient manager, and by the time I transferred, she had repaid almost the entire loan.

Later, I learned that the boy had also returned to the village with the girl he had married. The family gratefully accepted the boy and his wife. The loan was closed, but in the process, I underwent a protracted period of agony.

Fast forward 2023

The boy's hard-working parents have both expired. The boy established himself with his wife in a bigger town.

Even in this bleak world, I could see silver linings. Gulab Kshirsagar was a landless agricultural labourer from a family whose income was below the official poverty line. He had been working as a labourer almost since his childhood. Due to illness and old age, Gulab had lost the physical stamina to undertake strenuous work. He was under the IRDP, the pioneering poverty-alleviation initiative of the government, for setting up a goattery unit and purchased seven does and one buck. Gulab could repay the entire bank loan at the end of three years by selling goats during festival seasons, particularly Holi and Eid festivals, when goats are in heavy demand for sacrificial slaughter. He used his profits to enable his daughter to marry. One significant factor that enabled Kshirsagar to succeed was that he devoted abundant time to tending the goats. He grazed them personally and bathed them daily with soap and disinfectant. However, he could not afford supplementary food or veterinary tonics to stimulate their growth.

He fell in love with goats when he was a teenager. Now, when people ask, "How come you got into the business of goats?" he answers, "I didn't get into goats; they got into me." He now has 150 goats of varying ages on his small dairy farm, and he knows them all by name. Kshirsagar's flock of goats was much healthier than other villagers who had more money and could afford a servant to graze the animals and provide professional veterinary care. Kshirsagar is an example of what distinguishes successful goattery units from those that fail: the owner's commitment to his flock herd.

Small farmers need basic veterinary knowledge along with emergency veterinary kits. In the present case, the bank branch maintained this kit and periodically supplied medicine to the unit. I was cautioned that goats need regular doses of wormicide to disinfect their intestines. Worm infection is the most common problem with cattle, but wormicides must be given based on symptoms. In the case of successful units, I noticed that the owners were diligent and careful in sticking to proper medicinal schedules.

In the case of cattle loans, most cattle owners reported that they had either sold off the animals bought with the loan or that these animals were dead. In cattle loans, the adequate focus has to be on basic needs, including the availability of nutritious fodder, milk marketing, etc. Only those too old to work are turned loose. Buffaloes, whose milk has higher butterfat content than cows, are the mainstay of the commercial dairy industry. Today's dairy farm is mechanized, computerized and, above all, significant. The end product, however, is the same as it was a century or five centuries ago: all manner of cheese, yoghurt, butter and, in perhaps its purest form, the stuff you put on dry cereal or use to wash down a piece of chocolate cake—milk.

These stories show that development programmes, particularly dairy programmes for small farmers, can be counterproductive unless we provide fodder and veterinary allowances. Take the example of the much-discussed IRDP buffalo. It is easy for a farmer who already owns land and animals to use an additional buffalo well. The same animal can be a Damocles' sword for an asset-less household. The family can suffer heavy financial loss if the buffalo falls ill and cash is unavailable to treat it or grows weak during non-lactation periods when fodder is needed. I think it is time we stopped asking the BDO what villagers want. Perhaps it is time we ask people what they want. Or, better still, leave it to the people to ask each other what they want and then decide how they want to spend their resources.

In Yavatmal, for example, many poor individuals signed up to receive microfinance to purchase a cow to generate a little additional income from selling raw milk. While this was a sensible and compassionate intervention by the international donor and NGO community, the development outcome was highly problematic. The local over-supply of raw milk in many communities led to a general price decline. It undermined all incumbent producers, especially other non-client 'one-cow farms' who quickly saw reduced margins and incomes and were thus more likely to fall into poverty than before. It also had a negative longer-run effect by undercutting the day-to-day operations of potentially sustainable larger dairy farms. Like all other businesses, the onset of the internet and mobile phones has revolutionized dairy. Veterinary assistance is readily available. The story of the cow and the computer is a local parable showing that sometimes the most straightforward information is valuable.

Some months back, Sangita Kitey, a round-faced woman who cannot read or write, sat in the courtyard of her small home in Wanoja in Chandrapur with the family's only milch cow. For five days and nights, the cow moaned while in labour. Sangita grew ever more fearful that the cow would die. "This is the only good income we have," she said, explaining that the four gallons of milk the cow produced each day paid the bills. Word of Sangita's woebegone cow soon spread to Ashok, a public-spirited farmer who uses one name. The village's computer is in the anteroom of his home. The computer is operated full-time by Ashok, who uses it to call up a list of area veterinarians. A doctor arrived that night and, by the light of a bare electric bulb, stuck his arm into Sangita's cow, extracted the calf's spindly leg, tied a rope, and dragged the calf into the world.

One thing I admire in my cattle owners is their importance to their animals' health. If his milch cow or prized bull is ill, the owner will rush the animal to a veterinarian even though he may not take his child, who may be a victim of chronic diarrhoea. "A man can breed children. But if his bull dies, he loses his livelihood. What gives man bread should be cared for and worshipped," says Ledange, another farmer.

In villages, there is a specific day for honouring bulls. In the pola festival, the bulls are massaged and bathed, fed on eggs, and made to participate in a race. "He is my child," says Ledange, as his hand rests tenderly on the head of a sturdy white animal. He feeds his bull on wheat, and himself eats *ragi*, a coarse grain. And when his bull becomes a father, he celebrates the occasion in a manner that befits the birth of his son. "Do you know how to judge a bull?" he asks as his eyes glow. "You first look at its horns, then its hump and how it crouches down. When mine does, it deserves an *arti*(sacred ritual)." The bull is Ledange's companion. He brings him home in the dead of night. The bull is more than a wife he only sees at certain hours. His wife to him is a mere tool necessary to keep a unit complete and further a generation. He has no room for her. She finds room for herself in her motherhood.

After my bitter experiences with dairy financing, I vowed never to get into the nightmarish ordeal again. As I moved up the ladder of senior positions in the bank hierarchy, I came in contact with promoters of giant dairy plants, particularly in Western Maharashtra, who had modern salons and parlours for housing animals, state-of-the-art chilling plants and the required infrastructure in terms of veterinary care. These dairy plants were real wealth creators and sources of pride and revenue for the banks. This model, I realized, was the only viable route for dairy businesses: small dairy farmers need to be aggregated and linked up through a value chain to these sophisticated projects.

However, I found that the penchant of development agencies for high-yielding cows has never diminished. Long after I had lost direct contact with dairy farmers and the dairy circuit, no less a person than the Prime Minister announced a package of wagonloads of these Holstein and Jersey cows that were to go to farmers in the suicide-affected agrarian belt of Yavatmal and Wardha. The farmers were in great distress and were now supposed to feed these royal guests. Newspaper columns bled with morose headlines: 'Princely cows for measly families.' The results were on the expected lines. The farmers, unable to feed these cows, sold them off at paltry prices and were back to their original plight.

The stories of proxy purchases of animals and fleecing of clients for insurance claims continue, but the processes have become transparent and scrutiny challenging and rigorous. It is suitable for honest borrowers. Private veterinary doctors have increased, but people experiencing poverty are now more empowered and aware of their rights. Their innocence has gone.

Why do development agencies love modern cows?

The penchant of development agencies for high-yielding cows has never waned. Whenever relief work for drought-affected families in villages is undertaken, imported quality cows are considered essential in the official relief packages or self–help schemes. I have seen in my career that whenever a drought ravages a village, the crossed Holstein and Jersey cows arrive in wagonloads, and every family in these parched villages are a cow for each family;y. Regrettably, most beneficiaries are usually landless and use common property resources for pasturing and nurturing them. It defies them because they can't survive in a land scorched to dust by rainless years.

These generous gifts become burdensome since they have a voracious appetite and demand a rich nutrient diet. The only gainers are owners of cartels of cattle suppliers and the state's development staff, who usually love these natural tragedies because they ring the fortune bells for them. The families are generally in great distress as they are supposed to care for these royal guests. The apparent storyline that follows such government attempts is usually the same. Newspapers bleed with morose headlines: 'Princely cows for measly families,' and yet, the results are on the expected lines. The farmers cannot feed these cows; eventually, they have to sell them off at paltry only to return to their original plight.

It is easy for a farmer who owns land and animals to use an additional cow effectively. Meanwhile, the same animal can be a Damocles sword for an asset-less household. If the cow falls ill and the family cannot afford to take care of it, or if it grows emaciated during non-lactation periods when buying fodder is necessary, the family may not be able to afford the high costs. Therefore, to address the villager's needs better, we must ask them, not the development officers who spend their time in urban offices. Or, better still, leave it to the people to make decisions regarding the allocation of resources in their areas.

It may only be a coincidence that the development programmes have a more significant fascination for cows when several other alternatives could work better. My initial vitality and enthusiasm in my rural career suffered jolts, and I soon realized that financing cattle was not a simple apprentice's job. My notions of dairy finance being the simplest of all types of finance were based on my naivety and lack of exposure to rural realities. Soon enough, I realized it was the diciest finance wherein the laws of nature play a more significant role than our financial and agricultural skills. If the cows keep gushing out gallons of milk, yoghurt, and cream that keep padding the farmer's wallets with cash, the gravy train keeps chugging, and it is a happy, romantic situation for the dairy farmers. However, the problem starts when the cattle fall ill. An ailment, if left unattended, can lead to mortality, resulting in a heavy loss for the poor household.

In one district, for example, many poor small farmers signed up to receive microfinance. They decided to purchase a cow to generate additional income by selling milk. While this was considered a sensible and compassionate intervention by the international donor and NGO community, the development outcome was highly problematic. The local over-supply of raw milk in many communities led to a general price decline. It undermined all incumbent producers, especially other non-client 'one-cow farms' who quickly saw reduced margins and incomes and were thus more likely to fall into poverty than before.

In the case of cattle loans, most cattle owners report that they either sell off the animals bought with the loan or that these animals die due to improper care. Cattle loans do not adequately address other vital details, such as fodder availability and milk marketing, which heavily impact farmers' incomes. The stories of proxy animal purchases and client fleecing for insurance claims continue, but the processes have become highly transparent and rigorous. It has been beneficial for honest borrowers. Private veterinary doctors have increased, but the poor are now much more empowered and aware of their rights than ever before.

Basic veterinary knowledge, along with emergency veterinary kits, is necessary. The onset of the internet and mobile phones has revolutionized the dairy business like every other. Veterinary assistance is now readily available. The story of the cow and the computer is a local parable, which proves that sometimes the most straightforward information is the most valuable.

Sangita Kitey, a woman who cannot read and write, sat in the courtyard of her small home with the family's only milch cow in Wanoja, Chandrapur. The cow moaned for five days and nights while she was in labour. Sangita grew, constantly fearing that the cow would die. She explained, *"This is the only good income we have," implying* that the four gallons of milk the cow produced each day paid all the bills. Fortunately, the news about Sangita's woebegone cow reached Ashok, a public-spirited farmer who uses one name. The village's computer is in the anteroom of his home and is handled by Ashok, a full-time assistant veterinarian. Ashok used it to call up a list of area veterinarians, and a doctor arrived that night. By the light of a dim electric bulb, the doctor stuck his arm into Sangita's cow, extracted the calf's spindly leg, tied a rope, and dragged the calf into the world.

One thing I admire about cattle owners is their importance to their animals' health. If his milch cow or prized bull is ill, the owner rushes the animal to a veterinarian even if he may not visit the doctor for his child, who may be a victim of chronic diarrhoea. "A man can breed children. But if his bull dies, he loses his livelihood. What gives man bread should be cared for and worshipped," *says Ledange, another farmer.*

In villages, there is a specific day to honour the bulls. In '*pola*' (a bull-worshipping *festival)*, the bulls are massaged and bathed, fed on eggs, and made to participate in a race. "He is my child," says Ledange, as his hand rests tenderly on the head of a sturdy white animal. He feeds his bull on wheat, and himself eats *ragi*, a coarse grain. And when his bull becomes a father, he celebrates the occasion in a manner that befits the birth of his son. "*Do you know how to judge a bull?*" he asks, his eyes glowing. "You first look at its horns, then its hump and watch how it crouches down. When mine does, it deserves an arti (sacred ritual)." The bull is Ledange's companion. He brings him home in the dead of night. The bull is more than a wife he only sees at certain hours. His wife to him is a mere tool necessary to keep a unit complete, to bring the next generation. He has no room for her. She finds room for herself in her motherhood.

Veterinary services in villages are indigent, and the poorly equipped apprentices behave like sharks, trying to fleece people experiencing poverty even to treat common ailments. Some tribes think of their expertise as nothing sort of super specialists. The much-touted insurance of livestock is quite cumbersome. Techniques for increasing the quantity of milk are but one part of a vast repertoire of practices in which dairy farmers must be thoroughly grounded. They must have traditional and informal veterinary knowledge if they don't want to get jolted by these quacks,

After my bitter experiences with dairy financing, I vowed never to get into the nightmarish ordeal again. As I moved up the hierarchical ladder in the bank, I came in contact with promoters of giant dairy plants, particularly in Western Maharashtra, who had modern salons and parlours for housing animals, state-of-the-art chilling plants and the required infrastructure for veterinary care. These dairy plants were real wealth creators and sources of pride and revenue for the banks. This model, I think, is the only viable route for dairy businesses: small dairy farmers need to be aggregated and linked up through a value chain to these sophisticated projects, which carry the potential to transform the lives of all stakeholders involved sustainably. It is precisely why tiny dairy loans are now a sunset financial product on the banking shelves.

* * * * *

7. VIGNETTES FROM VILLAGES

At a time when rural banking was emerging as a strong sibling of other banking segments, I think it fit to share my experience in the theory, practice and academics of rural finance, which has been my abiding passion for well over three decades. The experiences have been diverse; some chilling, some amusing, some exciting, but they nevertheless serve as a prism that provides a view of every facet of rural society. The scenario has undoubtedly undergone a radical transformation in the last decade. Rural banking has lost its sheen because development bankers now feel that commitment has no relevance, especially when confronted with a rural society becoming more politicised with time.

On the institutional front, the greed for profits has diluted the original mission of Muhammad Yunus, the man who revolutionized the financial model for people with low incomes; the mission has shifted from serving the poor to skimming profit off people experiencing poverty. The banks needed to raise interest rates and engage in aggressive marketing and loan collection to ensure the small loans would be profitable for their shareholders. In some cases, especially in commercial microfinance, there were severe exploitations. The kind of empathy that had once been shown to borrowers when the lenders were nonprofits has faded away.

My new learning

During my first assignment at Aurangabad, my boss, R. P. Mehta, was a little bemused at the empathy for the clients, given the banks' approach to poor customer service. My colleagues gave Mehta the impression that I was liberal in my approach to borrowers, which customers could misuse. Mehta could be ruthless with errant staff and recalcitrant borrowers, but he also had a soft side whenever any staff member got into trouble because of a bonafide lapse. He would take risks to rescue him. His mantra was simple: be good with good customers, casual with routine customers, and wary of new loan seekers.

He did appreciate my gentle approach to compassion for customers. He was a little sceptical of my unbalanced approach and conveyed his feedback to me through our colleagues. Mehta was a great master in man management, and he would always drop subtle hints to ensure that his instructions did not demotivate the officer. When he found it necessary to counsel me, he would invite me to his residence for counselling. There was an occasion when I visited him and could get an accurate impression of his demeanour and temperament. He would be dressed in an impressive full-length coat and relishing a drink. A cigar was a part of his regular recipe. Mehta was a warm-hearted person but always expressed a stern glare that evoked a feeling of awe. I was slightly nervous when Mehta ushered me into his drawing room; he appeared slightly perturbed, disturbing me. He gave me a reproaching welcome.

As usual, Mehta raised his legs on the table and asked me what drink I would prefer. I knew he was not referring to a soft drink but the premium wines that adorned his small cellar. He laughed when I suggested lemon water but dispelled sarcasm and got into an everyday mood. He was a bit embarrassed by his innocence, "Do you know bankers are hard boozers?" I sulked for a moment but then controlled my emotions and feigned that I had not co; comprehended him. He gestured for his servant to fetch me lemon water with ice.

He then enquired about my personal experience in the city and interactions with the staff and customers. He complimented me for my sincerity and commitment at work and spoke about the positive feedback he had received. He then recounted how he had been flush with idealism and revolutionary zeal in college. He vowed to his teachers and friends that he would not marry till he cleansed the system of its veniality. But all his idealism vaporized after he experienced the tyranny of employers.

He recounted a fable of a millionaire who had to undergo a heart transplant. The doctors asked him to choose which heart he wanted to receive. The millionaire's fortunes were so vast that he could afford to buy anybody's heart: a film star, beauty queen, politician, sportsman, politician, scholar, astronaut, doctor and, if required, even that of a ruling king or queen. The millionaire wanted a heart that would be both sturdy and tough, one that could remain unruffled by emotions. He mulled over the suggestions of his surgeons and said, "I should be fine with a banker's heart. Bankers don't use their hearts; a banker's heart will be impervious to external emotions. I don't think that there could be a sturdier heart."

It was an apparent message for me. Mehta perked me up, saying there is always a way we can combine compassion with prudence since we were handling finance. Through his nuanced suggestions, he conveyed that, as a banker, I should have a hawk's head and a dove's soul. The hawk worries about the safety of the bank's money; the dove wants the maximum number of individuals to get access to banking and assistance through credit for setting up businesses as a source of livelihood.

A new experiment in rural banking

With the repayment culture contaminated and delinquent tendencies of borrowers so firmly entrenched, bankers became wary of extending rural credit. They started practising credit apartheid. Our planners responded to this situation with a myopic idea: target loans to women, the most important and stable constituency for vote-hungry politicians. Nobody wondered what the use of a loan could be for village women who played the triple role of mother, home-keeper, and wage earner, not to mention lacking business skills. Their only qualifications were reliability, honesty and trustworthiness, qualities which a bank's conventional appraisal methods cannot quantify.

It resulted in men using women as fronts for loans for a wide range of technical equipment: tractors, harvesters, grain mills and pump sets. The worst was to come when, on account of defaults, women started receiving court notices and became parties to lawsuits. It was happening at a time when the neighbouring countries of Asia were undertaking a sensible experiment in rural finance. Poor women trained with skills in bookkeeping, business skills and leadership qualities. When they could do business independently, they were given micro-loans for goat-keeping, cycle rickshaws, hair salons, basket-making, and other business activities. Women themselves serviced the loans and ensured that all conditions were complied with. Babkers waent on a fi;nancing binge. It took almost two decades for us to realise our folly and take lessons from experiments elsewhere .it was in the early nineties that we conceived of our indigenous Self Help Group model of rural finance.

Social banking

Most people believe that social control of banks was necessary to make banking accessible to the vast rural population that remained unserved by conventional banks. The branches of public banks were few, and villagers largely remained underserved. In 1984, additional private banks were nationalized in the second tranche of nationalisation after 1969 because the government perceived that poor people had no access to private banks. The politicians felt it necessary to impose social control in banking to give it a developmental thrust and emphasised extending banking to cover rural areas. Bank branches mushroomed at places of politicians' choice with scant regard to the viability of the bank branch and the availability of necessary infrastructure. The establishment of a new type of structure was needed, one specifically for the needs of the rural population. These banks needed low-cost employees familiar with the indigenous culture. It could increase both the efficiency and viability of the branches.

The Regional Rural Banks and District Cooperative Banks emerged in response to this thinking. A dedicated service philosophy initially drove them to that population segment that the formal financial system could not cover. But these institutions got so brutally politicised that they became tools for politicians. Instead of fixing the problem or learning lessons, our politicians moved to fresh territories and decided to use the mainstream public banks to achieve their socialist and populist agenda.

The problem with all the new development practices is the excessive haste with which the policymakers and practitioners peddle half-baked ideas without first piloting them to assess their suitability for scaling up across diverse geographies. We have professionalized and glamorized the strategic communication departments handled by experts who have mastered selling ideas. The most unsuspecting groups are usually the marginalized communities whose meagre incomes keep their raw minds groping for ways of getting rich the quick way. There is a scramble among the development scientists to score points. Development journalists always sniff for stories that please their editors and earn them by-lines. The rural economy underwent profound upheaval.

The disastrous end to the National Biogas Programme of India is a stark example of the monumental failure of the alternative energy model. Initially termed a revolutionary project expected to transform the economy of India's hinterland, the administrators allocated huge targets for installing biogas plants and doled out soft loans like hot snacks. They did not, however, make any effort to train masons or create a pool of service agents to ensure proper construction and maintenance of these plants. The programme was a financial tsunami for poor villagers with a legacy of unpaid loans. And there was no consideration of the implications of such blind waivers. The borrowers lost their eligibility for new loans as they fell into the defaulters' category. It was a typical case of a credit-worthy borrower becoming an untrustworthy e-borrower because of the over-enthusiasm of the staff of the development machinery, which depended on the juiciness of targets achieved. The result was that estrangement from the bankers deepened further.

This programme is the most glaring example of how a top-down approach can play havoc with the lives of people whose lot it proposes to improve. All households in Visakha, a village in Gadchiroli, within an eponymous *gram panchayat*, were covered under the programme. A recommendation that the concerned development officer should be publicly felicitated was pending at our zonal headquarters in Nagpur when a senior officer with vast experience in grassroots programmes insisted that all such recognitions must wait for two years to allow evaluation of the results. After two years, the ghost of the National Biogas Plan haunted the villages even as the spectre of drought sucked hundreds of farmers into its vortex of mass suicides.

Rural bank branches became the shrines of a failed rural revolution. In my bank branch in Chandrapur, I wrote off hundreds of loans as if ploughing a mountain of rotten potatoes just to rid the balance sheet of toxic assets. Every quarter, the concerned clerk would brand the yellowing dog-eared ledger sheets with a remark, *nonperforming asset*, so that interest income on these accounts would not classified as profit. The deadweight drained our staffing because the financial accounting exercise kept track of these dead accounts. They finally resulted in a vast sinkhole in the balance sheet.

The additional burden arising from the mass opening of rural bank branches adversely affected the resilience and viability of banks. The extension of commercial bank branches resulted from the need to fill credit gaps in the rural economy, which resulted from the cooperative movement's uneven and inadequate development. The politicians believe banks can bring economic revolution through rural credit, like expecting a midwife to deliver a baby. In a developing country, it is not enough to provide credit for production. Production must increase by adopting improved technology rather than pumping additional money into the system.

With the emphasis changing to security-oriented lending, the original banking canvas broadened into a social banking concept dependent on purpose-oriented credit for development. It called for a shift from urban – to rural-oriented lending. Social banking gradually evolved and became "better the village, better the nation". However, opening new branches in rural areas without proper expansion, planning and supervision of end use of credit or creating basic infrastructure facilities meant that branches remained mere flag posts. It was a make-believe revolution that would lead to a severe financial crisis in the years to come.

The Integrated Rural Development Programme (IRDP), the government's flagship programme for poverty alleviation, is a grim reminder of how mechanically trying to meet targets can undermine the integrity of a social revolution to such an extent that a new counter-revolution emerges. Arguably India's worst-ever development programme that stumbled India's development revolution, the IRDP, intended to provide income-generating assets to the rural poor through cheap bank credit. There was little support for skill formation, access to inputs, markets and necessary infrastructure. In the case of cattle loans, for example, most cattle owners reported that either they had sold off the animals bought with the loan or that these animals were dead. The programme lacked strategic focus.

Working for people experiencing poverty does not mean indiscriminately thrusting money down their throats. Unfortunately, IRDP did precisely that. The programme did not attempt to ascertain whether the loan provided would lead to creating a viable long-term asset nor try to make the necessary forward and backward linkages to supply raw material or establish marketing linkages for the produce. The essential data on the intended beneficiaries was not properly culled nor collated. Hence, there were no valid conclusions that could become guiding signals. The IRDP was an instrument for powerful local bosses to distribute their largesse opportunistically. The abiding legacy of the programme for India's poor has been that millions have become bank defaulters through no fault. Today, the people so marked find it impossible to rejoin the formal credit stream.

The IRDP alone accounted for 40 per cent of the losses incurred by commercial banks in rural lending in India. By the end of the 1980s, there was serious concern about the low capital base, low profitability, and high percentage of non-performing assets in public banks, whose revenues were invariably lower duc to losses from lousy loans. They required continual refinancing and recapitalisation by apex institutions. The final nail in the coffin was the official loan waiver in 1989, which destroyed whatever semblance of credit discipline remained. Some bold bankers responded with an eloquent retort to this line of thinking.

There are two essential prerequisites of a poverty eradication programme. Firstly, there was a need to reorientate relations among farmers so that more people could share land ownership. Secondly, no programme for removing poverty can succeed in an economy plagued by inflation and spiralling rise of prices.

A poverty eradication programme, therefore, must mop up the surplus with the elite classes. These two prerequisites a robust political will in the national leadership to implement the much-needed structural reforms. Besides, the government must aim at a strategy for developing the social sector: population control, universal primary education, family welfare, and job creation, especially in rural areas. These and other aspects of poverty alleviation have not been important in our planning, though we have always thought that economic development can eliminate poverty.

Expansion of bank branches

During the massive banking expansion phase in the 1980s, opening a bank branch was made to look as casual as punching a flag post. It lacked the soul of a genuine economic revolution. It was not conceived by the grassroots agents but assembled by starry-eyed mandarins who had picked up bits and pieces about financial inclusion from pompous, new-fangled and half-baked ideas generated at seminars and conferences. The district coordinators of the public banks who handled the process for individual districts were astounded by the strange-looking names of villages identified for the location of new branches of banks. As a district coordinator overseeing this expansion programme for my district, I saw how an unenlightened politician can wreak havoc with financial systems.

I was handling Wardha district, which was identified by the Planning Commission for overall development purely on Gandhian lines, emphasising Gandhian values and economics. It was impossible to locate a proper structure to house the bank. The staff needed primary but essential amenities, which were unavailable because of the immaturity and lack of appropriate understanding of the planners. When the expiry of the RBI licence for the opening of the bank branch approached without proper premises, banks were launched in a local temple or a community centre, marked by a small banner. A picture of the bank's banner adorning the premises was sent with excitement to the administrative headquarters as evidence of the launch of the bank's operations. The village had now been with access to banking.

Juicy numbers give musical resonance to the ears of all bosses. Numbers have been a great obsession with Indian planners in particular.

Number of men & women sterilized, contraceptives circulated, wells dug, toilets constructed, villages screened for polio, TB, or malaria, children enrolled in schools, and saplings planted. There is no accountability for fudged figures. Most rewards go to officers most adept at massaging figures. The game of numbers without a concurrent focus on social performance and evaluating the quality of assets created has been the bane of most credit programmes for poverty reduction and self-employment. The targets were always arbitrary;

The borrower on his deathbed

I remember the case of Manik Meshram, a progressive farmer from Charurkhati in Chandrapur, whose father had long taken a l loan for a bore well and an electric pump. The general complaint was that the bank-assigned contractors did poor work. The villagers could not benefit from the well, yet the loan continued to grow even after the final notice from the bank. I extended an olive branch and agreed to substantially reduce the repayment on account of interest. Still, Manik's father refused to pay the loan as a protest against the callousness of both the bank and the contractor. Our relations became highly strained. I decided to wind up the matter at that stage.

One day, I heard Manik's father was ailing and was virtually in the throes of death. I decided to visit him because I considered Manik the most decent farmer in his village. I found the venerable older man propped up in his hospital bed, monitors beeping and flashing graphs measuring his vital health parameters. His arms had needles pricked all over, and a tube ran through his mouth into his lungs. The room was illuminated only by the psychedelic images on the television screen, with blackout curtains drawn to block the sunlight. Manik briefed me on the health of his father, saying that his father's chance of surviving appeared quite dim and he was marking time. As I sat with Manik, I casually mentioned the outstanding loan of the failed well and requested that he pay at least some portion to demonstrate his credibility. I also advised him that his refusal to do so would demean him in the eyes of the bank and taint his father's high reputation.

It seemed the very mention of the loan aroused the olfactory organs of Manik's father and triggered the raw nerves. He jolted back to life and started accusing me of unnecessarily insisting on recovery of a loan that yielded no benefit. I was terrified that his very ghost would chase me after his death, so wild was his rage. He let loose a barrage of abuses against the bank. We mollified him and put him back to bed with generous assurances. Such was the sharpness of Manik's father's senses that my casual remark wrought a wonder that intensive medication could not achieve for almost two days.

Handling village wells

I remember we had tough, rocky soil in Wanoja's fields where most previous efforts at digging wells were failures. The region was rain-fed, and agriculture depended on the monsoon's vagaries. I received an application from a farmer for a loan of Rs. 1 lakh for digging a well, installing a pump and energizing it with an electric connection. The farmer was highly enterprising and wanted to make a serious attempt. He planned to dig it much more deeply than what was attempted by farmers earlier. He tried to justify the higher amount on the ground by saying that it involved excavation to a depth of almost seventy-five feet and entailed the deployment of heavy-duty pulverisers and dynamite. People in the village had cautioned me about the notorious record of the farmers and the mysterious trail of failed wells. However, the farmer's zealous enthusiasm led me to believe it would be worthwhile; if the farmer could achieve a breakthrough, it could open new vistas for irrigation in an arid region. I always had an open mind and greatly admired innovative and progressive farmers.

Since it was my first assignment, I didn't realize I had to inspect the site at every stage of construction and release the amount in tranches depending on the progress of the work. The farmer had informed me that the entire stock of cement and steel had to be purchased at wholesale rates from the original so that he could enjoy a decent discount. He assured me he would give me periodic feedback reports about the progress of the excavation and construction of the well.

In one of his feedbacks, the farmer informed us that water had been found after digging the earth to a depth of 120 feet. It involved a much deeper excavation and concentric concrete rings built along the circumference to reinforce the outer support for the well. Finally, the only formality left was the installation of electric poles to connect the transformer and the pump by wires. Meanwhile, I also sanctioned a temporary overdraft to meet the expenses due to the increased excavation depth. I insisted that the farmer plan my visit to the site as I had to compile a report for headquarters.

The farmer agreed to an inspection after it had rained heavily for almost three days, saying the project was an astounding success. The water level was so high that I smelled mischief. The village headman who had accompanied me saw my disbelief and brought a long bamboo and asked me to lower it into the well to get a rough idea of the water level. The bamboo hit an obstruction just eight feet below. I cornered the farmer and threatened to book him with the local police for fraud unless he coughed up the entire amount with interest. With the help of local farmers and assistance from the local police, we recovered the whole loss. However, the incident severely eroded my faith in the innate goodness of villagers. It is not to detract from the character of most poor and marginal farmers, whose reputation for honesty should be trusted. The ordinary peasant is still a paragon of great virtues.

Loans against gold

One of the critical businesses at rural branches was loans using gold ornaments as security. Suppose anybody opened the bank vault.

My lady assistant, Chandrabhaga would design and stitch tiny cloth sachets containing gold ornaments. In some parts of South Asia, there is a long-standing tradition of gold as a preferred form of saving. More miniature ornaments can accumulate at different intervals; they are not easily lost or destroyed; they are compact and lightweight compared to their value, and a portion could be slashed with the help of the goldsmith and then sold. When required, Indian families typically have an emotional attachment to the gold they own, usually jewellery, coins or bars. Thus, gold is one commodity against which the loan is usually not paid unless there is extreme financial distress and it is necessary to sell it. Loans against gold are periodically renewed and seldom sold because of cultural practice. However, pledging gold ornaments and other gold assets to local pawnbrokers and moneylenders to avail loans has been prevalent in Indian society for many decades, particularly in rural areas. Jewellery shops and pawnbrokers do brisk business in buying or pawning gold. The bankers have taken a cue and are also pitching in aggressively. I remember we had to sanction at least twenty to thirty loans daily during peak season.

The financial institution's primary responsibility is to safeguard the gold jewellery. It requires well-developed logistics to prevent fraud or tampering. Each jewellery item is kept in a tamper-proof sealed sachet, carefully labelled and tracked by meticulous inventory systems. During our days, vaults were ordered and imported from England, and the suppliers had enormous confidence in the vaults and their guarantee of durability that it took months fo;r them to manufacture, design, assemble and finally deliver. Most of them bore the acclaimed Chubb brand.

Loans against gold were popular at village banks because they required straightforward paperwork. Customers just had to walk in, wait for an hour or so and come out with the loan amount. Since most village borrowers were agriculturists, they could get the loan at a concessional rate. They just needed to produce proof that they owned agricultural land. It was not without its hiccups, however. In our village, no goldsmith could certify the quality of gold. Just imagine the plight of a bank manager who must assess the gold without any technology to assay its purity. Secondly, most jewellery had expensive coloured stones. The bank's instructions were to discount these external hedges and give loans against the net weight of the actual gold content. Weighing the gold and assessing its quality and the extent of purity were the exclusive responsibilities of the branch manager. When I started my career as a bank manager, I had not purchased even a finger ring; here, suddenly, I was an authority on gold. We had a bottle of nitric acid and some bleach chemical paper to help us assess gold.

My mantra was simple. First, we ascertain the borrower's character and technically verify the composition of gold. Our coordinator was a wonderful man with practical common sense, ideas and solutions. The first question he asked at a meeting of officials drew a lot of angry complaints. The core issue was ascertaining the genuineness of gold and how to detect it in case of spuriousness. We had little familiarity with gold, and no assistance was available to evaluate it. The coordinator came up with a simple solution: when a gold loan customer shows you his ornament, you should immediately put him on the defence, challenging the originality of gold. This haggling continues, but the borrower's response shows that he is honest in his claim. He said this simple rule of thumb held, and he had handled thousands of gold loans. Surprisingly, his simple advice appealed to the entire audience. I have never used this technique out of the fear that some sensitive customer may retaliate, but many people tell me that in those old days, it did work.

Tackling recalcitrant village farmers

Managing a farmer's credit requirements is tricky for a bank manager. It is a gut-wrenching exercise handling the farmers who have become seasoned in handling the bankers, particularly after being mentored by the new breed of canny politicians who have devised ingenious methods to flummox banks.

When the sowing operations begin, the farmers will start grumbling about the growing cost of farm inputs and try to get inflated sums sanctioned. When the crops reach the mid-stage and need fertilizer support, the farmers will be in an exuberant mood, telling the bankers of the possibility of a booming harvest provided a proper, timely and adequate quantity of fertilizers is available. But when the harvest season approaches and bankers start courting them for recoveries, the farmers put up grim and sullen faces, saying the crops suffered damage during harvest and it would be challenging to meet the repayment obligations. They would ask for relaxation in interest rates, rescheduling of their loans or waiver of the interest portion, adding their masterly histrionics and lamentations bemoaning the government's apathy towards them. They would then unleash a litany of complaints against farm input suppliers, accusing them of selling spurious products and cheating them on prices.

At first, I would get emotional and spend endless hours trying to work out relief packages. But later, I realised I was burning myself out for these undeserving farmers who were hoodwinking me just because they could.

The wily villagers

I remember a colleague doing his first rural assignment when confronted with a government programme for financial assistance for digging wells. This manager had spent his entire career in a metro region and carried the impression that villagers were saints. He worked very hard to ensure that all proposals for dug wells were processed speedily and the amount disbursed to farmers. He handed over the money to farmers as he felt that if he released it directly to contractors/vendors, they would exploit the farmers by inflating the costs.

A fortnight after the loans were released, the manager decided to inspect the sites to submit a progress report to his head office. He was shocked to find no indication of work having commenced at any of the sites. He met the representative of these farmers to question him about what he perceived as a big fraud. The intelligent and highly sophisticated farmer feigned total innocence. He asserted that all the farmers had dug their wells, but a mischievous contractor, who was jealous of the newfound prosperity of the farmers, had dumped waste material from construction sites in their wells.

The farmer's histrionics moved the compassionate manager so much that he immediately devised a relief plan. He consulted his bosses and gave an ad hoc bridge loan to help the farmers cope with the crisis. Experiences like these have the most committed bankers turning their hearts against the villagers they have come to assist.

Much later, the manager came to know the canny farmers beguiled him. The manager was highly demoralised and sought a transfer. The event tore the credibility of the villagers in the area and severely upset the implementation of the underway development programmes. After the investigation, an exhaustive training manual was prepared, highlighting the manager's experiences and how one could not exercise the necessary caution against such hazards.

Hazards of sympathy

I vividly remember the sweeper at our branch who would turn up religiously at dawn from his small but self-owned house near the bank building. I admired how the family portrayed resistance, tenacity and sincerity. I greeted him when I passed on my morning jog. I would give the family gifts on every festive occasion. Bose had a son, his only child, and they were keen that he should not suffer the disgrace and humiliation they suffered to make a living. The boy was not enrolled and could not qualify even for a menial job in the market. The only option was to set up a small business. It required capital, which Bose could hardly afford. The only option was a loan from a bank. It appeared a fair and workable alternative to Bose as he knew the staff of our branch quite well. I sympathized with Bose's sentiments and his intentions for his son. Still, I could not assure him of a definite solution because his son didn't qualify for government subsidies under our bank's loan schemes.

I contemplated extending a loan to Bose's son but couldn't figure out how. A perfect opportunity came my way when I came across a government circular I had skimmed over earlier and filed and forgotten, calling for applications. My curiosity is now piqued. I retrieved it from my slush pile of discarded correspondence. The scheme stipulated a non-refundable loan of Rs. 25,000 to scavenger families. That was in 1996. Today, the amount would be the equivalent of Rs. 2 lakh after inflation is incorporated.

I called Bose, filled out the application form, got Bose's son's signatures and other supporting personal documents organised and sent the application to the District Collector, putting in my strong recommendation for sanction of the loan. Bose purchased a wagon-load of stock, and his son's shop was overflowing with various commodities. No customer could turn back for the non-availability of any item. The shop became popular, and the Bose couple helped manage it. With the son well settled, the Boses started looking for a suitable bride for their son. With their reputation for honesty, they got a suitable bride from a well-settled middle-class family from nearby Nagpur. The girl was enrolled and was deft in handling household chores. She started helping the family manage the shop. She introduced some professional business practices, like maintaining the inventory of stocks, recording sales of every item and monitoring the cash flow.

Things went well for the family, and I was happy that I was part of his success story, but the glory was short-lived. One day, I heard that

Bose had sold his merchandise. When my colleagues confirmed the information, I was aghast. I visited Bose, who trembled as I confronted him.

"Sir, my only daughter-in-law was ill, and the local doctor advised me to get her treated at a multi-speciality hospital to avoid risks. I decided to sell the stocks to another shopkeeper and moved her to a high-tech hospital in the neighbouring city; we all had to stay for more than a month. I am broke, and I have run up debts. It is the will of God."

I was unmoved, even though Bose's tears kept rolling as he sobbed and mumbled in his plaintive voice. "What if you didn't have all this money?" I thundered.

"Sir, I would have taken a risk and treated her at the government hospital. But I thought I should not charge my daughter-in-law's parents for taking me to task since I had the resources." I was shocked by Bose's reasoning and logic and was guilty that I had become a tool for a wasteful drain of public money.

Events like this have been a routine experience in my career in rural India and have made me rethink the myths of innocence and simplicity surrounding the rural population. At the same time, I would not care to generalize these experiences. They are aberrations in an otherwise calm and value-driven rural society. When a development manager has undergone only a short stint in a rural area and most of his experiences are flooded with such events as I mentioned above, he is bound to become pussy-footed and pusillanimous in his approach.

The banking system stipulates filing a police FIR for the misuse of assets. Still, the police system is so slow to respond that a failed case can significantly harm the banker's efficiency more than simply leaving the case alone. It is better not to file an FIR at all. Threats, legal notices, and lawsuits have lost their bite after people have seen their inefficiency.

Handling bank defaulters

A bank manager's entry into the village sets the ferocious and swift word-of-mouth whispering machinery into action. The defaulters get alerted, and most disappear in the fields. The family members are seasoned in handling the broad array of lenders and know how to shoo away the visiting recovery staff. The inmates usually close the doors as soon as you knock on them. After sensing your arrival, they will open the door only after much persuasive tapping.

The lady of the house will emerge frowning at this act of intrusion, knowing full well the purpose of the visit and listing ou;t a litany of grievances in response to your enquiries about the l;oan. She will put up a deadpan expression, pleading ignorance about the matter. When you ask her about her husband's whereabouts and the fate of the loan, she will narrate the usual script. "I don't know anything about it. He alone manages it. He may have gone to the market, possibly to organize money. He is under severe stress as the crop has failed. We have not been able to pay our schoolchildren's fees for two months. Please show mercy to us."

If you are fortunate enough to meet the borrower, he will try to assure you of his intentions.: "I have already sold the stocks and am awaiting the payment. The first thing I plan to do is to square the loan." The confident and assuring tone of the borrower gives an impression of make-believe sincerity and may attract a neophyte manager. The farmer will go further. "Why do you unnecessarily waste your time coming to the village? I am more concerned than you. I have to safeguard my father's reputation for timely repayment of debts. His record is impeccable. Instead, He would pledge his wife.'s gold rather than be labelled a defaulter. I don't understand why God has been so cruel to farmers this season."

The lack of transparency in bankers' postings

The Personnel Department at our bank has officials with the talent to ensure that an official who is not in their good books is sent to a place where he would suffer great distress. Once, the department unwittingly transferred an officer to his preferred posting. Elated, the officer thanked the Personnel Manager and distributed sweets in his department. When the Personnel Manager realized what had happened, he cancelled the transfer and got him posted to a place he greatly abhorred.

I was also a victim of this cruel strategy. Commonly, a rural posting was a punishment. I chose it because I was passionate about working in rural areas, particularly with poor women. The government appreciated my performance, and the media covered my work. To reward my contribution to rural development, UNDP deputed me to the University of Manchester, Malaysia's Ministry of Rural Development and Grameen Bank, Bangladesh. Sensing that my wings were spreading fast and that I was enjoying my assignment, the Personnel Department transferred me to Kolkata at the bank's Foreign Department. It wasn't fascinating to reconcile mirror accounts of original transactions in overseas branches.

My posting was irrelevant to my expertise and would dislocate me and my family. This posting entailed a loss for the bank because it drained the experience I had gleaned in rural finance. Since I had voluntarily opted for the informal rural cadre, I had admitted my children to schools where the entire teaching was in a regional language. The officers in the Personnel Department defended their move and said it was a reward for my work with this post at the Foreign Department. The Foreign Department was a backwater in the bank's foreign business firmament accommodated in the lucrative postings at the bank's overseas centres. All my colleagues knew the department was infested with fraud and irregularities, requiring a sledgehammer to fix the problems there. I put up a bitter fight with the management and bounced back into my natural territory, development finance after the bank realized that the rural finance portfolio I had so assiduously built had begun to rot. This bitter experience warned me to be very careful with the Personnel Department lest I stepped on their toes and invited their wrath. I also realized that the Personnel Manager was an unanointed deity. We would refer to him as the jailor or the hangman whose noose was keenly waiting for new prey each day.

Risks for empathetic managers

I remember a woman client, Chandrabhaga Bhajne, in Bina in Nagpur, whose alcoholic husband had made life miserable for the whole family. He finally died on account of a failing liver. I appointed Chandrabhaga as a canteen worker in my office. Since she was staying in a rental house, she found her savings inadequate to meet the family expenses. I encountered a government scheme for a concessional loan to acquire a house. I negotiated the deal with the house owner and finalized it. I felt delighted that I could extend some concrete assistance to this widow. Unfortunately, my sense of fulfilment was short-lived. Chandrabhaga's two sons died within two months after the family shifted to the new house, both claiming their lives by consuming pesticides. The village believed that evil spirits inhabited the house, and Chandrabhaga made the mistake of buying it. It was then that Chandrabhaga started cursing me and continues to curse me even to this day, accusing me of trapping her in the deal involving the haunted house. A Good Samaritan becomes a devil. That is the tale of a poor rural manager. Banks have attempted to rein in recalcitrant borrowers who misuse funds. Still, considering borrowers' ingenuity (what has now become a local innovation or 'jugaad') bankers keep testing new ideas and discarding the old.

The system of making payments directly to vendors had also not worked. The vendor deducted twenty per cent of the payment and released only eighty per cent to the borrower, resulting in the asset for which finance had been provided not being acquired. Some vendors were not traders but agents who assisted the clients in encashing the fungible assets and earning huge profits. Ghost loans have been another bane of the development finance arena. Most ghost loans have been products of ingenious crooks in the financial system. Ghost clients vitiate most government development programmes, conduits for siphoning off institutional funds.

Shrewd farmers

In 2011, the farmers in northern Maharashtra suffered severely due to low cotton yields; additionally, the government procurement prices for cotton were pegged low. As a result, our loan recoveries plummeted. I conducted a detailed assessment of the farmers, realising their plight was genuine and needed a rehabilitation package.

In my report, I informed my bosses that because of the twin effect of low yield and low prices on the yield, the farmers didn't have enough money to service our loans and needed some concessions. No one from my head office came to meet the farmers and verify the situation. Our boardroom pundit's portfolio monitoring resulted from his meticulous reading of business newspapers. He came across a news item stating that the state government had devised a new plan to address the farmers' woes. Instead of raising the prices, the government compensated the farmers by paying subsidies based on landholdings. Our senior officers must have felt excited and believed they had scored a victory.

But I was not the one to get trumped by these armchair know-all toadies. I was familiar with this tribe and realised that the poor reading of the problems and unrealistic solutions were the root cause of anti-farmer policies in regal boardrooms, away from the grim realities in the farms. Moreover, most senior executives were out of touch with ground realities, their only source of information being the newspaper, where experts' opinions could be grounded in a suitable ideological theory. Also, these opinions take a macro view and do not account for the vast diversity of regional problems. I shot back a tart letter informing them that the government move was, in fact, a conspiracy against small farmers and smacked of outright feudalism; since eighty per cent of my farmers were either tenant farmers or sharecroppers, they would not stand to gain anything. Instead, the wealthy landowners would get this subsidy without cultivating their land or suffering any loss.

I had seen how the anti-poor-farmer lobby operated and how its policies impoverished the farmers rather than offering assistance. Had I not been aware of the pernicious implication of this policy at the ground level, I would have kept building pressure on the farmers. Such serious ethical dilemmas keep buffeting the conscientious manager's mind because of blatantly political exercises like this. I don't want to talk about how loan waivers have penalized and demotivated good borrowers and violated the credit culture in rural India.

Travel risks for bankers

Apart from routine occupational hazards, a severe security threat for rural managers looms when they must ferry cash by motorcycle without armed guards. Smaller village branches have a cash-holding limit. If the money exceeds this limit, excess cash has to be sent to the parent branch. If there was heavy demand for cash from customers, it had to be withdrawn from the parent branch and then carried to the paying branch. Money is sent in a concealed container that an armed guard can man. The logistical planning for this arrangement can take two to three days; an armed guard cannot be sought when cash is transferred at short notice. Any delay in handling cash can hamper banking services and cause hardship to the customers.

The only solution was to transport the cash on the bank's battered motorcycle through rugged, desolate terrains with no hope for any respite from bosses in case a tragedy struck. The bank's stringent punch line would be that the officer had violated the bank's instructions. If you were robbed or waylaid, you would have to reimburse the loss amount and face a volley of office memos seeking an explanation.

Guidance for handling dacoity

The bank's instructions in case of an attempted dacoity were quite strange and naïve. The circular said that when dacoits seize the currency vault, the staff should encourage them to fill the gunny sacks with small denomination currency notes to minimise the loss to the bank. Similarly, the dacoits' primary focus was usually on cash. We were cautioned to fill the bags of dacoits with low-value currency and spoiled notes. I always wondered whether Indian dacoits were such dimwits that they could get caught in such foolish traps. How did the management expect its unarmed staff to stand up to these professional thugs? I am sure the instruction was from someone who had not encountered dacoits.

Handling godown loans

In my early banking days, the most common loans were loans against stocks and mortgages of stocks in godowns. The godowns had two locks, one for the traders and the second for his banker. The goods in the warehouse were deposited to the banker, and the money was released after the stock inspection, after which the bank's representative computed its monetary value. Whenever the money was required to be released against the security of stocks, the padlocks were unlocked by the keys retained by the bank inspector in the joint presence of the trader and banker, and an inventory of the stocks was undertaken. The banker always preferred to take a gross estimate of the stocks by counting the containers. It was much later that banks found several of these containers empty, usually ones stacked in the rear, so they might not catch the bank representative's attention. Then, banks started shaking a few containers to verify whether they were empty or filled. Much later, we noticed that the witty traders filled these boxes with waste paper so they wouldn't appear empty when shaken. These loans have been closed, but retired bankers keep bandying about these stories when recounting their nostalgic memories.

An even greater fraud was traders taking out credit from two banks against the same stock. On one occasion, one of the two bank godowns and inspectors was taken in through the route, which displayed the second banker's name and bore his lock. We discovered that the same stocks were mortgaged to two banks simultaneously. It was then a fresh and ingenious innovation for deceiving bankers, and it took a lot of time for bankers to caution themselves against it.

Rural camaraderie

My friend from the World Bank, Gautam Ivatury, who was then a microfinance specialist, would regularly visit our village to study first-hand the impact of new models and policies at the ground level. When he arrived at the hall where colourfully garbed and decorated women waited to welcome him, Chanda the leader, stepped up to greet him. Gautam raised his hands in a 'Namaste'. He was stumped when Chanda beamed a loud hello and stoutly offered her right hand for a warm handshake.

I translated Gautam's words for the audience. My friend was so stirredby the enthusiasm and energy of the women that he answered he would learn Marathi, the local language, and speak to them the next time he visited them. It evoked a spontaneous comment from Chanda, who assured Gautam that she would talk in English if he spoke in Marathi the next time.

Managing complaints

One of the most agonizing roles in a bank manager's career is coping with frivolous and baseless complaints, particularly from political elements holding out threats when loan applications are declined if they don't comply with bank rules. It is laudable that the banks' customer grievances redressal machinery is sensitive to their complaints, but the whole process is demoralising for the bank manager. The job of the complaint cell at the bank's regional head office is to affix a pre-printed letter asking the manager to redress the complaint and obtain a letter from the complainant stating that he was satisfied with the settlement and was confident with our approach. A stereotypical reminder at periodical intervals follows this letter. In most cases, the complaint will be baseless or couched in aggressive phraseology that portrays the manager as a villain. The new semi-literate breed of leaders of villages and small towns have a lot of time and the sincere desire to project themselves as saviours. They are the real complaint factories, using the complaints as a blackmail weapon.

Seeking a letter from the complainant, even if the complaint has been closed, puts the manager in a highly vulnerable position. There will always be a residual problem animus in the complainant, and the fact that most will try to exploit the opportunity to extract concessions puts the manager in the dock. The banks must design a system whereby fake attract the *First Information Report* (FIR), the first formal complaint to the police. They must learn a lesson from the judiciary, which has started litigants filing frivolous lawsuits.

Most complaints are doctored or sponsored by disgruntled insiders who provide the bosses' precise names, job titles, and addresses. Often, even the various laws under which the complaint attracts judicial or police attention are not applied. Hence, the complaint is, in effect, a well-crafted legal petition. The insider may also go to the extent of drafting the entire complaint without writing in their hand to avoid suspicion. These insiders also follow up on the complaints by peeking into the correspondence between the local branch and head office. On several occasions, internal remarks on confidential notes relating to confidential matters are shared with the concerned clients, thus alerting them about the internal developments. The clients would also learn the name of the specific official instrumental in rejecting their loan cases.

The issue becomes thorny if the information source is a union leader. The industrial laws in our time provided union leaders such solid protection that, despite stark evidence of their wrongdoings, management would quail to take them head-on.

Another weapon akin to complaints is a hunger strike or threat of immolation. At the height of the agrarian crisis, which led to mass suicide in the Yavatmal district in Maharashtra, loan defaulters would sit in front of the bank manager's residence with kerosene cans in their hands due to restrictions from banks. Often, bankers gave in to unreasonable demands to escape the vicious and endless cycle of police enquiries. Several young bank managers in Yavatmal put in their papers, ruining their careers to save themselves from the orgy of arson and violence. Political leaders who prefer to use populist tactics keep sharing the fire with virulent rhetoric.

Torn and dirty currency

The Reserve Bank of India took a tough stand around 2002 to rid the banks of dirty, smudged currency notes and replace the entire currency stock of the country with crisp notes. Bank cashiers had had a tough time convincing customers to accept old notes. Customers would sometimes throw the packet on the cashiers' faces, muttering foul language. We had a senior cashier, Babulal Sondhiya, on the verge of retirement. He had spent his career at several places and was highly adept at handling customers. He designed a unique strategy. Whenever a customer threw the packet at him, he would raise a hue and cry, shouting, 'This person has insulted Laxmi (goddess of wealth), and people should condemn him!" The customers would then meekly apologize, hurriedly pick the cash up, and quickly escape before suffering somebody's wrath.

Allergy to media

One of the most significant weaknesses of public banks is their inaccessibility to the media. As one who handled this for my organization for almost a decade, my primary task was to keep the press away from bosses diplomatically. That is why most media leaks are due to sources that prefer anonymity. No one who reads it can be sure whether it is authoritative or authentic. Bosses always fear they will be misquoted or out of context to give a false and distorted twist to the controversy. Middle-level and even senior-level officials do not have the authority to speak, even if they are thoroughly informed. It was a funny situation from which I could not escape. I used to take the press delegation to remote rural places to build awareness among journalists about the revolutionary work being done in the hinterland by bankers. However, I could only share the innocent facts whenever they were curious about specific policies and wanted clarifications. If I allowed myself into a discussion, I would be overstepping my brief and inviting disciplinary proceedings.

On their part, the bosses always shied away from the media. Controversies would rage, and confusion over policies would run riot, causing immeasurable damage to the organization's image and brand. Still, the doubts in the media would be allowed to linger and fester. On several occasions, even when I had become uneasy and had made it strictly clear that I was not the official spokesman for my organization, the media would refer to me in good faith. But this innocuous act of theirs would lead to nightmares and make my job harder as bosses angrily questioned my priority. During my extensive travels in rural India concerning our rural finance programmes, I had to be cautious not to encounter the media. Whenever I conversed with them, I would always clarify that it was more informal feedback from someone working in the sector than part of an official briefing.

Risks of innovation

One of my most audacious acts as a rural banker was one that almost cost my job, resulting from the infamous Telgi scam, in which fake judicial stamp papers flooded the government treasury. The Government had no choice but to impound the legal stamp documents, which constitute a security document like a currency note and are also necessary for executing contracts, including loan contracts. Instead of stamp paper, the procedure complied on plain paper against the required fees paid in the government treasury, which attests to them and embosses them with revenue stamps. The Telgi scam was a flourishing racket of circulating fake stamp papers. With the dubious stamp papers withdrawn, loans were closed till the new papers were printed and relieved by the government.

Almost two hundred marginal and tenant farmers in the village attached to my bank branch were dependent on us for credit for farm inputs. The season had approached, and stamp papers could not be issued. The more prominent farmers elsewhere had several other sources of income, particularly dairy, and could meet the contingency. The farmers in my village had a perfect track record, and their credit history demonstrated an excellent credit culture and repayment ethics.

When convinced I couldn't help them through official channels, I disbursed loans on printed documents instead of the government-embossed security paper. I took a joint undertaking from the village headman, village officer, police and two prominent agriculturalists, one of whom was from the Dalit community and one from the Kunbi community, which happened to be the majority constituent of the village council. I got them to pass a resolution in the *Gram Sabha* (village assembly), taking full responsibility for the loans in case my action in releasing the loans on the strength of agreements on non-government security paper came under the scrutiny of auditors.

The outcome of my action was along the expected lines. The auditors were in a rage, my bosses were angry, and the gossip channels among my colleagues were abuzz with news of my mad action. I got telephone calls asking me whether I had been divested of all authority because of my flagrant violation of rules and was merely an official sans authority. My only weapons against my adversaries were my clients. I have never compromised on even the slightest injustice to my clients, mainly because most of my clients have been poor, unsettled and underpowered. My sincerity is visible through the warmth of the gratitude that my clients have evoked in their communication. Added to this has been my intense focus on proper documentation of facts and communication of my actions to all functionaries who are part of the loop.

I prepared a small dossier in which I filed the resolution of the village council, village assembly and representation of the critical local citizens. I scanned these documents and sent an adequately drafted letter to the revenue department of the state government, explaining the circumstances of my action, my intention and the hypothetical consequences of my non-action. I still firmly believe that all bonafide actions, if supported by proper documentary evidence and attestations by influential individuals, will sail through troubles. That doesn't mean you don't have to answer explanations or face enquiries. People misunderstand a call for explanations or holding of enquiries as vendetta. I think facing all these and coming out clean enhances one's credibility and strengthens the confidence required for decision-making.

Grassroots Wisdom

Most managers relied on the conventional wisdom of city dwellers, which projected villagers as meek, innocent and ignorant. They are not to be blamed; all anthropologists and public administrators from Metcalf to Shrinivas have hailed villages as self-contained republics. Their writings also bristled with noble characters who exemplified the fundamental human values of compassion, honesty and hospitality. These managers tripped like lame ducks when a new generation of villagers with extensive television exposure caught them off guard. Their predicament invited the attention of their bosses, and remedial measures soon followed.

When the managers visited the farms to inspect wells for the excavation and construction work out of the loan, the borrower wore a sullen expression and meekly admitted with moist eyes, "Sir, my well has been stolen. It was nearing completion when my jealous neighbours dumped stones and mud down the diggings. I am now planning to engage labour to remove the rubble." The manager usually did not have the heart to do anything but commiserate with the borrower. The villagers told me that the borrowers used similar tricks in cattle finance. They would take the manager to the field and show him a herd of cattle from a distance, indicating some of the beasts financed by the bank. These events became commonplace in banking lore.

The Integrated Rural Development Programme suffered a cruel end because of the ingenious but foul-minded villagers. The farmers are usually upbeat when they have easy access to initial loan tranches during the onset of the farming season: "Rain may not have been up to our expectations, but we are sure the crops would be better this year. We will be able to clear all bank arrears this year." Or "I don't want to remain a defaulter any more. I have decided to settle all my overdue and become debt-free." Buoyed by the encouraging sentiments of the farmers, the bankers also get into bullish gear and start releasing funds without serious inspection and assessment. Come harvesting time, and the smile turns into a frown. The farmers start wailing: "We were expecting this year to be better, but it may be worse. The government should create a relief package now that the harvest isn't good. Markets should behave well; good rates alone can save us".Indian banks received a frazzled shock from overbearing politicians who introduced the so-called cure in the form of socialisation, which was worse than the disease. There was a surge of cheap credit, which eroded the viability of banks. There was a distinctive blend of a variety of loans.

In most villages, the mountain of bad loans had turned larger than good loans. With the downturn in the rural economy, banks were looking far less inclined to add bad loans to their asset portfolio — unless they could snag them at a severe discount and have a guarantee of great return. At the same time, farmers were passing through such a critical phase that if the pain from taking action was great, the pain from not acting was even more significant. The late twentieth-century literature, which mainly consisted of polemic and counter-polemic rather than empirical investigation, did not answer these questions. So, all we could do was pass on the flavour of the debate to our practitioner colleagues. Most poverty-alleviation schemes wrote off loans. Banks' lending officers seemed more concerned with balancing their accounts than seeing poverty and injustice disappear from the countryside. They had been motivated to initially define their new mission in building the capability of villagers to navigate the present, prepare for the future, and reflect their commitment to excellence.

Encounter with the corrupt

When the government subsidy programmes for poverty alleviation were at their zenith, there was a spate of corruption charges against all local officials: the government officials, bank managers and local bodies handling these programmes. The officials had extracted hefty commissions on these loans on the pretext that they had to bribe their bosses to get subsidies released. The subsidies ranged from twenty-five to fifty per cent of the loan amount. The Anti-Corruption Bureau of the Police Department also had a field time laying successful traps and, in the process, helping its staff burnish its credentials in my district. The department surpassed its yearly target in just one quarter.

Since I had agreed to the bureau's suggestion to be a part of the team whenever it involved a case of corruption by bank staff, I got an insider's view of the entire operational exercises. The first case involved a junior manager of a minimal bank unit who had demanded Rs. 500 to sanction a loan to purchase a flock of ten goats. They appeared to have shared at a tea stall on the road traversing the village. The farmer visited the bureau office in the morning, where the currency notes he was to deliver were sprinkled with chemical powder and were kept for use as a court exhibit against the labelled criminal. The acts of bribery of public servants come under a law called the Prevention of Corruption Act, which stipulates a maximum sentence of seven years in jail. It covers bribes taken by the staff of government departments and government-supported institutions.

Our team stationed itself at a villager's residence near the tea stall. At the appointed time, the manager arrived at the tea stall, and the farmer handed over the amount, which the manager immediately inserted into the side pocket of his pants. The Sub-Inspector leading our team pounced on him like a crouching cat upon its prey and waited for us to join him in relishing the kill. The manager insisted the farmer had forcibly inserted the amount in his pocket. Still, the veteran police officer asked the manager to remove his pants as they would be seized and sent for a chemical examination of the powder that had stained his pocket. It looked like a hilarious scene, and life was severely embarrassing for the poor manager, but the tea stall owner came to the manager's rescue. He organized a lungi and then located a man whose pants somehow fitted him so he could accompany the police in at least tolerable dress. A panchnama (recorded statement by five witnesses) was noted n on a rough and almost waste paper, typical of discarded stationery in villages. However, the 'writer', as the police officially designated him, wrote it in highly technical Marathi in lovely handwriting, with every sentence in a perfectly straight line. With the *pahchnama* completed and signed by us, I was relieved. The poor manager tasted the flavour of how the police function.

I later heard that the manager lived along the same road as me. My curiosity piqued, and I decided to drop in at the bank branch whose manager's trousers we had seized. I introduced myself to the new manager and could sense his fear that I was perhaps on a hunt to flush out corrupt money from a new prey. I told him I had nothing to do with the unfortunate incident and was only a witness to the drama. He then told me the long ordeal he had to suffer while handling the whole affair. The primary modalities took place in the village with the help of village bureaucrats and local witnesses., but the bank's administrative office handled the more complex proceedings. The real problems arose when the police returned the pants to the bank after completing their enquiries. The manager asked his peon to get the file, which could give me an idea of the drama that unfurled in the aftermath of the return of the pants. The file was appropriately titled 'Correspondence relating to the seized full pants of the suspended manager'. A large stack of papers had already groaned the file. It was probably the first such case to be handled by the bank's regional headquarters, and it took a few months for the bank to decide which department should handle this matter formally.

It seems this became a high-priority matter at the office for several days, and the gossipmongers used their experience. The bank's manual of procedures was not very helpful as it was in arcane and technical language. l, and a forensics enquiry could decide the course of action. After the necessary journey of the trousers through several departments, they finally arrived at the branch where the branch manager and the staff torched them. A document confirming the procedure, signed by those present at the funeral of this unique branch customer, was sent to the administrative office. The matter was closed, but I could understand from the file the amount of human resources consumed to close an aborted bribe of Rs 500. Yet, the ghost of those pants continued to haunt the new manager and his colleagues! A nudge is not always enough to force change. Sometimes, a series of forceful shoves is required. The present system for curbing bribes is no longer effective and can't accelerate the eradication of corruption, as the real culprits know the tricks for getting away from the system. We need to do transformational work to ensure that the end of corruption ultimately transpires.

* * * * *

www.ingramcontent.com/pod-product-compliance
Lightning Source LLC
LaVergne TN
LVHW091146150826
845672LV00005B/1055

* 9 7 9 8 8 9 3 6 3 3 6 3 4 *